MW01295581

HERO'S LOOP
STORIES OF BOATING AND ADVENTURE

MIKE AND DENNIESE LILES

authorHOUSE®

AuthorHouse™
1663 Liberty Drive
Bloomington, IN 47403
www.authorhouse.com
Phone: 1-800-839-8640

Cover Design by: Jena M. Stilwell, Yellow Bird Studios, www.yellow-birdstudios.com

Published by AuthorHouse 02/04/2015

ISBN: 978-1-4969-0912-1 (sc)
ISBN: 978-1-4969-0911-4 (e)

Library of Congress Control Number: 2014907989

Any people depicted in stock imagery provided by Thinkstock are models,
and such images are being used for illustrative purposes only.
Certain stock imagery © Thinkstock.

Thank you

Thanks to all the people who had a part in this grand adventure. Jay and Tricia Liles, who took care of our properties and forwarded our mail. BJ, Tiffany and Nanny, who kept all our house plants alive. Jennifer and Hudson, who kept us up to date on the family. John, Beth and the boys, who gave us a much needed sabbatical along the river in Alabama. Jayne, Wayne and Gene who kept Nanny happy in our absence. Ronda and Nelson, who put together a beautiful wedding for BJ and Tiffany, and the angels we met along the way. Also, our friends Ralph and June Vaughn who encouraged us to write this book. We couldn't have done it without you.

We thank you all.

Credits

Andy Jones: photography

Chuck Williams: photography

Jena M. Stilwell: graphics

Frank Caperton: website design

DISCLAIMER
and
ACKNOWLEGEMENTS

This book is written for the entertainment of the reader.
It is not a navigation tool or an instructional manual for
safe boating. It tells the stories of a lifetime of boating
and the true enjoyment of being aboard a boat.

Exerts were taken from "*SOUTHWINDS*" Magazine, July 2005
issue, pages 28-31, "Race to Mexico: Regatta del Sol al Sol 2005,
Gulf Storm Brings a Rough Ride for Many" by Dave Ellis.

The travels of the Great Loop were taken from the log book of
Lifestyle II, the reflections of the author and depiction of the
events, happenings and feelings of the crew at that time.

The people, companies and organizations referenced in this book
are only part of the story and in no way endorse or necessarily
recommend any part of this book or the actions taken.

Every effort has been made to make this book accurate, but even
with sincere proof reader's effort, errors may be present. You are
welcome to report any such findings to the website; Herosloop.com.
They will be appreciated and corrected in future editions.

Boating can be a lifetime sport, hobby or source of income, but
it is not without some risk. A boater will gain competence with
experience and education and the practical application of good
practices. Lots of educational courses are available to a boater from
various sources and should be a continuous part of the enjoyment of
boating. In addition to safe and competent boaters, we need clean
water to enjoy and for that reason a portion of the sale of this book
goes to Boat U.S. Foundation, for boating safety and clean water.

Listed below are some of the organizations that
provide educational resources for boaters.

Boat U.S. Foundation
U.S. Coast Guard
U.S. Coast Guard Auxiliary
U.S, Power Squadrons
Tennessee Wildlife Resources Agency
State Resource Agencies
Boat Safety courses and other groups are available On-line

Contents

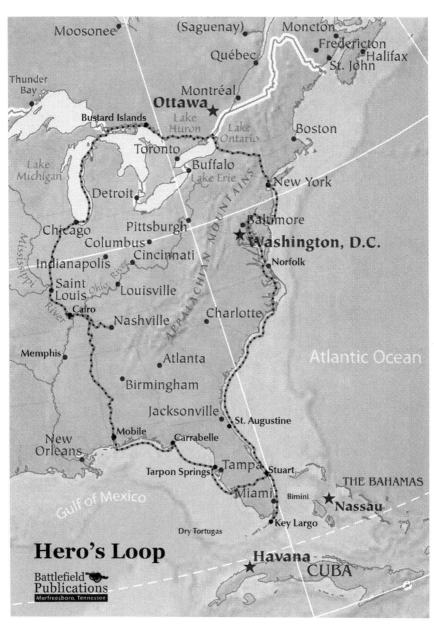

Map of our loop

Chapter 1

Hero's

Everyone has one or if they don't, they should. My hero is a boat!! I know, most people my age had a hero that rode a white horse and wore a white hat. If they didn't like Roy Rogers then they must have been a Gene Autry fan. Of course Sky King brought all of us together. He could ride a horse and fly a plane. What a guy! Our hero's were smart, good looking and always right. They shot straight but only winged their opponents which always converted the bad guy and he did wrong no more. Hero's are good or at least in the 50s they were. But how or why did I end up with a boat as my hero and is that the reason I found a HERO boat to do the Great Loop?

It all started in the fall of 1951. My mother took me to see a movie called *THE AFRICAN QUEEN*, an adventure film adapted from the 1935 novel by C.S. Forester and directed by the great John Houston. I'm sure the movie impressed others because it won lots of awards including best actor, best actress, best screenplay and best director. It was a story that took place at the beginning of WW1 in East Africa. The Germans were in control of the area and were clearing the place of any person or group that could slow their goal of world domination. In their path was a pair of British missionaries, a brother and sister by the name of Samuel and Rose Sayer. The little village of Kungdu where the pair called home was in the way. In the first few minutes of the film Samuel was shot and killed by the Germans and that left Rose,

1

played by Katharine Hepburn, as the sole occupant of the village until the captain of the *African Queen* came to her rescue. Captain Charlie Allnut, played by Humphrey Bogart, took charge. The choices were few so the missionary Rose joined the rough hued Charlie aboard the *African Queen*. The rest is one of the greatest boat stories ever told. The *African Queen* was an open cockpit, tiller steered, steel hull work boat about 30 feet in length. She was powered by a cantankerous steam engine and wood burning steam boiler. The weight of the boiler and steam engine added stability to the boat and was state of the art when she was built. The real boat was built in England in 1912 and was used to deliver goods and people in Belgian Congo and on Lake Victoria. In the movie, *THE AFRICAN QUEEN*, Lake Victoria was guarded by the German patrol boat *Queen Louisa*. The destruction of that German patrol boat became the object and mission of Samuel and Rose. The *African Queen* was going to destroy the *Queen Louisa*, good over evil and the ultimate success of the underdog. What a great story and what a great little boat, my hero?

Being reared in Florida, I was exposed to boats of all kinds from an early age. My family didn't own a boat. We were still making payments on a very used 1952 Hudson and rent payments came before recreation. As a youngster I didn't really have an opportunity to own or even enjoy boats other than to look at them sitting at anchor or docked at the Tampa harbor. I watched and enjoyed boats of all kinds travel up from the Gulf to downtown Tampa. Banana boats and shrimp boats were always in discussion by my buddies. I even had a buddy whose dad built a 40' shrimp boat in his back yard in the early 60's. I watched as he and his dad built the boat from keel up. Getting the finished boat to the water was a story that captured the attention of the Tampa Tribune and the evening paper, the Tampa Times for several weeks. But the banana boats held a special place in our imagination. The story would go that a banana boat had just docked at the Tampa docks and they needed help unloading all the bananas. We would talk it up and dream about all the money we could make carrying the bananas off the boat and setting them on a cart by the dock. We knew the way to the docks and the bus fare was only a nickel. So we would spend most of the afternoon planning the job of unloading bananas and thinking of ways we were going to spend all that money. Then, just as a bunch of skinny pre-teenagers were ready to set off for all this easy money someone would say, "What about the tarantulas?"... The next sound was "I ain't going down in no dark boat and get bit by a tarantula. Why those things are as big as a catcher's mitt". That ended the thought of going to the Tampa docks. Later I did have friends that owned a ski boat and I learned how to ski on the Hillsborough River. For fun we would ski all the way down the river to the commercial shipping lanes of Old Tampa Bay. Once I even got to handle the controls of the boat. I was smitten. "One of these days I am going to have a boat", I thought. Maybe even a big boat like the *African Queen* and go down a river bigger than the Hillsborough River. Maybe even as big as the mighty Mississippi, like Huck Finn.

After graduating from high school with no real desire to go to college and the draft looming, I joined the U.S. Navy, just like Humphrey Bogart did when he was that age. The difference was he was sent to serve aboard a ship. I was sent to Memphis. Navy, Memphis..? Well there was the Mississippi River. After I arrived at Naval Air Station, Memphis I found out that the base wasn't even in Memphis. The base was in Millington, a little town about 30 miles from Memphis. That's OK, I thought "because this is just for training and as soon as I graduate from the six week "A" school I will be transferred to an aircraft carrier and see the world". Not to happen... After spending four years at the same location I mustered out of the Navy, still at Memphis and had never served aboard a ship. The closest I got to a Navy ship was on one of my days off, I visited a mine sweeper that docked at Mud Island in Downtown Memphis. The mine sweeper was a wooden boat and reminded me of a larger version of the *African Queen*. I'm not sure where it was deployed or what it was doing at Mud Island. Maybe the Navy had some inside information on the capabilities of the Viet-Cong.

Boats took a backseat to the responsibilities of life. Marriage, college, children, mortgage and car payments all came before any thoughts of a boat. Our first house was a duplex in a nice quite neighborhood. My neighbor Steve owned a trailerable sailboat. It was a 23' sloop, meaning it had one mast, a head sail and a main sail. The swing keel allowed it to be driven on the trailer like a power boat. The good thing about having a sailboat on a trailer is you can take it to small lakes and enjoy your boating whenever you want. You also don't have to pay for slip rental which is important to save expense. The bad part is you have to step the mast each time you want to sail. To raise the mast you must attach the shrouds, the headstay, raise the mast, attach the backstay and then adjust everything. Sailboats are a lot of work to begin with even if the mast is already stepped. You still must hank the sails, run the sheets and hang a small engine on the transom, in case the wind stops, and you want to get back to the trailer. Also a gas can is handy. My point in this is, that Steve needed help each time he wanted to go sailing. He was an attorney and I had started my own business so we could arrange our time to go sailing. Before long I was using the proper terms for boat things. Ropes were now lines, left was port and right was starboard. The pointy end was the bow and the back was the stern. The stern had the vertical part known as the transom, which held the tiller. Attached to the tiller was the rudder. Sailing on the local lake, I was able to spot wind patterns and identify clouds which could be a forecast of potential problems. I had earned my private pilot license along the way, so Steve and I were a good compliment for sailing. At some point I decided that I needed my own boat. At that time I was either not smart enough to realize or had not heard that the best boat is a "friend's boat."

The advertisement was posted at the local marina "Sailboat for Sail". It was a 25' O'Day sloop. O'Day had been a quality manufacturer located in the Northeast and had produced everything from daysailers to coastal cruisers. By the late 80's O'Day folded as a result of the downturn in the economy and a luxury tax. The luxury tax was one of those bright ideas that seem to come from Washington every decade or so that goes like this…." We need more money,,..We'll just tax the rich". Of course those that could afford to buy a new boat stopped buying those new boats, airplanes, expensive jewelry and other items that our tax code identified as "luxury", and as a result many companies went out of business and the hourly worker was left without a job. O'Day was one of those companies. The boat on the ad's name was *OPHIS*, and the owner said he named it so when his wife ask where he was going he could honestly say he was going to the office (*OPHIS*). That seemed like a good idea to me and we soon settled on a price. Then as a proud owner of my first boat and a real sailor the *African Queen* came back into my mind with thoughts of "how would Bogie do this?". As my desire to know more about boats grew, I signed up for every course the local Coast Guard Auxiliary and the Power Squadron had to offer. I also read every book I could find on the subject. I even joined a local "Yacht Club". I had to apply for membership to the club and was surprised to find the main qualification for membership was the $100.00 membership fee and what brand of beer I drank. No blue blazer or white duck pants, just a bunch of folks that loved sailing and wanted to share that love. My little boat was possibly the slowest boat on the lake but I was having fun and learning boating. My family now included two boys that enjoyed watching me try to sail. The boys learned some new and interesting nautical terms, especially on those hot days with no wind and when the outboard would not start. That's when I found how friendly boaters were to each other. Every boater knows the feeling of needing help so the boating community helps each other, whether they be a blow boat (sailboat) or a stink pot (motorboat). At some time they will all need help so usually they don't mind giving it. Getting towed back to dock is the second most embarrassing thing that can happen to a boater. You can see why, there is no place to hide. You are on a small boat, it has it's name on the side and all of your friends are watching. It says to all THIS GUY IS A FAILURE!! Of course the one thing worse than being towed back to the dock is running aground. When you run aground you run the boat in shallow water less than your draft, also known to boaters as skinny water. There you sit high and dry with the name of your boat in large letters for everyone to see. It says to all, THIS GUY IS A FAILURER AND HE IS STUPID!! Both events have happened to me so often that I have grown immune to the comments and have eventually learned that the draft of your boat and the depth of the water are important items to know.

Novice sailboat racers usually start as crew. As a member of a racing crew you start at the rail. That means you are "rail meat" a term used to describe those sailors that sit on the rail of the boat and trade sides each time the boat tacks or jibes. Balance of a sailboat is very important so the captain usually yells for the rail meat to move forward or aft or port or starboard. When the boat tacks or changes sides of the wind, going upwind, the sailors on the rail must scramble to the other side. With all grace abandoned you must crawl over sheets, sails and fixed gear. If you don't skin your knee or bump a shin on a block or hatch, you will the next tack. A jibe is the same maneuver only the boat is going downwind and the higher the wind the more dangerous the maneuver can be.

After several seasons as rail meat I moved to other positions on the boat. Trimmer, foredeck, timekeeper and starter were all tried. The bigger the sailboat the more people required to properly man it. Sailing is very competitive and the story goes that if two sailboats are on the lake, one is racing. As a competitive sailor I always looked for ways to improve my skills or challenge my knowledge. Those opportunities were always there. Beer can races; those races that are usually held on a week night and with relaxed rules grow to weekend races and then multiply into longer races or regattas. Next, are the overnight races or long distance races. My first opportunity for an overnight race was arranged by a friend who lives in the Tampa Bay area. The race was to start at Clearwater and end in Key West. It was estimated to be about a 30 hour race. The start was great. Approximately 50 boats all jockeying for position as the cannon fired to start the race. The captain of the boat I was on was a novice to long distance racing, as was the crew, but we all had the desire. Being a lake sailor, I didn't have my sea legs and it was not long before I felt a little strange in the stomach. I didn't turn green until the next day. The long day turned to a windless night and then a front passed and we had four foot seas and a confused sea, which meant the sea had no pattern. Everyone on the boat was sick. Sea sickness is contagious and so if one person gets sick usually another person will get sick. Before long all the crew is hanging over the side. The only known cure for sea sickness is to hug a tree. So 30 hours passed and we were not even half way to Key West. Fortunately, we were not far off the West coast of Florida. I told the captain that if he would find us a port I would rent us a van and drive us to Key West. He agreed, and soon we were tied to a dock and all looking for that tree to hug.

We made it to Key West just in time to join in the celebrations for the race crews. The trip was not a total waste because I learned some valuable lessons about long distance sailing. I also learned that I had a propensity for sea sickness. As time would go on I would investigate methods to cope with my inner ear problem while on open water. I didn't like the medical solution because it made me feel medicated so I investigated the old sailor's methods of cure. Watching the horizon as my body adjusted to the movement of the boat helped. Most everyone will get their sealegs given enough time. Watching the horizon seems to help. Not going below deck was another way. By staying on deck you stay busy and your legs compensate for the movement and the body adjustment begins. My favorite natural cure is ginger. Ginger is a proven natural healer of seasickness. Ginger ale and ginger snaps are a part of my stores when boating on the open seas. On night watch I can consume a bag of gingersnaps. One crossing where I was a part of the sailing crew, the crew found the value of the gingersnaps and would not let them out of the cockpit. By the time my shift arrived the bag was wet to the point of disintegrating and my precious gingersnaps were soggy. Yes, the lessons we learn.

Joshua Slocum is credited with the first solo trip around the world. My ambitions never reached the point where I considered sailing solo around the world or even crossing the Atlantic. I have friends that have sailed the Atlantic. I admire their ambition but that's not for me. Many things have changed since Joshua Slocum made his 46,000 mile trip. He was 51 years old when he started the trip in 1895 and it took him three years to complete. He made the trip after the end of a career as a captain of a commercial sailing vessel. The advent of steam driven boats had put Captain Slocum out of work. A friend felt his despair and gave him a derelict sailboat. He took on the challenge, rebuilt the old boat and named it *Spray*. He recorded his trip in articles for several newspapers as he progressed around the world. Later he combined those articles in book form which is still regarded as one of the best sea stories written.

Maybe it was Joshua Slocum that influenced my decision to purchase a very used 35' sailboat that I spotted in a working yard in Port Washington, NY. The canvas covering the cockpit had long since worn away and the weeds had grown high around the once beautiful craft. Maybe it was what my mother said to me many times in my youth… "Waste not want not!" The broker was happy to receive an offer on the boat named *"Lifestyle"*. She was a 1984 Oday 35. She had great lines and a good sail inventory. The 30hp engine looked like new. I soon found out that it was new because the owner had failed to put oil in the original engine. It seems he had more money than he did a sense of responsibility. The boat had not been taken care of and once the owner found it in disrepair he just parked it and put it on the market. I had the boat trucked to Middle Tennessee and docked on the Cumberland River. With promises of great sailing adventures and wonderful times on the nearby lakes I was able to coerce family and friends into helping me redo the boat. The prior owner had removed the diesel cabin heater and even patched the hole in the overhead but had neglected to clean the oily soot that covered the interior of the boat. My future daughter-in-law was one of the helpers. She was almost overwhelmed when she first saw the inside. But like the true trooper she is, she just started cleaning and soon the boat was looking like the diamond in the rough I knew it to be. It took almost a year to redo all the neglected items and tune the rigging.

On a visit to the marina office I spotted a poster on the wall. It was a chart of the American Great Loop produced by Raven Publishing. The American Great Loop Cruising Association (AGLCA) is a group of cruising sailors, motor and sail that travel a circle know as the Great Loop. The chart shows the 6000 mile circumnavigation route around the Eastern part of North America. It has arrows pointing the direction of the course. This was my first occasion to see or hear of this year long odyssey. I studied the poster and thought "maybe I could do that". The seed was planted, but it would be several years before my Loop adventure would begin.

The Loop is a connection of intracostal waterways, lakes, rivers, and canals that create a circle around the eastern part of the US and the southern part of Canada. The Loop even requires a crossing of the Gulf of Mexico between the panhandle of Florida and the West coast of Florida. It was by the connection of these waterways that commerce was moved in the early days of this country. The Dismal Swamp Canal is one of the Country's oldest. It was surveyed by George Washington and connects Elizabeth City, North Carolina and Norfolk, Virginia. The Dismal Canal began as a route for commerce and was used to transport harvested wood to the rapidly growing northeast. Some of the original timbers defining the canal walls can be seen as you transit the canal. It was completed in 1805. Today it is a National and State park and a wildlife refuge. This canal made possible the transfer of commerce between North Carolina and Virginia without sailing around the Outer Banks and on the Atlantic Ocean. At the time I was looking at the poster in the marina office in Nashville, I didn't know the Dismal Swamp would be one of the many canals I would transit while on my loop adventure in the years to come.

After a year of cleaning *Lifestyle* and several thousand dollars in new canvas and rigging, paint and varnish, I stepped the mast and was ready to sail my new boat. The only problem was the marina was located on the Cumberland River. The Cumberland River at that point is narrow and sailing was limited to tacking back and forth across the river. A new home for *Lifestyle* was found on a lake upstream from the Rock Harbor Marina and I set the course for Harbor Island Yacht Club (HIYC). Nashville was only about 10 miles away from Rock Harbor and that was my first stop. We docked the boat at the foot of Broadway on our way to our new home on Old Hickory Lake. Nashville is known as Music City USA, but it now has much more to offer. Music is still a very important part of its fiber, but now the growing downtown offers an NFL stadium, a National Hockey franchise and the new Schermerhorn Symphony center.

Lifestyle was now ready for larger waters. Her new home was on Old Hickory Lake. Old Hickory Lake is 25 miles upstream from Nashville and is named for President Andrew Jackson (Old Hickory) who had his home and plantation on the river. The Hermitage is still available for tours. The Old Hickory Dam was completed in 1954 and impounds approximately 22,500 acres of water. Several marinas are located on the lake, but one of the yacht clubs is devoted solely to sailboats. It was Harbor Island Yacht Club (HIYC) where *Lifestyle* found its new home. The club is located on an island that was formed when the lake was dammed in 1954. HIYC is a sailing club but has part of its charter to educate sailors. The club also works from seniority and as a new member *Lifestyle* was assigned a mooring ball. Also, as a new member, I was expected to establish the mooring ball. The next weekend I was at the club early on a Saturday morning and I helped move a chain and float ball attached to a 55gal barrel of concrete to a place in the harbor. From the ball I attached a rope called a bridle to which *Lifestyle* would be secured and spend the next year. Everything was great! My new boat home had a beautiful little cove, not far from my home and a club with good neighbors and boaters to associate with. The only problem was the boat was moored to a floating ball about 100 yards from the dock. The next purchase was a boat to get from the dock to *Lifestyle*. One of the club members had a sailing dingy with a small trailer for sale. The boat was a Dink and in addition to being a great rowing boat it also had a mast and boom where a small sail could be attached. A small centerboard and tiller made it a great addition to my boat inventory. The Dink was a fun little boat that could carry two people with comfort and maybe a third person if all were careful. It was fun to sail, but I enjoyed rowing it even more. To me rowing was more enjoyable and great exercise. *Lifestyle* had transformed from the derelict I found on Long Island Sound to a fine looking sailing vessel. She sat proudly in the cove among many other sailboats. Like most sailing clubs, HIYC had a very active race group. I found a captain that would be a good fit and joined his crew. A good fit for me was a captain that did not yell.

Sometimes it is necessary to yell to be heard on a boat but some captains start yelling at the dock and continue till the race is over. Racing is good in that, in order to be competitive, you have to get the most out of the boat you are on. Most races are set up to make the boats equal but the crew makes the difference. So you can see how some really competitive captains can get excited. Larry the owner of a 30' Benetaue was mature and low key. I enjoyed crewing for him and learned a lot during the following year. Wednesday night races evolved into Saturday races and then to weekend regattas. I started out as rail meat and moved to a position on the mainsheet. Trimming the mainsheet required much attention to detail. The little ribbons called telltails attached to the leach, or back, of the mainsheet required all of your attention. A tack or crossing of the wind would require lots of work for a couple of minutes and then back to trimming and preparing for the next tack. A race could last a couple of hours or a couple of days or more. Our races were usually from 8:00am till 12:00 noon. We would race each Saturday and Wednesday evening. We raced summer and winter. In the winter months we would not sail on Wednesday because of the limited daylight hours and we would not race on the weekend if the high temperature was predicted to be less than 32 degrees. Several times we arrived at the boat to find the rigging and deck iced but the predicted high would be above freezing so we raced. Living in Nashville, we didn't find many of those days but sailing on a frozen deck is an unforgettable experience. While crewing on someone else's boat is good for your education, you are always second guessing the captain, thinking I would do that differently. One good thing is that you are able to watch and learn from others mistakes. I watched a friend T-bone another boat at a start line of a race by not allowing the boat to gain speed after tacking. Another friend sailed his boat in front of a commercial tow boat which was pushing about 12 empty barges. Empty barges sit really high and the tow boat operator pushing the barges thought he ran over the sailboat, panicked and altered his course which drove the barges up on land. That's an emergency stop for a tow boat pushing barges. No one was hurt, the barges were pulled off the land in a couple of hours and our sailboat race was completed. The following week we had educational classes on who had the right-of-way on the water. The local coast guard said that was the only way our club would again be able to have races on the navigable waterway. All the while I continued to work on *Lifestyle* getting her ready to take her to saltwater. *Lifestyle* was moored at the yacht club on the Cumberland River which led to the Tennessee River which now, with the completion of the Tombigbee waterway, was a short cut to the Gulf of Mexico. The picture of the Loop hanging in the marina office came to mind and the thought that maybe it really could happen.

One of the members of the club had sailed to Mobile and soon I was getting advice from him. The Loop was new to me but it had been an objective of boaters for a long time. The book <u>A YEAR IN A YAWL</u> was written by Russell Doubleday and describes the adventures of Kenneth Ransom and crew aboard the 30' yawl *Gazelle*. After reading this book two things struck me as unique. The boat *Gazelle* was a true sailboat, meaning it had no auxiliary engine, and the captain and crew were very young and had limited experience. In addition to that they started the trip from Lake Michigan in October. Had they been older and more experienced they would have waited until the spring of the year. But things were different in 1898. In fact, so many things were different, a hundred years later, it was hard to imagine these young guys making the trip at that time. As someone contemplating the Loop journey, I held them in high esteem and although their voyage only took a year to complete as compared to Joshua Slocum's around the world trip that took a little over three years, it has lots of similarities. Both Slocum and Ransom built their own boat. Neither captains had the use of modern navigation equipment that serves boaters today. A compass was the main instrument and in Ransom's case it was the only instrument on his boat. The *Gazelle* was seldom out of sight of land and didn't need a sextant where Slocum had to take his readings daily. Auxiliary engines had not been developed for small sailboats in the late 1800's and were not available for either boat. Both boats and crew were truly at the risk of the elements. The currents, the wind, the water depth, and approaching storms were all challenged without prior warning. Slocum had the benefit of a lifetime of experience but also had the handicap of being a solo sailor. Ransom had limited experience but had a couple of young friends to crew for him. Ransom also had the advantage of being close to shore or on a river. And as Captain Ron Rico said in the movie "CAPTAIN RON", "If we get lost we will just stop and ask someone." So Ransom had the advantage of being able to ask someone for direction or help. He did so many times along the way. Slocum was able to give talks along the way and as his notoriety grew it produced income and even more followers. Both individuals gave me inspiration and confidence that I could complete the Loop. In boating like other things in life, local knowledge is the best. A local author and friend possessed the local knowledge I needed.

C.B. Arnett and his friend Elvis Rushing were the first pleasure boaters to complete a small loop from Nashville to Nashville using the Mississippi going south and the Tombigbee going north. They were aboard a 24' pontoon boat named the *Lu-ce-bee* and completed the trip March 5, 1985. The *Lu-ce-bee* traveled some of the same route that Ransom took in his 1898 trip. C.B. Arnett wrote about his trip in a book The Saga of the *Lu-ce-bee*. His local knowledge was part of my trip preparation.

C.B. Arnett's trip was possible because of the opening of the waterway from Mobile to Paducah, Kentucky known as the Tombigbee or the Tenn-Tom. The route north from Mobile connected rivers, creeks and lakes to form a passage that connected the Tennessee River to the Gulf of Mexico, eliminating the need to travel the lower Mississippi River to complete the Loop. The Tenn-Tom was completed February 1, 1985 with the completion of the Aberdeen Lock but the idea began many years before. A letter penned to the King of France in 1792 by the French Explorer Marquis De Montcalm stated that he need be thinking of connecting the Tombigbee with the Tennessee river if he wanted to take over the new world. A Cruise Guide of the route by Fred Myers tells that story and others about the Tenn-Tom. The guide is; THE TENN-TOM NITTY-GRITTY CRUISEGUIDE. In addition to giving a mile by mile report of the river system it also gives some of the history of the system. Page six of the book states "Many years later and after many fits and starts, the Feds really got serious, particularly after the project was authorized by Congress in the River and Harbor Act of 1946." The Tenn-Tom is only 234 miles between the Tennessee River and Demopolis, Alabama. The Black Warrior River-Tombigbee waterway to Mobile is another 217 miles so the entire 450 mile waterway has come to be known as the Tombigbee. It is reported that the system cost over two billion dollars and moved more dirt than the Panama Canal. It has proved to be a worthy investment. It allows commerce from the Gulf to the Great Lakes and avoids the commercial and fast flowing lower Mississippi River. But to the pleasure boater its main purpose is to eliminate the necessity of traveling the lower Mississippi River where docks are few and the tows and commercial traffic are plentiful.

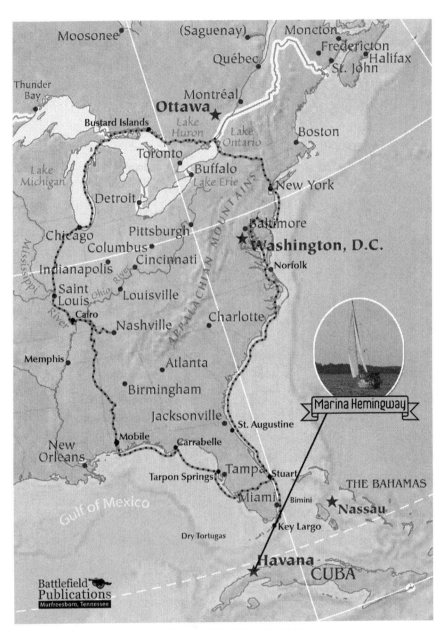

Cuba, the jewel of the Caribbean

Chapter 2

Cuba Calling

Cuba has been an interest to me for many years. In October of 1962, I was a junior at H. B. Plant High school in Tampa, Florida. We were in school during that famous 13 day standoff between the U.S. and the USSR over missiles in Cuba. At that time Tampa was the home of MacDill Airforce Base and The Strategic Air Command Headquarters (SAC) and we felt Tampa would be one of the targets if an attack occurred. At school we practiced getting under our desk in the event a missile was coming our way. Later, President Regan would want to spend billions of dollars for a missile defense system while we had the answer in 1962, just crawl under a ¾ inch maple school desk. After the 1959 revolution in Cuba and the overthrow of Fulgencio Batista, the Castro group nationalized almost everything in Cuba. The wealthy and those that could afford it departed the country quickly. The best and brightest of the population departed for Florida. Miami became a magnet for a large number of the immigrants and today is still a home for the largest Cuban population in the U.S. Tampa was also the recipient of many of the Cubans fleeing the communist. Most Tampa arrivals came without much more than the clothes they carried, and had to start over in a new country. When he arrived in our school, he, like many of my classmates, could not speak English. At that time there were no English as a second language classes. They just started from zero and were forced to learn the language. All the Cuban students whom

I knew then, and have been able to keep track of since, have done well in their new country. Cuba is only 90 miles from Key West and is just an overnight sail.

Bill Clinton was president in 1995, and talk among the sailing community was that the rules of the 1962 Cuban embargo were relaxed. Sailing to Cuba was again a reality as long as you didn't spend any money. At that time, the embargo was understood to apply only if money exchanged hands. If you were a member of a sailing club you could present your membership card at Club Havana and the club would comp your dock fee. So it was reasoned that if your boat was fueled and stocked before you departed Florida you could stay in Cuba without spending any money. Many sailing magazines carried articles about the relaxed embargo and the great things to see in Cuba, the jewel of the Caribbean. A friend in the Tampa area was the editor of a local sailing magazine. I contacted him with a request to introduce me to a captain that was going to sail to Cuba and needed crew. He made the introductions and plans were laid to meet and sail from South Florida to Havana. We were scheduled to set sail March 1, 1996. Airline tickets were purchased and it was all set, until I woke a week before the trip to read the headlines in the local paper that said "U.S. civilian planes shot down by Cuban MIG Fighters". The two twin engine planes were supposedly on a humanitarian mission and in international waters when they were shot down. President Clinton ordered the U.S. Coast Guard to search for survivors and protect the area. F-16 and F-15 flew over the search area while the Nantucket, a 110 foot Coast Guard vessel searched the waters. Not a trace of the two planes or the four people were ever found. The Cuban government had previously warned that anyone invading their airspace or territorial water would be shot down or sunk. The planned trip was called off and thanks were given that we were not in Cuba when all that occurred.

Soon the furor over the planes being shot down seemed to fade. It wasn't long before sailors started to talk about making the trip once again. This time the talk was more in line with who do you fear the most the Cubans or the U.S. Coast Guard? I called my editor friend and ask him to pass the word that I was still interested in crewing for such a trip. A few days later, he called to tell me that an informal race from St. Pete to Havana was being considered and would keep me informed. The St. Pete to Havana sailboat race traces its origin back to 1930 when Commodore Rafael Pooso of the Havana Yacht Club and George S. Gandy Jr. of the St. Petersburg Yacht Club organized the first race. It became such a huge success that Cuban President Gen. Gerado Machado presented the trophies. The yacht *Haligonian* set a record of 41 hours, 42 minutes for the 284 mile race. That time would stand for five years. During WWII the races were called off but after the war the races began again and became an annual event until Castro came to power and discontinued the race. But the tradition was still alive, especially in the bar and halls of St. Pete Yacht Club.

In early May of 1996 I got the call and my friend told me an unofficial St. Pete to Havana race was in the planning stage and wanted to know if I would be interested in crewing in the race. The major concern of fellow boaters was not the Cuban government, but the U.S. State Department. The official word now was that the penalty for any U.S. boat caught in Cuba would be confiscation of the boat and heavy fines for the captain. That got every boat owners attention who even considered going to Cuba. The real challenge for the State Department, was knowing who went to Cuba. The U.S. State Department and the Cuban government do not talk to each other and the U.S. Coast Guard did not patrol the Cuban marinas, so how were they to know. The result was a few brave boat owners got together and decided to make the race unofficially and on the QT. I said "Put my name on the list". The Commodore of the Havana Club, Club Natico, was notified and the race was scheduled. I was assigned a captain and on the recommendation of my friend I agreed to crew with little knowledge of the boat or the owner or much else. I wanted to see Cuba and felt this may be my only chance. After a quick SouthWest flight and taxi trip to the boat I saw my ride for the first time. From the dock she was impressive. A well cared for early 70s 41 foot Morgan OutIsland Sloop. Designed and built by the famous Charlie Morgan who had sailed the St. Pete to Havana race in 1957 and placed second. His 40 foot design won the SORC race (Southern Ocean Racing Conference) in 1961 and 1962. That design was the basis for the extremely popular OutIsland model sailboat. As far as boats go the Morgan 41 is hard to beat. In addition, my home town of Tampa held Charlie Morgan as a local hero since he had graduated from the University of Tampa. I knocked on the hull and asked if the captain was aboard. Up from the main hatch popped a head that was less impressive than the boat. The head said, "Who wants to know"? I said, I'm Mike and I'm your crew for the race"! He looked at me and I looked at him and he said without much enthusiasm "Come aboard". The interior of the boat was just as nice as the outside but was showing its age in places. But nevertheless, I had been on a lot of boats and this one would place high on the list of very good boats. The owner was Bill and he said he had been a CPA for the City of New York and had retired to the South. He was single and looked to be about 60, although, it appeared to have been a rough 60. He was about 6'3" and weighed maybe 180lbs. His balding head showed scrapes and scars from where he had banged his head on the overhead and maybe the boom. Like most fulltime liveaboards his attire was not much. A pair of old shorts, a tanktop and flipflops. What little hair he had was grayish brown/red and flopped one way and then the other as the wind blew. His gray beard was more of not caring to shave as one of design. If not being the owner of such a fine boat he would not be out of place on a busy street corner with a sign saying "Homeless-Need Food. Please Help!" This was my captain? He offered me a beer and we sat in the main salon and talked to get to know each other. He told me a story of a divorce after his retirement and sadly said "She took everything except his retirement check and the boat", and then smiled. He said he had made the trip to Havana several times and wanted to be part of the first St. Pete to Havana race since the late 50's. He told me he had friends in Havana and knew his way around. He said he would have a friend meet us at Marina Hemmingway as soon as we cleared customs and were assigned a dock space. Maybe I should have been suspicious with his familiarity of a place Americans are not supposed to go, but at this point I was just happy to have a boat to crew.

The next day we provisioned the boat and took on fuel and checked the weather. All seemed good. The race was without a start and was more of camouflage for a trip to Cuba than it was a formal race. Bill thought a straight shot to Havana might draw some interest by the Coast Guard if they happen to be watching from the sky or radar. So we would set sail for the Dry Tortugas, a small group of islands 70 miles west of Key West. We planned a departure for that afternoon. When I ask about the rest of the crew he just shrugged and said they couldn't get off work. Well, OK we can do this, I think? We cast the lines, raised the sails and set the course. After the sails were trimmed and the auto helm was set Bill fixed a great supper which we enjoyed in the cockpit as the sun was setting. The weather was perfect. A 15 kt breeze coming from the north gave us a beam reach to our destination. We agreed on a watch schedule of four hours on and four off starting at 2200hrs or 10pm. I always like to see the sun come up so I took the second watch and turned in. At 0200 I was awakened and given a brief update on the trip. Our over ground speed was averaging a little over eight kts. We were still getting a push from the Gulf Stream and the waves were about two feet. It's hard to get better than this. After I settled in behind the wheel and sipping on the mug of hot chocolate my captain had ready for me, I began to enjoy the moment. Sailing at night in open water is like nothing else. The sky is full of stars and without city lights it seems the whole sky is full of lights of varying degree of intensity. Occasionally you will see a falling star. The water even has lights. The bow wave stirs up fluorescent algae to make a green glow coming from the front of the boat. As the boat slips through the water, a few breaking waves can be heard. The winds in the sails have their own way of adding a pleasant sound to night. A rush of air from a dolphin breaching near the cockpit caught my attention, but then I realized it was just a friend saying hello. As daybreak nears, the sky will turn such beautiful colors that can only be seen on open waters. By the end of my watch I put the coffee on so we could share a cup of coffee before the daily routine began. The sun was full and the day was warming by the time we adjusted the sails and checked our position on the GPS. We then compared our latitude and longitude reading to the chart. Our ETA at the Dry Tortugas would be early afternoon.

Ponce de Leon is credited with naming the small group of Islands after the Turtles seen in the area, in1513. There is no fresh water on the islands so it was marked "Dry" on the charts and so became known as the Dry Tortugas. A light was added in 1825 and Fort Jefferson began construction in 1846 to guard the Gulf and protect the commercial traffic coming down the Mississippi and headed to the Atlantic Ocean. During the Civil War Fort Jefferson was used to house military prisoners and even held Dr. Mudd and three other men convicted of complicity in the assassination of President Lincoln. But the remoteness and design of the fort led to its abandonment in 1874. Today it is a national park and wildlife refuge. Float planes and fast ferries deliver tourist to the island from Key West. Overnight stays are only by boat and in selected anchorages.

The high six sided brick walls can be seen from miles out to sea. It is such an unusual sight, with water everywhere and then this huge brick fortress that consumes almost all the island. Navigation to the small dock and gatehouse is done over clear but shallow water and coral heads that seem to be just below the surface. We docked the boat and were told by a park ranger that docking was prohibited. We talked our way into a brief stay, long enough for a quick tour and a visit to the cell where Dr. Mudd was jailed. We had the entire place to ourselves. The hour long self guided tour was not long enough to see or appreciate the entire fort, but it was a special event, especially for a person who enjoys and studies the history of that era. Back on the boat we were getting ready to shove off when a commercial shrimp boat pulled up beside us. I hailed the captain and asked if he would trade some shrimp for beer. We quickly agreed a bucket of fresh Florida Pinks were worth a six-pack of beer. What a deal!! You just can't beat fresh Florida Pink Shrimp. I watched as the mate took my bucket and climbed down the ladder into the hole of the boat. I winced as he bumped his head on the steel hatch cover. He was gone less than a minute when he started up the ladder with a bucket full of ice covered shrimp and again bumped his head on the hatch cover. That must be a requirement for a mate on a shrimp boat, to have a head as strong as steel. We departed and set a course to the southeast and still within site of the fort when I had some shrimp boiling on the stove using only the gulf water for the boil. As the sun set on our second day we sat with our bellies full and a beer in hand to celebrate the day. Life is good!!

The next afternoon we spotted the tall buildings of Havana. OK, I admit I was nervous. There we were just off the cost of Cuba. I had wanted to see this site for many years, yet I had mixed emotions and some degree of fear. I asked Bill if he thought it was time to call the Cubans and let them know we were in their waters. He said "Not yet." Another hour passed and now I could see the walls of El Castillo del Morro, the aged fort at the entrance to the Havana harbor and the famous sea wall at downtown Havana and Malecon Highway. I asked again if we should call the Cuban Coast Guard. Bill didn't seem too concerned, so I said "They are going to send the coast guard out and sink us!" Bill looked up at me and smiled again and said "Not to worry, The Cubans don't have enough gas to come out and sink us". We turned to the starboard and took a heading that paralleled us to the coast. I kept a lookout over my shoulder, watching for a Cuban Coast Guard vessel with guns blazing. It didn't happen and in a few minutes Bill made the call for permission to enter Marina Hemmingway which is nine miles west of Havana. Marina Hemmingway is, yes, named after famed American author Ernest Hemmingway who lived in Havana until Castro took over. Hemmingway loved Cuba and the Cubans loved him and still hold him in high esteem. The marina was built as part of the Pan American Games of 1991. Those games are remembered for the upset the Cubans delivered to the United States by winning 140 gold to US 130 gold metals.

We stopped at the check in point and were told to stay aboard our boat. The Cuban government has a job for everyone. In the communist structure everyone works for the mother country. The mother country has full employment. The practical application of this means that instead of one or two custom officials coming aboard as we would have in the US, there are six Cuban officials taking turns to come aboard. First, two customs officials request the boat papers and a list of the people aboard and their passports. Next, the Army arrived with three officers, two came aboard and one stayed on shore. We had been told that these folks require a cold beer in order to clear your boat. While they drank their beer, we were asked questions about firearms and contraband. Also, they wanted to know if we had any pornography. I guess they wanted to maintain the purity of the country. After they cleared us a doctor came aboard to lift our quarantine. We were able to keep our clothes on during the questioning but were asked questions that would violate our HIPPA laws in the U.S. We were given our papers and assigned a slip and told we could take down our "Q" flag from our starboard shrouds. The "Q" flag is a yellow flag hoisted by foreign boaters to signify that they have not been cleared by customs. After customs cleared the boat the yellow flag was replaced by the Cuban national flag as a courtesy to our host country while our American flag still flew from the transom of the boat. We motored to our slip, which was a starboard tie with boats docked bow to stern along the concrete wall. The grassy medium between the channels was well kept and at a distance the area appeared to live up to the standards we would expect from this country's flag marina. An electrician met us at the assigned slip and wired our electrical cord to the dock box. At all the marinas to which I docked before that time the electrical cord was just plugged into the dock box. The reason an electrician was needed at Marina Hemmingway is that the Russians built the electrical system and nothing fits the Russian receptacles. The receptacle in the box had long since been snipped out and tossed in the channel and now just live wires were left hanging out. Like other dock boxes this one also had the water lines run to it. The water faucets were also built by the Russians and leaked like you would expect a Russian water spigot to leak. The water and the electrical wires were able to comingle. So we waited until the electrician had completed his work and he had wrapped all the electrical lines with black electrical tape before we thought about stepping off the boat and onto wet Cuban soil.

True to his word, Bill's friend, Roberto, showed up shortly after we had tied up and put the boat to bed. Roberto drove across the grassy medium and parked a small vehicle of unknown origin next to our boat. The car appeared to be 10 to 20 years old and must have been made in Russia, since U.S. vehicles were part of the embargo. It could have been French because it looked like a three passenger Fiat. Regardless, it was a set of wheels and we were ready to see the town. We loaded up and headed to Havana. What a strange and beautiful place. The Cuban people have very little. They have a saying that if you see a fat Cuban you have found a government official or a crook. The people have to be frugal and waste nothing. Remember, they work for the country. All the hotels have resident doctors who could probably pass the board here in the states, but yet they get paid the same as the person who cleans the guest rooms or sweeps the streets. It is said that they get $30.00 per month and all the beans and rice they can eat. As we were riding into town, we saw all the small children walking home from school. There were no school buses, they walked. Each child was dressed in the uniform of the school they attended. They were beautiful children in brightly colored uniforms and all were neat and clean. Motor scooters were as popular as cars and no vehicle carried less than its capacity. It was the law. No one drove by himself. If you didn't have a car, you could stand on the edge of the road and you would get a ride. It was required! Even a dump truck returning from dumping its load was required to pick up people. Everyone helped and did it with a good attitude. Frequently, a motor scooter would pass with the whole family riding down the road. Father would be driving with a small child in his lap. Behind him would be another child and then at the rear would be the mother. As we drew closer to town, we could see the disrepair that we heard about. We saw the crumbling walls and the roofs that had fallen in with large pieces of plaster missing from most structures and the faded paint. The streets were clean and the limited traffic moved with ease. But if anything beyond manpower was needed, then it most likely did not get done. Since everyone works for the government and got very little money for their efforts it is easy to see why everyone has a side job. The culture is based on the black market. If you owned a car you could use it as an illegal taxi. If you possessed mechanical skills you could fix taxies on the side. You could turn your apartment into a restaurant, and if you are a woman with good looks you would work the tourist trade. Everyone works part time just to survive. We parked the car and walked to a walkup apartment that had been turned into a restaurant. We were seated at Bill's favorite black market restaurant.

The tables had linen table cloths with linen napkins and we were waited on by several waiters. The food was very good and the service, the best. I was even able to buy a round of drinks for my new friends and was pleasantly surprised to find this little ad hock café carried Jack Daniels Black Label. We settled up and left a generous tip and everyone was happy. American greenbacks were the preferred money.

We took a tour of downtown and watched a man change the clutch of his 1957 Ford Fairlane 500 parked on the street in front of the Capitol building. If a car breaks down, it is most likely fixed at that spot. The Capitol building is a smaller replica of our own Capitol. Now the Politburo meets there. We drove back to the marina which was a controlled area. One needed to be a guest, or invited by a guest, to get in the marina. We checked into Club Natico and found a welcoming committee with the club Commodore and a representative from the Cuban government, dressed in the uniform Castro made famous welcoming the sailboat racers from Florida. They were welcoming the sailors who had braved to sail to Cuba against the wishes of the U.S. Government in order to sail a race that had been celebrated in Cuba for several generations. The race had attracted about a dozen boats from various ports. All were happy to be there and the Cubans were glad we were there. They made us feel welcome; we took pictures and bought souvenirs. So much for the economic embargo!

The next day was reserved for boat work and more site-seeing. The dinghy was launched and the marina was explored. The Cuban officials watch all boats and are skeptical of any craft that could be used to smuggle Cuban citizens to Florida. Pleasure boats do not come and go in the marina. Once there, you stay until you clear customs for departure. Riding around the channels in the marina was OK as long as no Cubans were aboard your boat. I returned to the boat and reported that the dingy outboard motor was not running very well. Roberto, who now seemed to be living aboard the boat, took to the challenge. Within a few minutes he had the carburetor disassembled and laid out in the cockpit. He went about meticulously cleaning each part with gasoline and a toothbrush. I climbed out of the cabin into the cockpit and to my amazement spotted him smoking a cigarette while cleaning the carburetor. I quickly said "Roberto, Roberto, "no smoke while cleaning with gas"!! He causally looked up and said, "No worry Miguel, this is Cuban gasoline". He kept cleaning and smoking and we didn't blow up, so I guess he knew what he was talking about. Plus, the engine ran great after his work. Later we all loaded into the car and decided to see some of the Island. We traveled the main roads but most were only two-lane roads. We didn't see many cars but Roberto was always on the lookout for the government car or local police who may stop him for carrying passengers for hire. Occasionally Roberto would make a detour to avoid a known traffic stop. Once we were riding down the road and we heard a loud bang and the engine started running rough and making strange noises. Roberto pulled over to the side of the road and shut the engine off. I just knew the engine had blown and was equally sure that we were in an area not serviced by AAA. Roberto did not seem too concerned. He walked back up the road about 50 yards and picked up something. He returned to the car and showed us a sparkplug. He then said something about "No problemo". He wrapped a piece of aluminum foil around the threads, and with a pair of rusty vice grips he reinstalled the sparkplug and off we went. "No problemo". We saw a lot of agriculture but not many tractors. We saw more horse drawn carts than tractors.

The highlight of our stop was Hemmingway's house. It is on the outskirts of Havana in a modest neighborhood and looks to be surrounded by 15-20 acres of mostly woods. It has been turned into a tourist attraction and has a rock wall surrounding the property. We got to the gate but found it closed. We ask Roberto why it was closed and he said he would check it out. In a few minutes he returned with a uniformed guard who opened the gate. Roberto told us to give the guard $5.00 and explained we could not use the restrooms. It seems the septic tank had stopped up and so it was closed until it could be repaired. The $5.00 allowed us a private showing. WOW! Just the three of us walked through Hemmingway's house; saw his bed, bathroom and writing tower. The best part of the tour was the Pilar. His famous fishing boat!! This is the real Pilar, the one he traveled from the Dry Tortugas to the Biminis and Key West to Havana. He wrote parts of books and articles, made love to women, hunted German Subs and helped survivors of the tragic results of the Hurricane that struck the Keys in 1935, all aboard The Pilar. Here she sat on the hard behind the house Hemmingway called "Finca", which is Spanish for estate. Pilar sat in a drained swimming pool at about deck to ground level. We were not permitted to go aboard because she was in disrepair and even with a patio type cover over the display she still had visible rotting in several places.

The boat was ordered from Wheeler Shipyard Inc. in New York, NY in April 1935. On the invoice she is described as a 38 foot twin cabin Playmate cruiser. She was designed with one Chrysler engine and a trolling motor. She had four 75 gal gas tanks, two copper lined fish boxes, and a live fish well. The hull was painted black and the name "Pilar of Key West" added to the transom before it was delivered to Hemmingway. The total cost was $7,455. The boat, as displayed, still had beautiful lines and a regal design. As I stood looking at this beauty, it didn't take much imagination to visualize Ernest at the helm or on the aft deck with his pole in the socket and a huge marlin at the end of the line. This was worth the trip. What a hero he was to so many and idol to others. Was this a hero's boat?

The next day we checked out of Marina Hemmingway and again the government group came on board, only this time to make sure we didn't have any locals hidden away. Captain Bill said we would sail up the coast before departing Cuban waters. "I'm just along for the ride." I offered. As the sun was setting we pulled into a little harbor that had one lone pier tucked in behind a small island. We tied to the dock with no help from anyone. We finally found a man dressed in the national brown government uniform and said we were here for the night and offered him the customary beer. We got the OK to stay but soon found out the generator for the small dock and island was broken and we would have to depend on our boat house batteries for our needs. With no electricity, there was also no power to pump water to the island, so we showered onboard the boat. Such is life in Cuba. The good part was an old man standing on the dock with a live lobster about 15 inches long, and he wanted to trade it for a beer. Trade done, we chopped the tail off this big boy and Bill and I had the delicious sweet lobster for supper. I turned in happy and full. What a trip this had turned out to be and it wasn't finished yet.

About 4:00 in the morning I heard a tapping on the hull just above my bunk. Bill had the forward vee berth and I had the aft watch berth. I got up and went on deck to see two Cuban men in a small rowboat quietly talking to me in Spanish. Since I don't speak Spanish I just watched. They didn't seem to be a threat, but did want me to do something. My first thought was they wanted to come aboard and I wasn't going to let that happen. Finally I saw they wanted to give me something. They handed me a sailbag full of something. A sailbag is like a big laundry bag where a sailor keeps his sail. Sailbags usually have a sewn on handle to make it easier to move about or carry a heavy sail. This one was full and I needed both hands to load it aboard. The men in the rowboat said "You take"… I put the bag on the rail and they rowed off. By the time I woke Bill the men were out of site. I told Bill of the incident and he went topside to inspect the sailbag. I watched as he opened it and exposed a full bag of assorted Coheba cigars, all neatly wrapped with the familiar yellow and black Coheba logo. I have to admit, I don't know much about cigars. I guess I have smoked less than a dozen in my entire life, but I know the Coheba brand. No telling how much money now rests in that worn old sailbag. Coheba is Castro's own brand of cigars. He started the state owned company in 1966 with the goal that it would be the best cigar made from the very best tobacco especially grown for the Coheba label. Since then the Coheba brand has grown to cult status and is always judged as one of the very best by cigar aficionados. And just think, two men in a row boat just dropped these off. My excitement waned as I started thinking about how all this happened and where I was. Then Bill smiled and casually stated "I deliver a few cigars back to the states when I come down here." O great! Now I am in the middle of a cigar smuggling operation. Bill said, "Don't worry, the only thing real is the Coheba label. The cigars are rolled in a farm house nearby and Roberto supplies the labels from the factory." O Great again!! Not only am I in the middle of a cigar smuggling operation, but it is the Supreme Commanders own cigar. In addition, we have stolen labels from his company. Now as I sat in the cockpit with coffee in hand I was thinking, "Which would be worse, getting caught smuggling Cuban cigars into the USA or getting caught in Cuba with El Generals counterfeit brand." I quickly decide the USA is where I want to serve my prison time. I yelled to Bill "Let's get outa here." We shoved off and as the sun peaked over the horizon we were headed back to Florida. Bill designed our arrival to coincide with the docking of the cruise ships and the thousand travelers disembarking and being cleared by customs. When I ask Bill about customs he said "They're too busy to worry about us, besides I didn't check out with them." We docked the boat and I made a hasty good- by and thanks for a memorable trip. And Bill," Please forget that you met me!!"

Sailboat *Lifestyle*
By: Chuck Williams

Chapter 3

Johnny Crash

Back on the Cumberland River on a mooring ball at Harbor Island Yacht Club, *Lifestyle* was taking shape and my knowledge had increased with the regular club races and thoughtful study. Although I still had many practical lessons to learn, I was gaining in confidence and felt my trip down the Tombigbee would be in my near future. The saying goes that there are only two types of sailors: those who have run aground and those that will run aground. One of my many grounding lessons would occur on the Cumberland River. My friend Chuck Williams and I decided to sail up the lake a few miles and see if we could spot the famous singer Johnny Cash's home. I was told it was a large white house that set in a slight cove above the river and had a curved room with lots of windows overlooking the river. The wind was coming out of the east at about 15mph and with warm temperatures it seemed like a perfect day for a sail. Sailors say when you think about reefing, that is the time you should reef your sails. We had the main full and the headsail rolled all the way out. We trimmed the sails and we were on a hard beat at hull speed up river toward Johnny's house. After a while the wind began to freshen (blow harder) and was now gusting close to 20mph.

One of my studies included the Beaufort scale of wind force. A scale devised by Admiral Sir Francis Beaufort in 1808. The scale grades the effect of the wind on the water. At the wind speed we experienced a sailor would see moderate waves with some spray. The wind on the lake was showing that effect. Was it time to reef? Maybe it was past time. But we were making such good speed, the boat was balanced and the rail was just about to touch the water so I held off reefing the sails. We were really going fast and it felt so good. I was unfamiliar with this part of the lake and had not reviewed the chart nor did I even think to glance at the depth finder. Then I looked up and saw the most scary thing a sailor can see, a bird standing directly in my path and his knees were above the water. Another clue that I was in very shallow water was the weeds and grass growing out of the water.

Lifestyle was a 35' sailboat with a deep draft that needed almost six feet depth with the keel straight down. On a beat the boat healed over and the keel was at an angle which required much less water. I now had a choice. I could tack the boat and in doing so, my keel would go straight down in the process or I could continue to sail the boat into Johnny Cash's back yard. I chose to tack and quickly came to a stop in the Tennessee mud. The sails were still full but the boat was stopped. When a boat is hard aground like this, your objective is to get it back in deep water. The motor was no help, the sails are no help. I didn't have a dingy so I could not take an anchor to kedge or pull me back into deep water. I couldn't lighten the load because it was just Chuck and me, so I did the next best thing I could think of. I called a friend. A fellow boater and friend found us about an hour later. We discussed the situation and decided I needed to configure the boat the same way it was when it ran aground only heading out. His plan was to attach a line to the bow of the boat and pull it around so that it faced deep water. That worked reasonably well and even though his boat was only a 30' sailboat he was able to turn the bow with several attempts. We then raised the sails and started the motor. We weren't ready yet. Next he attached the rope that he had used for the bow to an extra main halyard. The main halyard went to the top of the mast. That rope pulled from my mast head and allowed his boat to heal my boat over till my rail was almost touching the water. That angle resulted in reducing the draft to about three feet. That helped considerably since *Lifestyle* was in about two feet of water and four of mud. His boat had a strong motor but did not weigh as much as *Lifestyle* and the healing over would only be a minute or less.

He would head off in his boat at a 90 degree angle to get a good pull and I would rev my engine. Each effort would gain us about ten feet. After about an hour of this, we both looked for additional help. It came in the form of a 15' ski boat that was sitting close by watching these two sailboats struggle to not look stupid. I hailed the ski boat and ask the captain if he would offer a little forward tow and pull me out while my friend healed me over. The captain of the ski boat was, as it seemed to me to be a senior citizen out for an afternoon cruise with his wife. But being good boaters, they agreed and soon we had a line attached from his stern to the bow of my boat. With all my sails out, my motor running, a sailboat attached to the extra main halyard pulling sideways and a ski boat attached to a bow line pulling forward I gave the signal and Chuck revved our motor and all pulled. The wind was still gusting close to 20mph and just then a nice gust came along and filled the sails and bang… I was out… sailing in deep water again. The only problem was, *Lifestyle* was a much larger boat than the other two boats that she was towing. We were towing a 30' sailboat and 15' ski boat, both of them backwards as we started gaining speed. Chuck was at the helm of *Lifestyle* and I was trying to uncleat the tow lines and loosen the sheets for the sails. The ski boat couple was in the most peril because of the low freeboard at their transom. They were in danger of being swamped. In addition, he had his tow line cleated and locked. With the strain on the line he could not uncleat it. A knife or ax would have been helpful. I learned from that experience to never cleat a line you may need to release quickly. After a few anxious moments, we soon got everything under control but not before the speed and weight of *Lifestyle* had ripped the aft rail off my friend's sailboat and scared a couple of folks out for an evening cruise in their ski boat to the point of hyperventilation. Our nerves had calmed by the time we picked up our mooring ball in the bay. The cost of replacing the aft rail on my friends' boat was minor but I was never able to find the ski boat owner to thank him. My guess is, he decided that he did not want to have anything to do with sail boats or their owners every again.

Time was approaching when the stars would align so that I could move *Lifestyle* to warmer waters. I felt I knew my boat and she was, as most boats are, "much better than the captain". I had educated myself in boating and my experience allowed me to sit for the USCG six pack license. The six pack license is the first level of a USCG Commercial Captains License and gets its nickname "six pack" because it limits the number of passengers to six on the vessel. My two sons were out of school and on their own and I had taken an early retirement. In addition, my wife had filed for divorce and I was ready to spend the winter in Florida and be an official "parrothead". Also the fall of the year was approaching and I didn't want to winterize my engine again. I loaded the boat with supplies and with a member from the yacht club, we headed out.

The club was on Old Hickory Lake east of Nashville and our first stop would be at Old Hickory Lock and Dam. This is a TVA power producing dam which impounds 22,500 acres of water at an elevation of 445 feet above sea level and extends almost 100 miles into Middle Tennessee. I was excited about this adventure as we cast off from our mooring at Harbor Island Yacht Club. I had studied boating, learned racing and practiced getting off groundings many times and had a boat that would take me where I wanted to go, and so what could go wrong? The one thing that I failed to do was contact the Corps of Engineers, which control the rivers and locks, and request information on the condition of the rivers, locks and dams. With the dam in sight I contacted the lockmaster of the Old Hickory Lock and Dam on the VHF and ask permission to lock through. He opened the massive doors and signaled me with a green light. We pulled into the lock and tied to a floating bollard. There are about as many methods of tying or controlling your boat once inside a lock as there are locks. Old Hickory Lock has a floating bollard. It is a steel drum that has a place on top to loop a line. The bollard acts like a float and stays at the same location on the water as your boat, thus you don't have to adjust lines as the water raises or lowers. It is a great system and gravity does all the work. Well not exactly, the water rushing in or draining out will take control of your boat and you will think a demon has hold of it. I was told to reduce the action of the boat just tie a line from bow to stern, put a loop in the middle and loop it over the floating bollard. In theory and in the books it looks good but in actuality it is a thing of mystery. Later, in my years of traveling, I would have a boater tell me "Just tie a line to the bollard and cleat if off tight midship and let your fenders do all the work for you". But on this day I was using the bow/stern line method and fighting the boat to keep it from getting sideways in the lock. The water finally drained down and before the lockmaster opened the gates he strolled down from his watchtower to meet this green Captain in his pretty sailboat. Standing beside the boat, he asks "Whereya headed?" That's Tennessee for where are you going? I proudly told him I was going South for the winter! He said "Well ya know Cheatums closed!"?? Cheatum Lock and Dam is on the west side of Nashville and was between me and the warm South. Not to look too foolish I said "That's OK; we're stopping in Nashville for fuel". He opened the doors and off we went. Now, as the crow fly's we were only about 5 miles from downtown Nashville but a river seldom takes the straight route. It would take the better part of the day before we were tied up to the small transit dock at the foot of Broadway Street in Nashville. Our last trip here had been after we left Rock Harbor Marina. From our dock we could walk to some great places to eat or visit some of the great historical sites in Nashville.

This is the same waterfront where paddlewheelers made Captain Ryman a wealthy man in the 1800's. It is also the place where in February of 1862 Mayor Cheatham surrendered the city to a Union Captain and a dozen troops by rowing across the river under a flag of truce and delivered the city to the North without a fight. In that spot now sits an NFL stadium and home of the Tennessee Titans. Tootsies Orchid Lounge is a couple of blocks up Broadway and is known for the many famous country music stars, who got their start there, while working for tips. It's across the alley from the Ryman Auditorium which was home of the Grand Ole Opry until they moved across town in1974 and is named after Captain Ryman. High on a hill within site of the Cumberland River is Capitol Hill and home of the state capitol building. The construction of the building was started in 1845, and it was still under construction when the Civil War started. It is said that future president Andrew Johnson would watch for Confederate troops from the copula. The building is still used as the State Capitol and is one of a few still in use from that era.

The following day we departed for our fuel stop and the prior home of *Lifestyle*, Rock Harbor Marina. It is here she was launched and much of the cleaning and repairs were initiated. A call to the Cheatham Lock and Dam gave me the bad news. The lock was still closed for repairs and they were not sure when it would open. Since the boat was provisioned and fueled, I thought I would check back in a couple of days. Thirty days later the lock was still not open and with winter just around the corner I called the trip off until spring. I took the time to add a tee in the water cooling system so I could flush the water and winterize the engine in one quick step. The water tanks also needed winterizing and I used a method that a fellow boater told me would get the job done. I drained the tanks as best I could and then added a half gallon of cheap vodka to each tank. The vodka kept the lines from freezing and also had other benefits. When spring came and you needed some water from the tanks it would be free of any algae.

Spring did finally come but by that time my crew had long since departed and I could not find anyone that wanted to take on the challenge. I decided to go it alone and departed Nashville on a spring morning. The spring rains had been heavy and lots of trash had washed into the river. The current had also increased because of the large amount of water that was shed into the Cumberland. I reached the Cheatham Lock by noon and had to wait for a tow with barges to clear. I got my first lesson on the power of these tows by getting in the wake of his props. My deep draft sailboat was in no danger but I got bounced around to the point that I broke out in a sweat. I am a solo sailor now and there was no one to take the helm or solve problems except me. I did have an auto helm and could use it on at straight-aways for head calls or to grab a quick snack. The river requires more attention to the helm than open water and with all the trash in the river it was not a good idea to leave the wheel for even a 30 second break. My lunch became a can of beans or a sandwich that I would prepare before I departed for the day. The concentration needed was so intense that my eyes would be burning at the end of the day. At noon on the third day I reached the cut that allows a boater to jump off the Cumberland River and onto the Tennessee River. I was finally sailing south but now against the current. I had motored from east of Nashville to almost Paducah, Kentucky before turning south onto the Tennessee River which would take me to the Tombigbee.

The Tennessee River is almost a mile wide at this point and it felt good to be able to raise the mainsail and let out the roller furling headsail. It is a wonderful thing to have a gentle breeze at your back and your sails trimmed and the engine off. A quite gentle spring day on the lake and a sailboat under your command is very special. During the week this area is almost void of recreational traffic. No sound could be heard except the few birds and the gentle splash of the bow sliding over the waves. After an hour of pleasant sailing, I spotted a cove on the east side of the river and sailed into it rolling my headsail in as I approached. I was watching my depth finder closely but I had studied the chart and I knew this area had plenty of water. I turned 180 degrees and dropped the mainsail. Letting it fall onto the deck. As *Lifestyle* settled to a stop I was ready at the bow to shove the anchor overboard. Everything had worked out perfectly. I was in about 15 feet of water and knowing I had soft mud for the bottom I chose a 25lb Danforth anchor with almost 100 feet of rode. A good tug back and the anchor was set. A snubber, or line, connected to the rode and then to a strong cleat meant I could sleep well and not fear the anchor dragging in the night. Sailors hate to drop the anchor, go to bed, wake the next morning only to find they are in a different place, or even worse to hear a large bump in the night. Designing a good ground tackle system is basic to good boating. It starts with an anchor designed for the boat and the bottom and then the rode or line is attached. The preferred rode is chain. Most sailboats use a combination of chain and three strand rope in order to save some onboard weight. If they are going to be anchoring out often and in unfamiliar areas, then an all chain rode is preferred. At the same time, a good Captain should not scrimp on the windless or the retrieving mechanism. An extra strong windless will last longer and may save your boat if it runs aground and no one is available to tow you off. To pull yourself off a soft grounding, take the anchor out by loading it into your dinghy and dropping it as far out as needed. Set the anchor and use the windless to kedge or pull the boat to the deeper water.

The cove I chose to anchor in that day is called Land-Between-the-Lakes. LBL, as it is known, is a nature reserve. It is the area between Lake Barkley and Kentucky Lake which was formed when the Cumberland River and the Tennessee River were impounded to form the lakes in 1963. The area has 170,000 acres of mostly undeveloped land and over 300 miles of pristine shoreline. It is considered the largest inland peninsula in the United States. Development of any kind is strictly regulated by the U.S. Forrest Service. Since there are few lights around, the night can be fully enjoyed. The sounds from the woods are without the sound pollution we are accustomed to in the city. With a nice warm breeze from the south, it was a great end to a hard day of boating. Only six more days to Pickwick State Park and a break to go back home and catch up on some business. It would take me over two weeks to get to Pickwick by boat but only about three hours to get home by car.

The leg after this is the Tombigbee, the river system between Pickwick and Mobile. The rains had continued and the rivers were high but I was going with the current on this leg, and the travel would be fast. I now had my son, Andy, with me and the trip was much easier with a mate aboard. Andy is a hard worker and loves the outdoors. We shared duties and the trip was smooth except the few occasions when I could not find a good place to anchor or I ran aground. We stopped in Demopolis, Alabama on a rainy Friday night and were amazed by the amount of trash in the water at the dock. It seems that all the upstream logs and debris stops in the curve of the river at Demopolis. They even had a 14 foot John boat with a board across the bow to push the trash back into the river. It worked like a road grader on water. The marina was old and rundown and it was not a pleasant place on a rainy night. To make matters worse, we were docked beside a liveaboard couple in a 50 foot houseboat who we all agreed needed a mental evaluation. We were warned by the dock hands to put out lots of fenders, so if our boat touched his boat it would not hurt his house-trailer on the water. We were careful but uneasy. We heard later that he had been a meter reader on the south side of Chicago and received a medical retirement after he got locked in a basement for a couple of days by a gang of punks who thought he was snooping around for the police.

After a night and a day in Demopolis, Andy said we either had to leave or he was going to hitchhike home. We refueled and headed south. *Lifestyle* had a 47 foot mast and I had been worried about my ability to get under certain bridges. All the rain had raised the rivers to flood stage and the distance between the water and the fixed bridges was significantly reduced. I called other boats on the VHF and ask about the bridges I was unsure of the clearance. Just past Demopolis we were approaching a sailboat with his mast down headed our way. I hailed the captain and ask about the bridge up ahead. The chart showed the bridge to be a fixed railroad bridge with a height of 50 feet. That is the minimum height for the waterway. But with the rain and high water I was not sure we could make it. He called back and said we would never make 47 feet. We looked at each other and wondered if we were going to have to stay in Demopolis till the waters receded. We were both sad that our voyage could end in a town that Andy called "the armpit of the south." I said "We've got to try the bridge." We motored on and soon spotted the bridge. Then I saw to my relief that the bridge had a tower. It was a swing bridge and I called the bridge tender to open it for me. All was good once again. Four days later we arrived at Turner Marine after a bumpy ride across Mobile Bay. Supper that night was at a local restaurant to celebrate our voyage. On our return to the boat the cab driver hydroplaned and almost hit a bridge. Would this rain every stop? We were safe now with *Lifestyle* at its new home, Turner Marine. Andy had to return to work and I needed to round up a few friends to crew across the Gulf, so we rented a car and drove back to Tennessee.

A few weeks later with Thom and Ceile Garrison, friends from Harbor Island Yacht Club, and a sailing friend, Robert Buzby from Tampa, we set out to cross the Gulf. At that time the weather patterns were two bad days followed by three good days, meaning a front would pass and you would be able to ride the winds across the Gulf. We started across from the Pensacola cut and set a course for Tarpon Springs. We figured it would be about a 30 hour sail. With a full mainsail and full headsail we were making hull speed and having a great sail. We assigned watch duties and established rules for doing work at night. Anyone in the cockpit would wear their Personal Flotation Device (PFD) and anyone going forward would snap a lanyard to a jack line and their PFD. Tom and Ciel had sailed the Atlantic and back and shared their experience. Robert had sailed in many club races. I wanted my first crossing of the Gulf to have a lot of experienced sailors. Although *Lifestyle* was my boat and I felt everything was ready for the crossing, it was good to have Thom and his lovely wife Ceile, give it their blessing. Soon we were off-shore and Thom proposed a salute to King Neptune. Since no virgins were available to sacrifice, we settled on a beer toast. No one liked it when Robert laughed at our toast to King Neptune and refused to pour a portion of his beer in the water. Bad JuJu!!, no way to start a trip! We had a nice meal and watches were assigned and the crew went to bed. Robert came on watch at 0600 and the wind started to pick up. What had been a nice sail with a fresh breeze from the south became a mild squall with gust above 20 knots. Before we could reduce the sail area we heard a loud bang and the mainsail was blown to shreds. We turned into the wind and started making reductions and repairs. The main had ripped at the first seam so it was just reefed at the ripped point and with the headsail rolled in about a third, we turned back to our heading. Later, after things had settled down a little, the captain, as well as Thom and Ceile, voted to sacrifice a crew member to King Neptune for calmer seas. Robert was selected and just as we told him we were going to toss him overboard, we spotted the light at Anclote Island at the entrance to Tarpon Springs. He was saved by the bell or light in this case.

We docked at the city docks and found a shower and good place to eat. Both were within 50 feet of the dock. Robert did earn his worth by having a vehicle ready for our use waiting at the dock. The first item on my list was to locate a sail maker. I was lucky to find a good sail maker just a few miles down the road. I delivered the blown head sail to him for a repair. After a few minutes of evaluation we both concluded that a new sail was needed. I ordered the new sail and gave him a down payment. The cost would be about the same as changing out an engine. So why am I sailing? I guess at this point in my life I didn't know any better. I delivered Thom and Ceile to Tampa International Airport and

Robert to his house. When I returned to the city dock, I moved *Lifestyle* to a nearby marina and signed a long term lease. This would be a good place to have work done on the boat, enjoy Gulf sailing and the city of Tarpon Springs.

Tarpon Springs is a tourist stop to land travelers but for sea goers it is an important stopping place for boaters of all sorts. It's a direct route from the Florida panhandle or any place along the coast. For slow boats like a sailboat or a trawler, it is an overnight cruise to most of the popular ports. Once you arrive, you have many marinas from which to choose. The City dock is a favorite because it is downtown and cheap. From there you can choose a better marina, like I did, or move on down the coast of Florida staying in the intracostal waterway. *Lifestyle*'s new home was on the Anclote River and a short drive to town or over to Tampa. Since I was now a live aboard, I had the time to take care of many of those time consuming items, like cleaning and varnishing all the teak. That is not a job for a lazy person or a person who needs immediate gratification. Cleaning and scrubbing with brushes and bleach comes first. Then sanding and next, cleaning again and then, finally you start applying the varnish. To get the true deep honey color and the protection needed for the Florida sun, seven coats of varnish are required. Good quality varnish requires a slow drying time. You are lucky if you can apply two coats in one day. When you finish, you have to remove all the blue tape and even the best painters tape will want to become part of the gelcoat after spending a few days in the Florida sun. Another job on my to-do list was the starboard side rub rail. I smashed into a dock the first night I docked on the Cumberland River and needed to replace the rail from bow to stern. I had the boat lifted out of the water to replace the rub rail and also repaint the bottom. Now that I was in salt water, a good anti-fouling bottom paint was a necessity. And while I was at it, the bimini and dodger were looking pretty ratty. By the time my year was up at the marina, I had spent enough money on this old boat to buy a new one. I now understand the old saying, "A boat is like a hole in the water where you throw money." If I'm going to be a real parrothead, I've got to have a real boat and *Lifestyle* was a real boat with great lines and now beautiful looks.

Andy Jones and Andy Liles at Saint Thomas Airport

Chapter 4

Andy Jones & Steve Robin

After a year in Tarpon Springs, I found a new marina in St. Pete that I liked and my neighbor at the Tarpon Springs marina helped me move *Lifestyle* to it. Andy Jones, is a professional photographer who at that time lived aboard an old Hunter 28 sloop in the next slip. The boat had not had the bottom cleaned in such a long time that I was sure new life forms were developing on the hull. He was a joy to be around and had a dry sense of humor that continued to amuse me. He was a dependable sailor and became a good friend. When we first met at the Tarpon Springs marina, he had recently separated from his young wife and was hoping things would work out for a reconciliation and the boat living would be a short respite.

It was not long after that, one afternoon, he came walking down the dock with a huge microwave oven and a coffeemaker. The microwave oven was the style of the time and was about the size of a console TV. It was so big he had trouble getting it through the hatch of his boat. Once he had it inside the boat, it was so big that he had to either eat on it or sleep on it. I asked him what was going on and he replied sadly, "I guess it's over!!" Soon the divorce was final and the Hunter became his permanent home.

The new marina we moved *Lifestyle* had all the comforts of home and more. I could park my car next to my boat and even walk to town if I desired. A swimming pool was part of the package and so I signed another one year lease and parked *Lifestyle*. A bicycle ride across a couple of bridges and I could enjoy St Pete beach. On rainy days, there was a winery next door where I could sample their product until I felt guilty and usually purchased a bottle of red and paid more than I should have. Sailing was good. I was about 30 minutes from Johns Pass and the Gulf of Mexico.

One of my favorite places was Boca Ciega Bay. From my slip I would motor to the channel and then sail to Boca Ciega Bay. It is a good size protected bay with lots of good places to anchor. Gulfport is a little city on that bay. I found lots of good places to eat, several bars, a dance hall and a hotel with a large veranda where drinks were served and music was played. Gulfport had made a successful transition from a cheap sunny spot in the 50s and 60s for the snow birds, to a biker's refuge in the 70s, to a developing art community by the end of the century. A high school friend that I had stayed in touch with over the years lived there with his best friend, his dog. Steve Robin was a hero without question. We both graduated from H. B. Plant High School and joined the U.S. Navy in July of 1964. He sailed off on a little ship named the *USS Pueblo* (GER-2) while I was stationed at Millington Naval Air station. On January 23, 1968 the *USS Pueblo* with Steve Robin aboard was sailing off the coast of North Korea in international waters when it was surrounded by the North Korean Navy and fired upon. The unwarranted attack killed one crew member and wounded several others. Steve sustained minor wounds. The *Pueblo* had only two 50 caliber machine guns and the new crew had only practiced with them on one occasion before the capture. This was the first mission off the coast of North Korea for the *Pueblo*. It had been refitted from a WWII supply ship at the Navy shipyard in Bremerton, Washington to a research ship. The equipment on board was state of the art listening equipment for the time. There was no defending the ship against the heavily armed North Korean PT boats and sub chasers. The North Koreans raked the ship with 50cal machine gun fire and fired the 57mm cannon into the hull, mortally wounding Duane Hodges. Next, the sub chaser opened a torpedo tube. The air temperature was just above freezing and the water was so cold the crew would die from hyperthermia before they could be rescued, if an attempt was even made to rescue them from the frigid waters. Captain Lloyd A. Butcher ran up the flags of surrender and surrendered the *USS Pueblo*. It became the first US Navy vessel to be surrendered in modern history. Steve and the other surviving crew spent eleven months imprisoned by their ruthless and inhumane North Korean captors. After his release, Steve was able to work for the Navy, the VA and even do some security work, but his health forced him into an early retirement.

At his duplex in Gulfport we would share stories of fishing in the Gulf or boating in general. On one occasion a hurricane was passing not far from Tampa Bay and I elected to stay aboard my boat. As the storm bands neared, the water in the marina got bumpy. Several of the boats in the marina were damaged. Only a couple of us liveaboards had stayed on our boats through the storm and we were kept busy adjusting dock lines and tying off flapping sails and canvas. As soon as the storm calmed, Steve drove up to my dock and asked if I wanted to go over to his house and get a cup of coffee. After about 16 hours of bouncing on my boat, I was ready for the solid ground, warm friendship and a good cup of coffee he offered. The ravages of being taken prisoner, living in an unheated barracks in North Korea without any medical attention and a constant diet of fish head soup with stale bread had so destroyed Steve's body that he died sooner than he should have on July 29, 2008.

After spending a little over a year in the St. Pete area, I was once again thinking of moving to another marina. This time it was the expense that forced a move. The marina was charging me for a 40 foot slip even though *Lifestyle* was only a 36 foot boat. In addition, the marina would increase the price every chance they could. Everything connected to real estate in Florida was soaring in price and this was just one way the marinas could get their share. Their argument was, "We can put a 40 foot boat in that slip and if you want to stay, then you have to pay the maximum price." Everyone was on the band wagon of profit margin. The local governments were happy with the inflated cost because they received more tax revenue and it seemed everyone was getting fat except the poor guy paying the bill. One thing about a boat different from a condominium, is a boat floats and it can float somewhere else. At the time, there was a true real-estate boom in sunny Florida. People were buying marinas and shoving the boats out and developing waterfront condos. It seemed the builders couldn't build enough. Everything was selling. I was in the local bicycle shop getting my bike repaired and noticed the building across the street was for sale. I asked the owner of the shop, who was very vocal and outspoken, and never hesitated to share his opinion no matter the subject, whether asked or not, about the property. He was overjoyed when I asked if he thought the asking price was good for the building across the street. He said, "HELL NO!, Those bastards are asking way too much, but someone will buy it." I was thinking, what did he know? He works on bicycles. Then he said, "I feel sorry for the poor guy who is the last one to buy, when it all comes crashing down." Looking back, I can safely say he may have been one of the smartest people I met while in Florida.

One day my friend Andy, from Tarpon Springs, called and asked if I wanted to crew in the upcoming race from St Pete to Isla Mujeres, Mexico, also known as the Regatta Del Sol a Sol. This is a popular race that starts in Tampa bay in front of the St. Petersburg Yacht Club (SPYC) and ends outside the harbor at the island of Isla Mujeres. Isla Mujeres is a small Island only about four miles long and just over 2,000 feet wide. It is across the bay from Cancun and adjacent to the Yucatan Peninsula. In the mid 60s it was a desperately poor area and it was felt a sailboat race would bring American dollars into the area. Mexican officials organized a series of races starting from cities such as Houston, New Orleans, Mobile, Pensacola and St. Pete with the finish line in Isla Mujeres. It worked so well that each April a few racing sailboats start first in ports somewhere in the Northern part of the Gulf of Mexico and race to St. Pete to join the fleet for the start of the official race. SPYC has partnered with the local Mexican sailing club to help the children of the island and the local islanders to entertain the sailors. Lots of food, drinks, dances and even a basketball game have become a part of the celebration. The basketball game has evolved to be more than just a pick-up game between the sailors and the locals. One of the highlights of the trip is when the sailing captains and crews take all the locals for a sail around the island. So when Andy asked the question if I wanted to crew, I referred back to my childhood in Tampa and remembered my Spanish class and ask, "Doesn't Isla Mujeres mean, island of women?" His hesitation meant to me that he didn't remember his Spanish or never took the course. Anyway I said, "Not yes, but Hell yes." He next introduced me to Curtis the captain and owner of our boat.

The boat was sitting in the same slip *Lifestyle* had occupied in Tarpon Springs just a year or so before. *High Cotton* was a pristine 40 foot Jeanneau sloop, outfitted to sail fast. The owner was an experienced sailor who had completed several Gulf crossings but never sailed in this regatta. Nevertheless, he had a very competitive nature and set his goal to win the race. The crew was supposed to be six but two people backed out at the last minute and so those positions remained vacant. We departed Tarpon Springs early Friday morning and motored to the ICW just around the corner from Anclote Island. The captain had a friend along by the name of Bob. So the crew was Andy, Mike, Bob and the Captain. As we motored along behind Clearwater Beach and waited for the bridges to open, we discussed our assignments on the boat and the strategy for winning the race. The starting gun was set for the next day at 0800.

We made it through the many bridges and under the connecting bridge to the Sunshine Skyway and around the point to downtown St. Petersburg. A weather briefing was to be held that evening and our boat had to be inspected by the race committee. Most long distance races have requirements that must be met. We were required to have an evacuation plan and life raft to hold the crew. The boat must meet certain safety standards and crew must have certain sailing experience. Andy and I had sailed together and I trusted him and he trusted me. Bob and the captain had sailed together and were good friends so all was good. Although the crew was the minimum for such a race, we all felt good about the race. The weather briefing was quick. The weather man said we would have light breezes not more than 15kts from the north. It would be a run, meaning the wind would be from the north, all the way. We were cruiser class and did not carry a chute or spinnaker. If we had wanted to sail with a spinnaker, it would have been necessary to have two extra crew members. We were given instructions on how to use the new item this race required, a satellite phone. Each captain was to check in at certain times and our position would be posted. Of course this was a sailboat race and engines were not to be used except in an emergency or for safety concerns and then it must be logged. The prop shaft was not wired off or sealed as is done in some races.

With all the business taken care of, it was time to eat and drink. I had learned from other crossings that on the night before a race it is tempting to over indulge, but until you have your sea legs it is best to keep both eating and drinking to minimum. We had a few drinks and talked to other sailors, some I had met before in other races or marinas. I was talking to a crew member from another boat and he asked if I had sailed this race before? I confessed that this was my first. He then said, "You'll have some stories to tell." Now what does that mean, I thought. Is the island really full of women, do they go bare breasted, or was he referring to the race? Whatever, it's not like this is the first race they have put on. This was the 37th race and I didn't think they had lost a sailor yet, although I heard a lot of talk about the race in 1988!! It seems a weather front passed with winds at 50kts and seas around 20 feet. The results of such a storm was, about half the fleet of 37 boats had to drop out of the race. For a while nine boats and their crew were unaccounted for. Finally, all were found in various ports from Florida to Cuba to Mexico.

Photo of Yawl *Seraphim* taken in high winds: by Andy Jones

Chapter 5

The Race

A sailboat race start is a thing of beauty. Some starts are by class, some races start everyone at once. But no matter, if you are one of the starting boats, you are working hard to get the right sail hoisted and trimmed and jockeying for position. The crews are moving from side to side of the boat, sails are flapping and people are yelling. Large boats bear down on smaller boats and all boats are demanding right of way. Captains man the helm and plan their position for the start strategy. I was in the cockpit with a stop watch in hand counting down the minutes. The wind was blowing at about 15kts and the water was choppy from the wind and frothy from the boats. At about three minutes to our start, I asked the captain if he wanted to hoist the mainsail but he wanted to wait. Since the wind was blowing at the max for the sails we had started out with, just the head sail was used until we approached the start line. The headsail was a large jib on a roller. It moved the boat with ease by itself and could be rolled in if needed after we got our start. With about one minute before our start, we were in a great start position. We were making our run for the start line when the captain called for the main halyard to be hauled in and the mainsail raised. The winch was singing and the sail started up the mast. The Captain was falling off the wind and the start line was in sight. With about 30 seconds to go, we were approaching hull speed. Suddenly the mainsail stopped its run up the mast. I looked up from my watch to see the main halyard wrapped around the starboard shroud. A real rookie mistake!! We had connected the halyard to the mainsail without checking to see if it was clear and the captain had elected to wait till the last minute to check it. We needed to take the pressure off the main in order to unwrap the halyard from the shroud, and to do that we needed to turn into the wind. So there at the starting line, with all the boats headed west, we had to turn east. We got the line unfouled and crossed the start line about three minutes late. Not a big deal in a three to four day race, but it sure did make us feel bad to be sailing in everyone's wake.

Shortly we had the Sunshine Skyway Bridge in sight and the boats were finding their groove. We had made up some time but could see several of the boats making way somewhat better than us. We worked to balance the boat by moving the crew. We worked to adjust the sails to get the maximum performance out of each inch of sail. By noon we were past the bridge and sailing in fresh air. The wind had picked up and outside the protection of the barrier islands the sea was becoming a little on the choppy side. "Where were those gingersnaps?" We were still pretty busy so the crew was gaining their sea legs without the ill effects of malaise. The wind was now coming from the south at about 20kts and we had reduced the sail area but were still making hull speed. Hull speed is the maximum speed a displacement boat can go in the water and is based on its waterline. In order to go faster the boat would need to raise out of the water or plane the boat like a ski boat would do. We were doing the best we could. The boat and the sails were trimmed correctly. A very light supper was had by all. I think I had a handful of dry cereal and some more gingersnaps. Bob was the worst. He ate nothing. He had found a spot in the main salon on the starboard settee against the bulkhead and he wasn't moving. Moving around on a boat that is healing at about 10-15 degrees and bouncing is not easy anyway and Bob was a large guy so it was best that he wedged himself in the corner and stayed put. If he had been dislodged and fell, he could hurt himself or someone else. Watches were assigned as night approached and soon it was another beautiful star filled night on the Gulf of Mexico.

The next morning the wind was coming from the north at about 20kts. Like most times on the Gulf, the seas were confused, meaning there was very little pattern to them. For breakfast I had a hand full of dry cereal, gingersnaps and a ginger ale. Andy and the captain were doing OK. Bob was in the same place as the day before. I'm sure he stood his watch but I can't remember him moving. Just off to our port side was a yawl that was racing to the same place and seemed to making the same speed. The boat was the *Seraphim*, a Mason 53 foot double masted yacht. We were about a quarter mile apart and experiencing somewhat stronger winds than had been predicted. He had his mizzen sail furled and covered. He was just sailing with main and headsail. The *Seraphim* was still over powered and was healing over significantly. In addition, when crossing a wave she would just about come out of the water. Many times we saw 50% of her keel. The sky had grayed but the visibility was still very good. Andy was always looking for that perfect picture and, having a trained eye, he had his camera ready and started taking pictures of the yawl. We spent most of the day watching the yawl. We would adjust our sails and he would adjust his sails but we stayed side by side. As we approached the tip of Cuba the yawl set a new course, a few degrees closer to true south. After an hour or so, she was out of sight.

Our location was now approaching an area where the Caribbean Sea and the Gulf of Mexico meet. The warm waters of the Caribbean are funneled through that gap between the Yucatan Peninsula and Cuba. Weather patterns are affected by the temperature of the water and the funnel effect of the large land masses which reduce the area the water must flow through. Storms are extreme in this area and can be devastating to sailors as we would see. Earlier we had made a course correction and were now sailing in a westerly direction in order to cross the Gulf Stream at a perpendicular approach. We calculated that a perpendicular approach to the Gulf Stream would save valuable time toward the finish line. The new course would reduce the drag of the north flowing stream on our little boat. At supper I was able to eat a banana with my gingersnaps. Bob will still wedged in the same spot in the salon. Watches were assigned and I turned in.

Sunday morning as the sun came up we were able to see the reason for the bumpy ride. The rollers had increased and the wind was now blowing in excess of 25kts. We had a double reef in the main and the head sail was rolled in one third. The boat was handling the wind with ease. Our boat speed was holding at the hull speed and increased as we surfed down the waves.

I was on watch at noon while Curtis was at the helm. We were both tethered to the boat and had our PFD's on. My choice for a PFD was a lightweight auto hydrostatic inflatable with a built in safety harness. That allowed me to clip my safety tether to the "D" ring on the PFD and to the boat at the other end. Without the built in safety harness, a sailor would need to put on the safety harness and then put on the PFD. The hydrostatic inflation device allows the devise to inflate with only a four inch submersion in the water. Of course the best way to keep from drowning is to stay on the boat. That is the reason for the tether. The tether is a high strength nylon webbing line with a snap hook at the boat end and a quick release snap shackle at the "D" ring. The idea is to keep you from falling overboard and allow you to move about the boat with ease. Jack lines run from the bow to the stern and a crew member can snap onto the jack line and move about the boat. Curtis was snapped on to the grab bars at the helm.

I watched as a large squall line developed to the northwest. It is hard to tell the distance, direction, or the strength of a squall line from a boat in open water, but this one looked big. This squall line had it all, lots of wind, lightening strikes on the water and a curtain of rain. There is no way to outrun a squall line in a small boat. They will be moving at speeds equal to a car on an open highway, not a slow displacement type boat. We watched the storm, hoping it would pass to our east and discussed our plans if it did not. Curtis was looking ahead of us and watching the waves. I was sitting in the cockpit looking aft at the approaching weather. I told Curtis I was going forward to take the main down and stow it. At the same time Curtis turned the boat into the wind and started rolling in the headsail. The boat was equipped with a sailpack with lazy jacks for the mainsail. That meant when the mainsail was released it would fall down the lines called lazy jacks into a sail cover called the sailpack. The zipper on top of the sailpack secured the sail and protected it from the weather and sun. I released the main halyard and controlled the fall of the main into the sailpack. The sail was almost entirely in the sailpack when the microburst hit us. The wind was over 50kts. Had it hit us on the beam we would have been knocked down and I would have been tossed into the water. I would have been dragged along through the water by the tethered line. The wind from the storm was bad but the rain was even worse. The rain was blinding and put welts on any bare skin. Minutes passed and I was still holding onto the sail with my arms wrapped around the boom and holding on with all my might. I knew if I let go of the sail it would be caught in the wind, causing the boat to veer and I would go overboard. Curtis always used the sailpack, so he had never cut any short lines for sail ties. Because of the force of the wind, the sail would not drop into the sailpack and it would not close over the sail. I couldn't let go of my grip on the sail for fear it would be sucked out of the sailpack and we would broach. Lucky for us, Andy knew he was needed on deck even though he was off watch. As he came up the hatch and slid the cover back, I hollered for him to bring up some sail ties so I could secure the main. Andy ducked down into the boat and started digging through lockers looking for sail ties. Meanwhile Curtis was trying to control the boat and keep it from broaching. The rain and the wind were still the strongest I had ever been in, on land or sea. Now the lightening was striking the water close to the boat and not just every once in a while but almost constantly. Here we were sailing along in the storm of a lifetime with a tall lighting rod, or mast, attached to the boat. Earlier in the day Curtis had attached car jumper cables to the stainless steel shrouds and let them dangle in the water. The shrouds are the support lines that go from the top of the mast to the hull of the boat. The thought was, the jumper cables would neutralize the electric charge and reduce the chance of a lightning strike. It must have helped because we didn't get a direct hit. Andy slid the hatch back and attached his tether to the boat and came up on deck to help me secure the sail. Andy could not find any sail ties but did find a half inch 50 foot utility line. It was not what I wanted but with lots of wraps and a dozen or so knots I was able to let go of the sail and rest. I dropped down onto the floor of the cockpit and sheltered myself from the rain and wind. Andy went below to get out of the weather. Curtis had turned the boat and we were now running with the storm with bare poles (no sails up). The hood of his rain gear was covering his head and he was peeking out to maintain our heading. We were only able to communicate by hollering. The storm lasted the better part of an hour. After that the rain and wind were only a mild discomfort. I looked at Curtis and his eyes were still large and set on the horizon. I broke his stare by asking him if during the storm he could hear me praying. He said, "No, I was too busy singing hymns." A second squall line passed but we were ready for it. During the storms we had recorded surfing down the waves at 12kts and winds in excess of 50kts for almost an hour.

By 1630 most of the storms had passed and we were only 135 miles from the finish line.

Daylight Monday brought more storms and lots more lightening. We heard the Coast Guard calling for boats to render aid to a boat in distress. We were several hours from the boat in distress when we heard the call and turned to head in that direction. Another boat was answering the call and was even closer. *China Doll* had turned to intercept the boat in distress. A Coast Guard helicopter was on station and a Coast Guard cutter was on the way. With help on the way we turned *High Cotton* back to the race course.

After the race, the captain of the distressed vessel (*Luan Two*) made the following report of his decision to declare an emergency; "I keyed the DSC MAYDAY button on the VHF radio. *China* Doll answered! *China Doll's* captain asked me if I had set off the EPIRB (emergency position indicating radio beacon). No, not yet I answered. I was trying to locate vessels nearby. He recommended I go ahead and set it off, which I did. About midnight I heard the USCG call *China Doll* asking them if they were in contact with *Luan Two*. I could hear the conversation but my batteries were weak and could not make contact directly with the Coast Guard. *China Doll* was roughly 30 miles behind us and headed our way".

China Doll, which had also lost a sail, arrived about 1100 hours on Monday and the USCG Cutter *Drummond* arrived around 1200 hours. The USCG boarded *Luan Two* and determined they were helpless and had been drifting in the storm and rough seas for the past 20 hours. The sails were shredded, someone had fallen into the wheel and broken the steering and the engine was inoperable, due to fuel problems. The crew and boat were in peril. The USCG took *Luan Two* in tow and headed for Key West.

Another boat caught in the storm was the sailing vessel *Maltese Kross*, a CYS 37 cutter. The captain became seriously ill, seasick, dehydrated, hallucinating and suffering heart problems. The crew decided to abort the race and activated their EPIRB. The US Coast Guard helicopter was sent to the scene and safely removed the captain. Two boats were hit by lightning, but no one was injured. On another boat a sailor was sitting on the head when the storm hit. The force tossed the sailor and the head down the passageway. A 40 pound toilet and a 200 pound sailor bouncing around the interior of a boat in a storm is a dangerous thing. The head was captured and secured and the boat sustained no further damage. The sailor had a good story to tell.

In *Southwinds* magazine, a magazine that covers sailing in the Southeast U.S. July 2005 article written by Dave Ellis reported the race and the storm in part with the following:

> "Soon the fleet was experiencing increasing wind. Then it became scary. Winds were reported at a steady 40 knots with higher gusts and with steep seas to 20 feet. Naturally, this was between midnight and dawn. Mike Boom who was on the yacht *Mi Vida Loca* reported "We watched lightning strike all around us for seven hours. It was the most intense storm I have ever seen. We hove-to for two hours in wind gusts that exceeded 65 knots".

> "There were many knockdowns, and most in the fleet had sails blown out. Two boats were struck by lightning. There was a dismasting. Two other boats were disabled. Roller furlers took a beating. A successful Medevac rescue off a yacht saved a crewmember who had become ill. Seven boats returned to their Florida ports."

By Monday afternoon we were in better weather. The sun was out and we were cleaning and straightening our floating home. Our boat had survived the storms and the crew had done most everything right, at least enough right to get us safely through the storms. Curtis had as a goal to finish the race on Monday and we knew it would be close. Our official time was recorded crossing the finish line at 2359 hours Monday. We were escorted to the dock to clear customs and check in with race officials. By 1:30 am we had straightened the boat enough to leave it for a few hours and check into our reserved hotel room. Since none of us had been to Isla Mujueres before, we called a cab and all loaded into the cab for what turned out to be a block and a half drive. Our disgust for calling a cab to take us a block and half was elevated by the fact that the night manager was asleep and the cab driver who was his cousin knew how to locate him. We found the room that Andy and I shared. The room was small by U.S. standards and seemed to be decorated in the original motif of the 60s. We were on the top floor of the hotel, the second floor. The street in front of the hotel was typical for the town and was about as wide as most driveways. We had a small balcony that overlooked the shops and restaurants below. The shower was the most wonderful thing in the world. All that was required was running fresh water and a floor that didn't move. It was so good to wash the salt and grime off our bodies. The warm water was oh so great. After a long shower, we crashed and had sweet dreams of hugging a wonderful green tree on a nice firm grass lawn.

By ten in the morning we were ready to cross the street and have breakfast. We had most of our meals in that little open air restaurant and became so familiar with the wait staff that we would just yell from our balcony our order and then walk the 50 paces to pick it up or grab a table. The little town had become successful from the tourist trade from the mainland and boaters. Most of the shops sold the same stuff but some good deals could be had on leather goods and high tax items. The big event of the stay was the "basketball game". Years ago the sailors took on the locals in a basketball game and of course beat them really badly. The game evolved and became a festival where the town feeds and entertains the crews and the support people. School girls dance on stage and awards are given for the best performance. Beer and food are free for everyone. All the town officials are introduced and the sailors for one night can do no wrong. Everyone has a good time with dancing and merriment. The basketball game is not the sand lot game you may imagine. It is now as sophisticated as a college game and may equal a pro team. The Mexican people of this region are mostly descendants of the Incas and are small people. Boy, was I surprised when the Mexican team walked out on the concrete park court and the shortest player was over six feet tall. Needless to say the Mexican team beat the sailors by a large margin. But it was all in fun and everyone departed happy and content.

The island was so small that we took a gas powered golf cart to every place on the island. A nice sandy beach was reported to be on the east end of the island so Andy and I boarded our cart and headed out to the beach. As we arrived, we were pleasantly surprised to find it was a topless beach and a couple of beautiful young ladies were taking advantage of the sunny weather. The young ladies were not shy and even posed for pictures. Andy was a professional photographer but on this occasion he had left his camera in the room and asked to borrow mine. I said "Not so fast sailor." It was time to lay down some ground rules and negotiate a good deal for the use of my camera. While we were negotiating, one beautiful young lady was standing under a palm tree with the Caribbean Sea gently lapping the sand. The slight breeze would lift her sun bleached hair and her breasts were oh so nice. What a picture this would make. As the seconds passed, the value of my camera increased. A deal was struck and one element of the deal was that we would share all the pictures of the trip and all would be equally owned. As an amateur photographer, this had value to me. Andy was a very good photographer and I knew his professional eye would capture some quality moments. Several good pics were taken of the bare breasted nymph and then we seated ourselves at the outdoor bar where we were offered such deals by the sailors for a copy of the pictures. At least we didn't have to buy any beer for a while.

After a couple days in paradise it was time to go back home. This time we took a plane. Curtis was staying a while longer and had another crew lined up to help him return the boat to Florida. Andy and I boarded the plane to Tampa and, like the guy at St, Pete Yacht Club had predicted, we had some good stories to tell.

The July 2005 issue of *Southwinds* magazine was published and we had been told it would have the race results and coverage of the race and the unusual weather we encountered. I found a copy of the magazine and, as reported, the Regatta del Sol al Sol story was listed on the front cover. The story on page 28 told the whole story with quotes from crew members and damage reports from captains whose boats sustained damage. It was a good story but one of the pictures told a big part of the story. It was a picture of the 53 foot yawl, *Seraphim*, coming out of the water as she crested a wave in 30 plus knot winds. It was a quality picture and one that seemed familiar. Yes, it was one of "our" pictures. It was one of the pictures that Andy had taken on that day that the yawl stayed off our port side for the better part of a day. One of the pictures that Andy had agreed would be shared when he forgot his camera at the topless beach. My excitement grew. But to my astonishment, there was only one "by line" and it gave the credit to "Andy Jones"! I grabbed the phone and called Andy and vented my frustration. When I asked, where was my credit line? He said, "I was hoping you wouldn't notice." We both laughed and I congratulated him for the great picture. Now, every time we get together, I ask him, "When am I going to get my credit line", and we laugh again.

Trawler *SUEME* at dock

Chapter 6

When Sailors Grow Up, They Buy Trawlers

I sailed *Lifestyle* to Mobile and thought about taking her back up the river to Nashville but instead I put her on the market. I listed her with the brokers at Turner Marine and within a month she was sold. I was boatless! Freedom! No maintenance fee, no dock fee, no boat!!

I had been dating a lady who was not as boat oriented as I, and after all, I felt I had sailed enough to last a lifetime, so selling *Lifestyle* was less traumatic than I had expected. Denniese and I were married within a year and we started talking about boats again. We joined the local yacht club. Percy Priest Yacht Club had a sailing program that taught members sailing in six weeks and gave them the confidence and knowledge to sail the lake in a club boat in that short time. I volunteered to teach the classes and Denniese helped. By that time I had upgraded my Captains license to Master with a sail power endorsement. The club was happy to have a captain with my credentials and experience volunteer to teach the classes. Denniese and I enjoyed the classes as much as the students did. Summer evenings on Percy Priest Lake with a light wind to our backs and a full moon shinning on the water and the students thought we were saintly. Many times we would be sailing downwind with both head sail and mainsail full out on opposite sides of the boat. Sailing wing on wing with not a sound except the ripple of the water as we glided over, it was magic. We taught the classes for two years and took other classes as they were offered. One class we took was "Suddenly in Command". A course about what to do when the captain falls overboard or is incapacitated and the wife must take the helm. What were we thinking; we didn't even own a boat. I think in the back of our minds we were both thinking that club boats were fun but someday we were going to be boat owners again.

Meanwhile, I had other interests. I had to stay busy even in retirement and what can keep you busier than building a new house. We broke ground on a new house and each day after Denniese got off work I would show her the progress of the day. We would talk about colors, countertops and bathroom fixtures. All was good but building a house didn't allow time to teach sailing classes so regretfully we stepped down from our teaching position. We both enjoyed the water and, even without a boat, we designed our vacations on or around the water. We chartered a sailboat in Tortola, British Virgin Island and later sailed onboard a tall ship in the West Indies. It has been said, people like to be on the water because it takes them back to the time they were in their mother's womb. I can't remember that far back but I do like being on the water as long as the water is easy.

One day Denniese came home after a stressful day at work and tossed her purse on the table and said with disgust, "If I didn't need the insurance, I would quit this job and we could go sailing." I said, "I can put you on my insurance." Before that time, we had not even talked about insurance. She had her insurance from her work and I had my insurance from my retirement. But now we were married and she qualified for my policy. The seed was planted and I had called her hand. She went back to work the next day but she had a different attitude.

Denniese had seen the Great Loop poster on the wall of my office and had made mention of it in the past, but it seemed as just a passing thought until she made that statement about "going sailing with me". A week later she came home and I gave her a copy of the book "Honey Let's Get A Boat...", by Ron and Eva Stob. They were a couple who bought a boat and did America's Great Loop, the same loop that the poster depicted. I told her to read the book and then tell me if she still wanted to sail off with me.

A couple of days later she tossed the book on the same table and said "I'm ready". I said, "OK, but we need a boat". Now remember, we had a new house under construction and a limited budget. We evaluated our situation and determined that if we were going to do the loop, we needed to do it soon. We joined the America Great Loop Cruising Association (AGLCA) and started reading everything we could on the Loop. The Association was founded by the Stobs who also created the chart which was the original inspiration for this trip. We also took the money that was designated for the upstairs of the new house and budgeted it for the boat. After all, what is more important, having a couple of rooms for potential guests, or a real boat. Also, since I had become a home body, I had adopted a pound dog. Some dogs love water, it's in their DNA. The dog I adopted was a hound, a scent dog and part Beagle. She did not like water except to drink. What were we going to do with Maggie? Denniese had trained dogs in the past and she felt it would all work out. So we made a list. It went something like this:

1. Finish the house
2. Find someone to take care of Lesley (Denniese' Mom)
3. Show my oldest son how to handle my rental units
4. Train Maggie
5. List the old house and, oh yes, buy a boat

I was the person who did not have a full time job, so I started looking for a boat. Every morning I would start the day on the computer looking for the right boat. In addition, I had to educate myself on boats that would be good for the loop. The Loop is such an unusual adventure and demands so much from the crew and the boat. The boat must be livable, self-contained sea worthy and able to take the rigors of a 6000 mile trip. The power plant must be dependable and as maintenance free as possible. A generator, a substantial house battery system and a good refrigerator is a must. Navigation, visibility and dual steering stations must also be considered. My past boating experience had been mostly with sailboats, slow boats that could take a lot of abuse. So trawlers were a natural transition.

Trawlers are slow roomy boats that have displacement hulls. Displacement hulled boats are designed to displace their weight in the water and push the water instead of riding on top of the water. The speed of a trawler with a displacement hull is limited by the length and weight of the boat. The simplified accepted formula of the speed of a displacement hull boat is approximately the square root of the water line of the boat X 1.34. For a 40 foot trawler with a water line of 36 feet the hull speed would look something like this: The square root of 36 = 6 X 1.34 = 8.04kts. Convert this speed to miles per hour and it would look like this: 8.04kts X 1.15 = 9.2 mph. or about the speed you would drive your car in the Wal-Mart parking lot, not very fast!! But this trip is not about speed, it is about the adventure and the sights to be seen.

As a sailor I was accustomed to slow speed and lots of work to get the maximum slow speed. Adjusting the sheets, trimming the sails and the balancing of the sailboat was a constant activity. Driving a trawler was much less work. Turn the key and if the engine starts you have it made. 2010 was a great time to buy a boat and terrible time to sell one. The market was saturated with quality boats of all sizes and shapes and there was very little money available to loan for a used boat. The Florida market was especially full of boats. Other than being a trawler and in the neighborhood of 40 feet and a few of the other things I listed, we really didn't know enough to make a decision. But this was the time to educate ourselves on the market and the best boat for us. The first boat I found and presented to Denniese was a Monk 36 and it was close by. Another consideration for us was the location of the boat. The Loop has a time line. It is not hard and fast but most Loopers start in Florida in the early spring and ride the warm weather for the entire Loop, arriving back in Florida in the fall of the same year. By buying a boat on the Tennessee River, it would give us time to get to know the boat slowly and then catch up with the fleet in Florida in the spring. I arranged a ride on the Monk which was being moved from one dock to another, a day ride away. The boat was nice and within our budget. But after a day on the boat, we decided it was not exactly right for us. Besides, it was a little early in the boat looking process so we passed on the boat even at a reduced price.

In the next months Denniese continued to work hard studying boats that I presented to her in the evening. On the weekends we would drive to boat docks and walk the docks looking for trawlers with "For Sale" signs. We were looking for deals, so bird poop and spiders didn't deter us. Fuzz or growth on the bottom was a plus. We traveled from our home in Middle Tennessee to Knoxville, Grand Rivers, Kentucky, Chattanooga, Pickwick, Fulton, Iuka, Mississippi, Charleston, South Carolina, Tampa Bay, Sarasota, Bradenton and finally the Keys. We used up every favor we had established with friends and family for places to stay. The phone call would go something like this… "Hi, this is Mike, Mike Liles… You remember, we were in the Navy (college, worked, attended that seminar) together. We were going to be in your area and wanted to stop in and say Hi, Yea, we are in the neighborhood looking at a boat and will need a place to stay?"

During the week, I was hard at work with the house. As the general contractor I had to stay on top of every item in the house and make sure the next item was ready and on time. In addition, I had the added necessity to save money for the BOAT! Besides putting a hold on finishing the upstairs, I nixed the paved driveway and left it graveled and as the deadline for the boat purchase loomed and money for both a boat and a house seemed to be getting less and less, drapes and a new washer and dryer were also put on hold. Denniese did her part. She found a three door stainless steel refrigerator advertized on one of those Black Friday specials. She arrived after sunrise to find the store had only one of the four specials remaining. She was able to purchase it only because the lady in front of her hesitated. Denniese snapped it up saving us $1000.00. The house was coming together and I was proud of our effort. We were close to a finish date and our check list was getting smaller. We were not able to spend Christmas in our new home but the bad weather had held off until we were finished with the outside and were working on the trim and painting on the inside. Soon the inside painting was done, the floors sanded and finished and the granite countertops would be installed.

The New Year was underway and we were getting close to a sail date for our Loop adventure and still didn't have a boat. We had made offers on two boats but could not make a deal work. We had gone from the preferred size of 36 feet to a minimum of 40 feet. We wanted a boat that had been taken care of and we could trace its ownership. While making my morning perusal of the internet, I found a 40 foot Marine Trader located in Key Largo. I called the broker and got the questions answered that I could not find on the listing information. One key piece of information appealing on this boat; it was being offered by the original owner. She was a 1984 Sun Deck, Marine Trader. A Taiwan built boat with a great reputation. They have lots of fiberglass in the production and lots of teak in the trim. They are stately looking and have great lines. This boat had possibilities!! Plus it was a single screw (one engine) with a Ford Lehman 120hp engine and a 24" prop. The Ford Lehman diesel is a workhorse of an engine and won its notoriety as a tractor engine. The engine is low maintenance and very dependable.

The electronics were acceptable with a GPS/chart plotter, 24 mile radar, two station autopilot, depth sounder and two VHF radios. The owner had ordered extras such as extra 120 volt AC wiring and receptacles as well as additional 12 volt DC wiring throughout the boat. An 8 KW generator was strong enough to run all the appliances and charge the house batteries.

The pictures showed a boat that appeared to be in top shape and had been taken care of by a loving owner. So what was the next step? I called Jim!! Jim Hooper and I had worked together in Nashville for the Department of Labor where I had served as Director of Tennessee OSHA, Consultative Services. We had become great friends and enjoyed boating together. We even planned our early retirement together. I was turning 55 and he was a year younger and we both had the philosophy that you can always earn more money but you can't make more time, so we were cutting our ties with our jobs. He now owned a 40' Sea Ray with twin 350hp engines. We both enjoyed boating and I felt somewhat responsible for his decision to buy this large "go fast" boat. When we first met I owned a sailboat (*Lifestyle*) and he owned a pair of jet skis. When he found out about my love for boating, he asked if we could go boating together. My love for boats does not extend to jet skis and it showed when I jokingly said, "Yes, as soon as you get a boat." Well Jim, being the good person that he is, forgave me for my smart-ass remark but immediately went out and bought a 30 foot run-about. He and his wife enjoyed it so much that just about the time he retired, he upgraded to the 40 foot Sea Ray. It is a great boat with all the extras. He ordered it from the factory in Tennessee and watched it being built. After his retirement, he trucked it to Florida. We even took it to Bimini to enjoy the warm waters of the Caribbean during one cold winter. Jim was now living in Key Largo and kept the Sea Ray behind his house. I got him on the phone and asked if he was doing anything the next weekend. He said, "No", so I said we were flying down to look at a boat and wanted to know if he would put us up for the weekend. I told him I needed a place to stay because there was a fishing tournament in Key Largo and the closest available room was in Miami. I'm sure there was a fishing tournament going on that weekend (there is always a fishing tournament going on in the Keys).

We booked a SouthWest flight and flew to Lauderdale and drove to Key Largo to see Jim and Beverly and the 40' Marine Trader. I found out from the broker where it was docked and told him I wanted to drive by and look at it before I scheduled an appointment to go aboard. We found her at the Fishery. The Fishery is a small commercial dock a couple of blocks off Highway One. She had great curb appeal, as we say in the real estate business, and she had great lines and appeared to be well taken care of. But Wait!! What is that name on the transom - "SUE-ME"? The owner must be an attorney. A name like that could cause you problems. I mean that's like giving everyone you pass the finger.

Changing the name on a boat is a very serious decision. Some people say it brings on lots of bad JuJu, bad omens, and bad luck. Oh my!! We had a planned trip of over 6000 miles and we didn't want to start off by making the King of the Sea, Neptune, mad at us. I still remember the trip across the gulf when Robert said bad things about King Neptune and the result was we ran into strong winds and blew out the mainsail. Not that I am superstitious, not in the least!! But that name? Could we live with *"SUE-ME"*?? I had my doubts. The next day we scheduled the walk-thru with the broker. She looked good, *"SUE-ME"*, not the broker. The broker was about my age and had spent a life in the sun while boating the Southern tip of Florida. The boat had plenty of room, a walk around queen size bed, a fly bridge, foredeck and sundeck. A walk around deck with access to all points of the deck is a must. Access to all parts of the deck is important when locking through the more than 100 locks we would access in the Loop. Strong cleats and capable dock lines and ground tackle was equally important. She had a heavy duty serious windlass capable of pulling close to 2000 pounds with a gypsy for chain and drum for rope. Remembering the times I had run aground and used the windlass to pull me off, made that item attractive. The boat also had about 150 feet of 3/8 inch hot dipped galvanized chain and about 500 feet of 5/8 inch rope for ground tackle. The primary anchor was a 45lb CQR. The CQR anchor is a plow type anchor that is a favorite among many boaters and has a reputation for good holding in a wide range of bottoms. A couple extra smaller Danforth anchors, which are favorable for mud and sand, were also included.

At this point in the purchasing process, the buyer is expected to look and not touch. The broker will go over the listing and make sure items listed are explained. It is assumed that all items that are on the listing sheet are present and are in working order. The broker shows everything in its best light. Even understanding that the broker is the eternal optimist and it is unlikely that he will say anything negative about his listing, this boat showed well. Remembering that the boat is a 1984 model, it still looked new in most areas. There was some water damage on the teak paneling in the master stateroom where a hatch did not seal. In that same room the teak and holy sole needed a fresh coat of varnish. There was also a green chair in the main salon that was worn and needed to be replaced or recovered. Some of the coverings were dated but overall the boat looked just a few years old. The superstructure had been painted but looked professional. The hull was ready for a new coat of wax but also looked good. All the brightwork(wood) was varnished and fresh. Some people consider varnished wood on boats a negative and a lot of work. Some people like their boats to look like Clorox bottles, all plastic and white. I like wood. I like varnished wood even better. This boat had teak everywhere. If we bought this boat we would be buying varnish by the gallon. But as a traditional sailor I consider seven coats of urethane varnish "LOVE"! Overall, at first look, it appeared we had found our boat. We didn't let on to our excitement and told the broker we would get back with him. We had lots to consider, evaluate and pray over.

We returned home just in time for Denniese to go back to work and for me to call a couple of sub-contractors and schedule their work. During the return trip, we had decided this was our boat. It met most of our requirements and we both felt it could serve as our home on the water for the better part of a year. I would negotiate the best deal and hope we could close on this one. Of course the name thing was still bothering me, so at my first opportunity I opened my favorite boating reference book, "Chapman Piloting". My 62nd edition had very good instructions on naming a new boat, right down to suggestions to score the bottle of Champagne with a glass cutter if you plan on breaking a bottle of Champagne on the bow, but there was no mention of re-naming a boat. Maybe it can't be done, maybe we will have to live with the name "*SUE-ME*" or maybe we should continue our hunt for the right boat with the right name. Maybe I should check the Internet. I Googled "Re-naming Your Boat" and found many sites that discussed re-naming a vessel and most gave pages of instructions. Most sites had a lot written about the superstitions and legends of taking a new name. This is serious stuff!! BoatSafe.com had three pages of instructions for the name change process. Another site had a one page short version. One site required virgin urine. With all the young girls watching MTV these days I'm not sure we can locate any virgin urine, so that one was out. All name change ceremonies required Champagne and some acknowledgement of Neptune. Well at least the name change can be done. We can work out the details as we need to. So with that information, I will be able to give "*SUE-ME*" a fair evaluation. I began pouring over the listing information again and comparing it to other Marine Trader 40s that had sold recently. By this time in the boat buying process I was pretty familiar with prices and the value added for extras or subtracted for the lack of a needed accessory. This boat was equipped for such a trip as the Loop but didn't have many extras. One thing it did not have was a bow thruster. As a sailor I was accustomed to having only one engine. But a sailboat has a large rudder and usually the keel will allow it to swing a turn without much effort. A trawler has less keel and a smaller rudder, plus the single prop is a 24 inch prop as opposed to the 10 inch prop on my 35 foot sailboat. The result would mean significant "prop walk". Prop walk occurs when the prop turning acts as force that pushes the stern of the boat to one side. With a single engine and no thruster a captain is at the mercy of the elements and the prop walk. Another thing that was missing was an AIS receiver. The Automatic Identification System (AIS) is an automatic tracking system required on commercial vessels and larger ships. Your AIS would transmit your name, heading and speed to other vessels in your vicinity and you could receive their data so all vessels could avoid collision or track vessels close by. On the inland waterways where we would be traveling this would enable us to see around the bend to see that commercial tow approaching and he could see us. AIS transceivers are not that expensive, so if we felt the need for one, it could be added. The listing did not include a dinghy and a motor. We would need a dinghy and a motor and that potentially could cost a lot of money. I would have to think about that need and see how to fill it.

A week after our return, we felt we were ready to make an offer on "SUE-ME". The price of the boat had been reduced a couple of times before this latest listing to reflect the market and I felt it was now in the proper range of other quality boats. However, I am one who doesn't like to leave any money on the table so I offered a price that was 10% below the listing price. Usually, a price offer of 10 -15% below the listing price will result in a sale and I felt this boat was worth the list price and hoped this contract would work. The contract on a boat should always be contingent upon the survey. The survey is paid for by the potential buyer and that should include pulling the boat out of the water. A 10% earnest fee will accompany the contract if it is accepted. I included in the contract that all batteries be replaced with the same type new batteries. The broker countered my offer by a few thousand dollars and I countered that with a split and it was accepted. The surveyor was contracted and scheduled. The survey was completed and the results were returned to me on January 25, 2011. Everything was coming together and it looked like we were going to make the Great Loop adventure after all. The survey was done by Jonathan Howe of Nautical Services Group, Inc of Ft. Lauderdale. It was nine pages long and was very thorough. Some surveys are full of fluff but this one was factual and complete. As suspected, the boat did very well. Jon presented me with about twenty items that were below standards. Jon and I discussed the items and he was excellent in offering his years of experience to the discussion. I divided the list into thirds. Five that had to be corrected or were deal breakers, five that needed to be done by the owner but could be negotiated and five that needed to be done and I could do. The biggie was the bottom. A boat that is approaching 30 years old and has spent its entire life in the water will have bottom issues. They will range from minor blistering to a waterlogged bottom. The surveyor listed the blistering as "superficial in nature" and did not affect the structural integrity of the hull. The contract was rewritten and included soda blasting of the hull, repainting with two coats of moisture barrier paint and two coats of anti-fouling paint. The closing was subject to my inspection and approval and set for February 20, 2011. My friend Jim lived less than a mile from the boat and was able to check on the progress for me. He was able to give me good reports and we were pleased with the progress.

We booked the flight and the rental car. Our plan was to close on the boat while on the hard and splash the boat and take it back to the Fishery dock. Jim, the owner, agreed to come back the following day and give us an orientation of the boat and teach us handling and docking techniques. After the day with the prior owner, we would leave the boat in Key Largo and return to Tennessee, finish up the house, pack for our planned move to the new house and our move to the boat.

February 20 came and we arrived at the boat at Harbor Marina in Key Largo. She was a beautiful site. She sat in the back of the yard on the jack stands. Sitting out of the water on the jack stands she looked like a mountain of a ship, much bigger than she looked in the water.

We took pictures and admired the new bottom paint, shinny hull and teak. We found a ladder and climbed inside and discovered tiny white specks on the teak and holly sole. It was the result of the sand blasting of the hull. The company had failed to tape off the through-hull fitting in the galley and the result had been a blast of paint chips being sprayed into the boat. They had cleaned the inside but the small chips of paint had embedded themselves into the teak and holly sole. It was a mistake that was more annoying than disfiguring. The owner, Jim, had hired a crew to clean the inside of the boat but some chips of paint were going to remain. We still had a few cosmetic items that were to be done after the boat was in its slip and we would evaluate the sole again at the dock. I had agreed to some additional work while out of the water and had been given an estimate by the manager of the Harbor Marina. I went to the office and looked over my invoice. The estimate had inflated by 50%. I complained that a courtesy phone call should have been in order. I got a shrug of his shoulders and a take it or leave it attitude. At a dry storage rate of about $50.00 per day and the possibility of holding up our closing, I reluctantly agreed to the inflated charge. I soon found that it was the way they did business and because they were the only working marina for about 50 miles they were able to get away with it.

"Active Captain" is a cooperative online service that is free to boaters and is based on the promise that boaters will share information about marinas, anchorages and local knowledge as they travel the waters of North America. It is a wonderful service for all boaters to share and one I use often. At the first opportunity I called up Active Captain on my laptop and wrote a scathing report on the Harbor Marina in Key Largo. That was my first lesson, "always read Active Captain" because there were several reports that reported the same experience as we had. We splashed the boat at 1200 hrs after a delay of an hour and a half waiting for the marina to repair the travel lift. We moved the boat to the slip at the Fishery. It was such a grand experience, owning our own 40 foot trawler, our home on the water and a ticket to the grand adventure of the Great Loop.

We had paid cash for the boat but the cost of the boat is just the down payment on the total cost of boating. We still had a long list of things the boat needed and we thought we needed in order to make the Loop. First on our list was a dingy and motor, next was a new mattress and some interior remodeling and of course that issue of the name "SUE-ME" had to be addressed. We made a trip to the grocery store and bought enough cheap merlot to last us the five days we were going to be aboard before we returned to Tennessee to pack and officially move aboard.

Logbook: Monday February 21, 2011

Key Largo, Fishery Marina. Weather same as Sunday. Breakfast onboard. Denniese went for a 30 min. walk. "Prior" owner Jim arrived at 1030 as promised for the boat handling lesson and familiarization of the boat systems. We took the boat out to a small island and practiced short turns and backing to get the feel of the boat. Practiced man over-board drills. We returned to the marina after aprox. one and a half hours. We successfully docked the boat for the first time. Jim walked Mike over the entire boat with instructions for all systems.

Friday we departed our new home on the water with a list of instructions for Tucker the maintenance man to complete. Tucker had worked for the prior owner for years and knew the boat inside and out. We gave him a list of items to be completed in the month before our return. He had his list and we had ours. Our list had grown from the few items that we had our first day to a couple of pages of needs and about the same for wants. We had a lot to do in the next 30 days and everyone needed to do their part. The new house was just about complete and the old house was listed. Boxes of household goods were everywhere and that was after two moving sales. It was all coming together and our plan was working. We still needed to get the landscaping done and the driveway smoothed at the new house but that would have to wait until the weather cooperated. I divided my time between finishing the new house and hunting down items for our boat. Denniese and I talked over all decisions. After all, she was the Admiral and I was only the Captain. I presented her with a name change idea. My 35 foot sailboat was named *Lifestyle* by the previous owner and I, of course, kept the name the same.

What about if we named our new boat *Lifestyle II*? The original *Lifestyle* had taken me to lots of places and even kept me safe several times when things got bad. The name had served me well. She agreed and I contacted a sign maker in Key Largo with instructions for a quote for the name change. Denniese offered her resignation at work for April 1, 2011. That was the official start of our Great Loop adventure starting at Stuart, Florida. Our plan was to take the boat from Key Largo to Stuart with Jim and Beverly as a shakedown cruise in late March and then come back home to conclude our business and say good-bys for the last time for a while before our start on May 1, 2011. To our surprise Denniese's employer did not accept her retirement letter, but instead offered her a leave of absence in order to do the trip. They had been following our progress and were supportive of our adventure but did not want to lose a valued part of the work team. That worked perfectly and we readily agreed to the one year leave of absence.

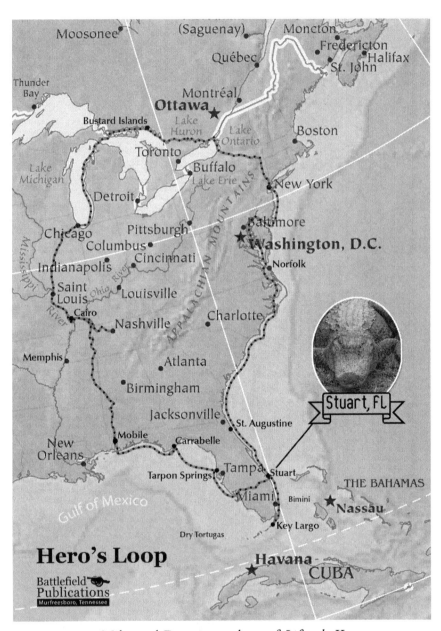

Hero's Loop

Battlefield
Publications
Murfreesboro, Tennessee

Mike and Denniese at bow of *Lifestyle II*

Chapter 7

Ready, Set, Go

The house was finally completed and the final inspection was done on March 14, 2011. The movers had us from the old house to new house within a couple of hours. The move did not include un-packing the many boxes we had, just to placement in the room marked on the box. Several of the boxes were marked "BOAT". Those boxes were placed in the new garage in the staging area that was designated for boat items. That staging area was growing larger and larger. We were cutting all this very close. The closing of the boat, moving the boat to Stuart, the move to the new house, the listing of the old house, the transfer of business obligations and the assignment of mail drops. We were committed to making this happen and were working toward that start day of May 1, 2011. Lots of distractions had been put in our path but we were determined to do this trip and with lots of effort and many prayers this would happen. This was the time and this was the boat, so we were going to make it happen.

One week after moving into the new house we departed for Key Largo, pulling an eight foot U-Haul loaded with tools, household goods, new furniture coverings made by Denniese, and 100 lbs of used charts which included several *Skipper Bob publications* plus other books for the trip. The *Skipper Bob Series* of cruising guides consists of 11 titles featuring the waterways of The Great Loop. We also had two bicycles, a new mattress, clothes and, oh yes, in the back of the SUV a beagle dog named Maggie Mae. Denniese, in addition to working, packing, moving and making new coverings for the furniture for the boat, had been training Maggie to use a piece of indoor/outdoor carpet for potty. Most of our work with the house and boat was being rewarded with positive results. The dog, not so much. Maggie was not going to poop on a rug, no matter what color it was or what we called it. No matter, once on the boat she would have no choice so we felt this small problem would reconcile itself, after all, Denniese was an official dog trainer! How naive we were about the determination of a small brown dog and the efforts we would make to try to convince this animal to poop on the boat. In addition, we had no idea of the crazy things our Maggie Mae would do or the wild things we would be involved in as a result of our decision to bring a beagle dog aboard our boat. Even with all the negatives about this dog, she became a constant source of entertainment and companionship. We loved our little brown dog Maggie Mae.

We arrived at the Fishery Marina in Key Largo at 7pm on March 26, after a two day drive from Middle Tennessee. We unloaded the U-Haul into *Lifestyle II*. By midnight we had our boat home in order and were ready to sleep a well deserved sleep. Sunday we awoke to a beautiful sunny south Florida morning. All was well in paradise. Grocery store and more cleaning took up most of the next couple of days. Jim and Beverly arrived at 6:00pm for supper and to witness the first official duty of the admiral and captain, the christening of the vessel. We had purchased a modestly expensive bottle of Champagne, and with the proper verbiage in hand, we moved to the bow of the boat. The words were spoken, the Champagne consumed and a large portion was poured over the side in order to satisfy King Neptune. The name was now *Lifestyle II* and *Sueme* was no more. We drank the remaining Champagne and, just to make sure all bases were covered, we said a prayer asking our savior Jesus Christ for blessings on our little boat, our voyage and our crew, including the official boat dog Maggie Mae. We consumed a large supper with our guest and enjoyed the mild Florida weather on the aft deck. Jim and Beverly departed and we turned in with the promise that we would start our shakedown cruise in two days, Wednesday, March 30, 2011 at 0800.

We still had one major item to purchase before we shoved off. We had looked for a dinghy that was within our budget of under a $1000.00 and felt sure we could find a used one without a problem but with two days left before our departure date we still did not have one. I did have a lead on one in the area and I contacted the person and arranged a meeting. The dinghy was a 12 foot RIB (Rigid Inflatable Boat). This was the type of inflatable we wanted because it had the solid bottom that was needed to beach the dingy on all kinds of shores; the deep vee hull needed to cut through the chop and the inflatable tubes added stability. The dinghy looked good and seemed to hold air in the tubes so a compromise on the price was made and we now owned a 12 foot RIB. The three of us loaded it on the roof of our Trailblazer and off down Highway A1A we headed. I'm sure the people who passed us on the road saw the Tennessee license plates on the car, just shook their heads and said, "Typical!!" Getting the dinghy off the car and into the water was going to take some thought. The solution came as I drove to the boat. There was a small dry storage marina next door to our boat that had a forklift for launching small boats. The owner of the marina agreed and soon our dinghy was resting behind *Lifestyle II.* Now, all we needed was a motor for the dinghy. We had time for that purchase since we would be going back home after the run up to Stuart. I would try to find a used motor that had been used on one of the many Tennessee lakes. Our trip was going to include as many anchor nights as we could arrange. That meant we would dinghy to shore for dinner or for Maggie, so a good motor was necessary. For now I would row the dinghy, or so I thought?? After all, I like to row and it is great exercise. My daily run to West Marine included a yellow Polypropylene rope; a ski rope for the dinghy? The rope to tie the dinghy is called the painter and the painter of the dingy should float and ski ropes float. With a new painter, a new foot pump and a bailer made from a milk jug, we were ready for our trip the next day.

Tucker was a liveaboard and he and his wife had a small boat dog that they had trained to climb on his shoulder to board and disembark their boat. His boat was similar to ours and he showed me how it was done. By standing on the swim platform he would tell his dog to climb aboard his shoulder from the sun deck. The swim platform was about five feet from the sun deck and it was easy for Maggie to climb onto my shoulder from the sundeck and then for me to squat down to the dinghy and let her jump into the dinghy. The only problem with this plan was that Maggie was afraid of the water and was reluctant to reverse the procedure. Several times on the trip, the return side of the potty walk would result in a wet dog as she would fall off the dinghy or the swim platform or from my shoulder into the water. The result would be several anxious moments as we pulled on the leash to retrieve the dog from the water. We eventually started using a choke collar and a leather leash instead of the flex lead.

The next morning everything was ready as Jim and Beverly brought their bags aboard. I turned the key to start the engine and nothing happened. I tried again and nothing happened. It took about an hour and a visit from Tucker to realize the gear shift was not in dead center neutral. This would prove to be just one of the many idiosyncrasies of *Lifestyle II* that I would discover during our Loop Adventure. After a few minutes warming up, the Ford Lehman was purring like a kitten so we took in our dock lines and we were on our way. Trailing behind *Lifestyle II* was our "new to us" battleship grey RIB dinghy. By 1230 hours we turned into Biscayne Bay from Angelfish cut. We were officially underway on the Loop. Jim took the helm and Denniese and I made our way to the bow to mount our white AGLCA burgee. Beverly took pictures of the event. The white AGLCA burgee shows membership in the association and displays to the world that you are attempting the loop. After a boat and crew completes the loop, or the circle, from start to finish, they are eligible for a gold burgee. If a crew completes the loop more than once, they qualify for a platinum burgee. This is all on the honor system but certain protocol is exercised. At the start of the Loop, a boat announces on the AGLCA web site that they have begun. At the conclusion of the Loop and the boat crosses her wake, the crew announces on the web site the crossing event. By that time the boat and crew are familiar with many other boaters and have become friends with lots of fellow Loopers. Congratulations are in order and are posted on the web site by friends, family and fellow Loopers.

After lunch, Jim was still at the helm and as captain, I evoked **BOAT RULE #1: When opportunity presents itself and it is needed - TAKE A NAP.** So I found a soft place in the fly bridge and eased into a peaceful sleep. Maggie was asleep at my side and the gentle rolling meant all was well in paradise. By 1700 we had dropped the anchor in 15 feet of water just behind the Miami Stadium. The anchor was allowed to settle onto the bottom and the required five to one scope was let out and then a pull in reverse set the anchor. It was now time to put into action the plan to walk Maggie. She had been on the boat since morning and had been a very good boat dog. We had walked her to the bow a couple of times during the day and showed her the square of indoor/outdoor carpet that had been retrieved from the back yard and carefully packed in the U-Haul for transport to Florida. The carpet had been purchased at Lowes on one of the many occasions when I was shopping for building supplies. It had been placed in the back yard near Maggie's favorite poop places and still had the smell of our backyard. Upon our arrival to *Lifestyle II*, the carpet had been carefully placed on the bow and tethered to the boat. To this day the carpet still remains unused. Maggie would not potty onboard, no matter what kind of carpet we offered. So, if she would not go on the boat we would have to take her to shore. The Maggie walk plan consisted of me taking her to a small island that was about 30 yards to our port side. It should be an easy row for me. Denniese got Maggie ready with leash and collar. This would be my first time to row the dinghy and although there was very little wind, there was an incoming tide so I decided to practice for a few minutes before I took on the official boat dog. Denniese and I had taught in our sailing classes to always wear your PFD and plan for the unexpected while on the water. I climbed into the dinghy and with my PFD and my sailing gloves on I sat and mounted the oars in the oarlocks and cast off the painter. The incoming tide was a little more than I expected and I started drifting down toward another island. With a couple of strokes from the mighty Mike, the dinghy was headed back to *Lifestyle II* and the waiting crew. I think it was about the third stroke when the starboard oarlock tore completely off the battleship grey inflatable tube. With only one oar my options were limited. I moved to the bow of the dinghy and started paddling like I was in a canoe. The only problem was the bow of the RIB is about 2 feet off the water and it was difficult to paddle effectively. I was losing ground fast. Denniese, Jim, Beverly and Maggie were standing on the sundeck watching but unable to help. Denniese told me later that she considered jumping in the water but thought better of it and it is just as well she did not. It would have just meant two people would be drifting off toward Miami. Even as bad as it looked from the boat, I was not as worried as Denniese was. There was a small island about 50 yards west and in my drift path. I felt I could at least direct the dinghy to the island. Also a couple of boats were tied to the island so I felt I was not in danger of being lost at sea. A sailboat was anchored to our starboard and the owner spotted my dilemma. He jumped into his dinghy and quickly rounded me up and took me back to *Lifestyle II* to the delight of my wife and friends. We still had the issue of Maggie. I asked my rescuer, whose name was also Mike, if he would tow me over to the island to walk Maggie. He agreed and Maggie was given her first of many boat-ride dog-walks. Mike was the first of many people who would come to our rescue along the way. In fact there were so many who helped us, we started calling them angels because we seemed to be receiving divine intervention. So I guess it is appropriate that Michael should be our first angel.

LOGBOOK: Thursday, March 31, 2011 - At anchor in Stadium Harbor near downtown Miami. Mike and Denniese up at 0645 - Jim and Beverly sleeping in. Temperature 70 degrees, cloudless sky, slight breeze. Jim and Beverly cook breakfast. Waffles on Jim's antique waffle iron after a quick electric cord repair. Anchor away at 0800.

The Great Loop reference books recommend going on the outside (the Atlantic Ocean) for the next 30 miles because of the many bridges that require an opening for only the smallest of boats. We were not ready for the Atlantic Ocean and besides we would miss seeing some of the most costly real estate in the nation and that is the reason given to Jim and Beverly, not that we are afraid of the mighty Atlantic. Bridges are nothing new to me. I have sailed through many bridges. After all, I did own a sailboat with a 47 foot mast. The difference between a powerboat and a sailboat when it comes to bridges is that in a sailboat there is no doubt if you need a bridge raising. In a powerboat, if you ask for a raising and it is not needed, you may be subject to a $250.00 fine. Bridge tenders like to see that you are doing your part by lowering your antennas. If you ask for a lift and your antennas are the only reason you needed a lift, you may find a letter from the State in your mailbox saying you owe them for an unnecessary opening. The first couple of bridges were scheduled bridges, meaning they only open at a certain time and other boats were waiting so we were one of many. I was at the helm and Jim was reading the names of the bridges and the height of the bridge. A bascule bridge is one that opens or raises from the center. A lift bridge is one that raises like an elevator; all of it goes straight up and is counterweighted like an elevator. A swing bridge is one that usually pivots in the center and revolves horizontally 90 degrees. All bridges that move have a couple of things in common. One is a name. They are called by their name. The other thing is a bridge operator that hates boaters. Now you can understand the operator's point of view. The bridge tender is sitting up there in his little air-conditioned house with such a great view, watching the seagulls and the girls in jogging shorts and getting paid for this cushy job. Then a boater comes along and makes him work. When a boater makes a call on the VHF to the bridge operator, they must use the proper frequency and call the bridge by its proper name. Sometimes the name of the bridge is hard to find on your chart or book. Sometimes you just have to guess, like the name of the highway, road or community it goes to. Bridges usually have the names attached to the bridge but are so small you have to be standing on the bridge to read the names. Additionally, since you will be close to the bridge when you make the call, you should use the lower power on your transmitter. This will prevent you from calling the bridge by a similar name 15 miles away. If you do all of this correctly, use correct terminology, pronounce the name of your boat and the bridge name correctly, you may get lucky and find a bridge tender that will be courteous, helpful and even raise the bridge for you in a timely fashion. If not, you may get S-I-L-E-N-C-E!! This is understandable. A bridge operator should not answer a call unless he is sure he is the one being called.

Jim advised me the next bridge was a scheduled bridge and we would get to the bridge about 10 minutes before its scheduled opening. "No problem", I said. "I'll just slow the boat and time it so the bridge opens upon our request at its scheduled opening". BOAT **RULE #2: Nothing on a boat is as simple as is seems.** I pulled back on the throttle, and like a car that has lost its brakes, it seemed to speed up. What's wrong, I thought? An incoming tide was pushing our boat, which has a height of 26 feet with the antennas up, toward a bridge which has a 20 foot clearance when closed. In order to stop a 30,000 lb boat zipping along at seven mph with a favorable tide, the prudent captain should put the boat in reverse. Did we talk about prop walk?? Just as I slowed the boat, the incoming tide and the 24 inch prop turning at about 750 rpms turned the boat to port and there was nothing I could do about it. Jim and Beverly ran forward with fenders to cushion the blow to the starboard bow of the boat where it would hit the bridge. Some of the people at the nearby waterside restaurant ran to the railing to see the big boat hit the bridge while others held there forks in midair. I was about to wet my pants just as the boat stopped and just barely touched the bridge foundation. I think the bridge operator felt sorry for me or maybe realized if I got stuck under his bridge, he would be required to fill out a lot of paperwork. So magically the bridge lifted and we were able to coast past it with a minor scratch on the railing. I learned **BOAT RULE #3: On a boat, it is never too early to prepare for the next event.**

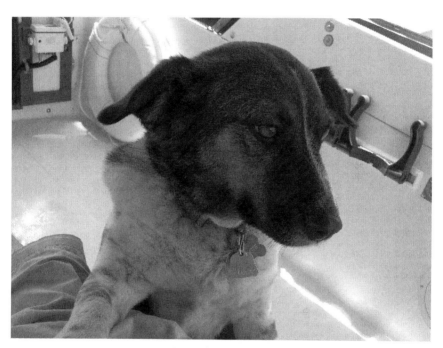

Boat dog Maggie

Chapter 8

Stop that Dog!

By noon we had calmed our nerves and the bridges were getting further apart. Lunch was served in shifts and all was well in the Florida sunshine. Maggie was pacing the deck and looking at the large green lawns as we motored past. We knew what our little brown dog was thinking. She had not been off the boat since the evening before and was not due to be off the boat until the day's end. I know with all the excitement and the new environment she probably had to go badly. We had the grass carpet on the bow which was yet to be used. We had even walked her forward with the leash just like going for a walk in the park, but she was having no part of peeing where she lived. So she knew the carpet was there and it gave us comfort that it was there if she really needed it. Beagle dogs are scent dogs. They are guided by their nose. They are very particular about where they poop and pee and love to smell new areas. This was going to be a matter of wills. Who could last the longest? Could we outlast the dog? This was a test and we were determined to make her use the carpet or just wait. Our veterinarian had told us that she could go 72 hours or longer without harm. WOW, can you imagine going 72 hours. Not me!! But at the same time I'm not a dog.

Denniese noticed a long green grassy park with a seawall. We were in Hollywood, Florida and the channel was deep up to the seawall. Denniese asked me, "Do you think you could pull over to the seawall and I could walk Maggie?" Seemed like a good idea to me. I told Jim and Beverly to get the fenders and lines ready and we were going to pull up along the seawall. From the upper helm, I eased the boat over to the seawall and all was going well until I noticed a blur of a brown furry object jump over the bow of the boat. Maggie had jumped from the bow of the boat over the fence and was now running north at full speed up Highway A1A. The grassy area beside the highway was the wonderland of grass and smells that she longed for. Our first trip, our second day and our crew was already jumping ship. I yelled to Denniese and told her that Maggie had jumped ship and was headed north. Denniese was off the boat, onto the seawall and over the fence within a couple of seconds. Denniese with the leash in hand, in her best sundeck outfit, was running at Olympic speed in her cute little boat shoes, the ones with the pump heels, after the blur of brown fur which by now had a hundred yard head start. I heard Denniese yell to the geriatric citizens walking along the sidewalk, "STOP THAT DOG!!" No one seemed to notice the beagle dog or the yelling woman. Life seemed to go on as usual in Hollywood, Florida. Meanwhile, back on the boat, the remaining crew was trying to keep the boat in its new and unlikely dock space. By the time I got off the boat I could see in the distance Denniese walking a happy and relieved Maggie back to the boat. She was able to capture Maggie (the wild beagle dog) when Maggie stopped to poop. All was good again. Our crew was safe and intact and we quickly shoved off before the Hollywood police came to ticket us for not picking up after our dog or walking our dog without a leash or docking our boat in a city park.

By 1400 we had dropped anchor in Lake Worth and were sipping wine and unwinding from the stressful day. This shakedown cruise was living up to its name but we were growing in experience and meeting each challenge and determined to make this trip happen. We could do this Loop thing.....I think!! We figured that since Maggie went to potty in Hollywood, we could forgo the evening poop run to shore. But by the next morning we were thinking of our furry boat dog and how she must need to go again. This time we spotted a small floating dock by one of the several bars located around Lake Worth. This bar and restaurant had been a lively place the night before and we were almost sure no one would be around this early and if someone was there, surely they wouldn't mind us docking our boat for a few minutes for a poop run. I glided our new boat up to the floating dock and noticed that, with the boat beside it, the dock looked very small. Then I noticed the sign that read, "For restaurant customers only". It was a dinghy dock and not for large boats. By the time I noticed the sign and the screaming restaurant manager, Maggie was standing ready with her leash on and her eyes wide. I explained to the manager that I just needed to walk my dog and would only be a couple of minutes. She told me my boat would destroy her dock and for me to leave, "Now!" All the while, I was walking Maggie toward some fresh green grass just a few feet away. The manager turned and headed back to the restaurant as Maggie found the right spot. I'm not sure if the manager was going to find a phone and call the police or a gun to shoot me. But this time I hurriedly took my poop bag out, cleaned up the evidence and headed back to the boat. Like the Hollywood stop, we hadn't even turned the engine off, so we were gone in a flash. We were getting better at this because we even made the next scheduled bridge opening on time.

The next few miles we passed some of the most beautiful homes along the way. The homes were like castles in size and the lots were multiple acres. It seemed like all of them had a good sized boat parked behind the house. The boat house for most of their boats would cost more than *Lifestyle II*. The good thing was we were on our boat heading for the Loop adventure and they were most likely on land working to pay for all that stuff.

We pulled into our slip at Loggerhead Marina in Stuart, Florida at 1715. The Marine Trawler group was having their annual meeting in Stuart and we found most of the marinas were full and were not accepting any transits. Loggerhead was convenient and had lots of slips available. Jim and Beverly headed off to the shower while Denniese walked Maggie and I readjusted the dock lines. The domestic water pump had stopped working on our first day out so we had been without pressure water since the start of the trip. A good boater will always have backup water in the event a pump fails but a shower is hard to accomplish with a gallon jug. I always store a gallon of potable water per person per day for a trip. Salt water can be used for some things such as the anchor wash down, some cooking and even a bath if Ivory soap is used, but it is always a good idea to rinse everything with fresh water. With all hands off the boat, I updated the log book and started the list of "To Do" items for the next leg of the trip.

LOG BOOK: April 1, 2011
"Maintenance and items needed:

1. Repair aft head.
2. Replace water pump.
3. Replace broken VFH antenna (broken on the first bridge that I thought we could clear without a lift).
4. Repair a scrape to bow rail when I hit the bridge structure.
5. Replace two chrome engine vent louvers (smashed while docking).
6. Find out why the anchor wash down did not work.
7. Add a12 volt fan to the cock pit.
8. Need a soap dish for shower.
9. Need rain gear for Denniese and me.
10. Need kitchen towels.

Engine hours for trip from Key Largo to Stuart = 30.5 hours.

Before the day was over, Maggie would take her second spill of the day into the water. Her dislike for the water meant she was always ready to get back on board each time she fell in. Usually the accident would occur when she was disembarking for a potty run which meant she had her leash on and we were able to pull her out without much difficulty. Even so, it made us very nervous. We would continue to think of ways we could get her on and off the boat without her falling into the water.

Before we departed Key Largo on *Lifestyle II*, we had already moved our car to Stuart. The day after we docked *Lifestyle II* in Stuart, we drove Jim and Beverly to the car rental to pick up a car so they could drive back to Key Largo. They both had been a tremendous help with the boat and their knowledge would help us to be better boaters. The remaining time that day was spent getting *Lifestyle II* ready to be left alone for about a month. During our time away, we would conclude our business in Tennessee and complete our "To Do" list for our long stay onboard. Our next leg of the trip would be the long trip up the east coast of the United States. Our friends back home would ask how we knew where to go on this Loop adventure? I would say, "Easy, just go up the east coast until we get to the Statue of Liberty, then turn left. When we get to Canada, we turn left again and when we get to Lake Michigan, we turn left again, and from there it's all downhill." I would be joking when I would make that statement, but looking back it did show how naive I was about the complexity and sometimes even hazardous endeavor we were undertaking.

We arrived back in Stuart, Florida on May 1, 2012. We had rented a SUV from Alamo car rental in Murfreesboro. The vehicle was full of all our needed items and many we felt we would need. Tupperware, clothes hangers, cable for the TV, electric toothbrush, sewing machine and our passports were all stuffed into the car. Maggie had her own box of supplies and her bed. Squeezed in the very back of the SUV was an almost new Johnson 6hp two-cycle outboard motor for our very used battleship gray dinghy. I had found the motor on Craigslist and paid $400 for it. Additionally, I had it serviced and tuned and spent another $300 for that work. Remembering the event off Miami on our first night out, I wanted a dependable motor for our many trips ashore. When a person or crew decides to make such a trip as the Loop, lots of things have to be taken into consideration. Many decisions have to be made and it takes a great deal of determination to make the trip. Many people put a trip like this off saying, "The time is not right, Mother needs our help, the kids need our help, our finances are not right, the time is just not right", and thus it never gets done. We had many obstacles placed in our path. We took each as a challenge as it came and our determination and faith carried us through. One such event stopped us in our tracks and almost forced us to cancel the trip.

We had a good friend who was also a Realtor. He was going to take care of our new house and forward our mail to us. He had been going through a difficult divorce and he and his son lived behind our house. Ten days before our scheduled departure he committed suicide. It stopped us cold! His son and wife were also our friends. They needed our help. During the first few days after his passing, we considered postponing our trip. We had a new house that was full of unpacked boxes from the move and we had friends and relatives that needed our attention. We had many reasons to delay our trip. As the time for our departure grew near, the obstacles in our path tugged at our hearts. After lots of prayerful discussions and some rearranging of responsibilities, we decided to stick to our schedule, so we departed Murfreesboro on April 30th. After the long drive to Stuart, we unloaded only the items needed to fix the bed. We climbed into bed at 1:00 am and within minutes we were asleep in our beautiful boat home.

Log Book May 1, 2011, Loggerhead Marina Stuart, FL. It took 2 additional trips to unload the car. I cooked a breakfast of grits, eggs and bacon. We started projects and continued to unpack and redo everything in preparation of our scheduled departure in two days.

Log Book May 2, 2011, Repairs done, car returned by noon. Discovered the Johnson 6hp outboard motor had been stolen. Seriously considered going back home.

When we unloaded the car the first night in Stuart, I sat the outboard motor on the dock beside *Lifestyle II* and continued to work on projects of higher priority. We were both tired from the trip and just trying to get the boat in a livable condition had taken all of our energy. The dinghy and the outboard motor were last on our "To Do" list. When I finally got to them, I walked to the place on the dock where I had set the motor and it was gone. I notified the dock master and she was very little help. It was my fault because I left it on the dock. However, this was a gated dock with only fellow boaters and I made the mistake of thinking the motor would be safe. What were we going to do, now? We needed a motor for the dinghy and could not start the trip without one. Should we pack up and go home? It seemed many things were pointing in that direction. It all came crashing down. We were in the lowest of the lows. We were still tired from all the work and now this. It was just too much. Our budget had been stretched to the breaking point by all that had to be purchased and arranged just to get to this point in our journey. I was ready to go home. Denniese in her wisdom said, "We need to sleep on it."

May 3rd was a better day. After a good night's sleep, we both agreed that we could overcome the problems of the stolen motor. We were going to do this trip!

Earlier, I had met a fellow boater from St. Johns, Newfoundland and we became friends and enjoyed talking about Newfoundland. I had visited there a few years before and told him how nice the people had been to me. After hearing of my dilemma, he volunteered to take me to West Marine where I purchased a new Mercury 6hp 4 cycle outboard. Next, he took me to a gas station and I purchased fuel for the trip. Neil Adams was another one of those angels that came to our rescue. He even refused gas money for his car. The log book reads, "For all the bad things that have happened Neil's kindness made this a good day."

By noon we had cast off the dock lines and were on our way after putting a $2000 charge on our Visa card. We made good time on the ICW (intracostal waterway) and the weather was great. The high that day was 85 degrees with a light breeze from the south. By 1630 we were close to Ft. Pierce and dropped the anchor behind a little spoils island. This would be our first trip ashore in our dinghy with the new motor. We talked through the event with the emphasis on how to keep Maggie from falling overboard. Everyone had their PFD on and Maggie had her leather leash attached to the choke collar. All went so well! Maggie stayed dry and as I cast off the dinghy painter, I felt maybe I was getting the hang of this. There was very little wind and current so we drifted only a short distance when I realized I had failed to load the outboard motor fuel tank. "No problem, I'll just row back to the boat" except for the dinghy oar was on *Lifestyle II* also. What should I do? Denniese was still onboard *Lifestyle II*. Could she start the engine, raise the anchor and come get me? "Not likely"! Then I remembered when Neil and I started the Mercury to check it out, we did not run the engine dry when we stopped it. Just maybe it had enough fuel left in the carburetor to get me back to the boat. The brand new Mercury started on the first try and I motored back to *Lifestyle II*, which by now was only about 20 feet away. (Thank you Lord) I loaded the tank and the oars and I took Maggie to the island for her walk. The return trip was without incident. Realizing the potential hazard that I had once again escaped, I vowed to make a check list for launching the dinghy and the Maggie poop walks. Back onboard and after supper, Denniese and I developed a checklist for launching the dinghy.

Dinghy Checklist:

1. PFD's
2. Handheld VHF
3. Fuel tank
4. Oars
5. Bailer (cut out milk jug)
6. Dinghy anchor and line
7. Maggie
8. Leather leash
9. Poop bags
10. The correct footwear for the landing.
11. Later for a birthday present Denniese gave me a throttle extension which was added to the list.

The outboard motor stayed attached to the dinghy for most of the trip and was only removed to flush the water, change the oil and when we put the dinghy on the swim platform for the Gulf crossing. The very old and used dinghy held air remarkably well and we only needed the foot air pump about three times the entire trip. Therefore, we kept the pump stored onboard *Lifestyle II*.

By May 7th *Lifestyle II* and crew had motored all the way to the St. Augustine Municipal Marina, where we purchased 75 gallons of fuel to replace the fuel we had used. The trip to this point had put 81 hours on the engine and we were getting great economy out of our 120hp 6 cylinder Ford Lehman power plant. St. Augustine is advertized as one of the oldest cities in America, established in1565 by the Spanish. The Spanish built a fort at the entrance to the harbor and named it Castillo de San Marcos. Later, when the British took over the fort, they renamed it Fort Marion. Today the fort still stands and is a popular tourist site. Unfortunately, the fort would not be on our list of places to visit, even though it was just across the bridge from our slip. After spending a week traveling, including the driving from Murfreesboro, we needed to restock the boat, do laundry and I had an ever increasing boat maintenance list that needed my attention.

BOAT RULE #4: Love your Engine. Our planned two day stop would include an oil change, fuel filter change and a list of minor things. I was also watching the port water tank. I felt sure we had a small leak in that tank. The tank was important, not just because it held half the needed water for our trip, but that tank was needed for ballast. The boat had a tendency to list to the starboard and I had been using the port water tank to offset that leaning tendency. We developed a pattern in St. Augustine that would follow us the whole trip. Of course, Maggie would come first at any stop. When she saw land, she would start running around the boat, barking and threatening to jump overboard. So the first thing we would do was chain Maggie to the boat in an out of the way place on the sun deck. There she could jump and bark and all her excitement would be contained. After the boat was secured to the dock, Denniese would walk Maggie. I would tend to the dock lines and hooking up the electric or check in with the dock master. Next, the grocery list was developed and the laundry was gathered. While Denniese was shopping, I would do the laundry. After the groceries and laundry were put away, we could start on the maintenance items. A glass of wine was always a must on the aft deck at the end of the day. Supper was fixed and served, the dishes were cleaned and stored, and then we would take a shower and get ready for bed. Every day was intensely busy. If we were on the water, we had just as busy a schedule with navigation and planning for our next anchor spot or marina. Our friends at home thought we were sitting around getting suntans and drinking cocktails. They would ask, "What do you do all day long?" We would say, "You wouldn't believe it".

Saturday afternoon we allowed enough time to search out a church for the next day. By doing that, we could also walk around St. Augustine and visit some of the tourist spots without feeling guilty. Our laptop had an AT&T air card so even if the marina did not have Wi-Fi we could find a church or a marina by looking on the Internet. When it came to marinas, we depended upon the advice at www.activecaptain.com. It is an interactive site that depends on the boaters to grade and comment on each place they visit. There is nothing like local knowledge and that is the backbone of the information on that sight. The experience a boater has at each location is written to that website. My first review at that website had been the report on the marina at Key Largo that had over charged me. The second was the low grade I gave Loggerhead Marina in Stuart, Florida. It told of the theft of the Johnson outboard motor and what little help the staff at the marina gave me. The St. Augustine municipal marina received a well deserved favorable report. These reports and evaluations would become a part of our research for future stops and impressions of the places after we departed. Each time an entry is made, points are given to the presenter and after an accumulation of points they can be cashed in for gifts or prizes. I proudly wear a hat awarded to me for my remarks and contributions to the site. This day, we used the computer to find a church and then walked to it to make sure we would allow enough time the following morning.

The crew of *Lifestyle II* had been together almost constantly for a week, but on this trip ashore, we would leave the official boat dog Maggie locked in the salon of the boat. The beagle part of her was a problem when she put her nose to the ground because she would run until she caught a rabbit or ran out of energy. During that time she would not stop for anything. Her famous beagle voice was also a big problem and it could be heard for miles. Even while she was locked in the salon, her barking could be heard at the end of the marina. Upon our return, we found two things that convinced us we could not lock her in the salon again. The first was a neighbor boater who was so mad about the continuous barking that he wanted to fight. I quickly diffused the situation by my sincere and continuous apology at his every statement. The other was that Maggie had torn all the blinds off all the windows in the boat. For the next couple of weeks, we would have to watch what we were wearing while we were docked at marinas.

Sunday, we attended services at the Ancient City Baptist Church. The people were very welcoming and friendly. The service was very good and several boaters talked to us about their boating experiences. The church claimed to be the oldest church in the oldest city in the U.S.

The day was turning out to be a great day. By the time we returned from church, the temperature was nearing 80 degrees, so after lunch I dived into the maintenance items. The oil change for the engine and the injector motor was easy, although I lost about a quart of oil by not putting the drain plug back in the engine before adding the clean oil. The engine has a pan under it and after draining the oil into the pan it is then pumped out and back in the gallon jugs that the new oil came in and they can be deposited at the marina. Next was the fuel filters. This would be my first time to change the fuel filters and my anxiety grew as I started working with the small "O" rings, slippery diesel fuel and potential air leaks, which I had been told could stall the engine.

Two hours after completing the work, I still could not get the engine to start. By that time I had been working on the engine for almost 4 hours and I felt I was at my limit. I told Denniese it was beyond me and I needed help. We looked in our AGLCA membership list and found a volunteer who made their home in St. Augustine and called him for help. He picked up on the first ring and told me he would love to help but was out of town for the week. He did help by giving me the name of a trusted mechanic not far from our location. The next morning the mechanic arrived and within a few minutes had the engine purring like a kitten. I watched carefully and he explained the sequence of bleeding the engine of air. Changing the fuel filters is a maintenance item that I would do frequently as required by the maintenance manual and prior owner Jim. I even got so good at it, the engine would start the first time. But unlike some other diesel engines, the Ford Lehman in very sensitive to air in the fuel system and I would deal with that peculiarity for most of the trip. By the time the mechanic departed and the boat was cleaned, we decided to just stay put for the day. We could get an early start the next morning.

White flag to celebrate our start

Chapter 9

By-By Florida, The Loop is underway

Since closing the sale of our boat, we had been on a schedule to have the boat out of the state before the 90 day clock ran out. Florida law states that if one buys a boat in Florida the new owner must pay sales tax on that boat if it is to be kept in Florida. The boat must be out of Florida waters within 90 days to avoid that tax. Florida has no income tax but does have a high sales tax and since we were not going to keep the boat in Florida and it was a "documented boat", we had the option of leaving Florida waters before the 90 day window was up and not have that large expense. But we had left the boat in Stuart while we went back home for 30 days, so the clock was ticking and adding an urgency to our trip. The subject is so complex that books have been written on it. One popular book was written by Captain Mike Maurice. The book is titled, "A Yachtman's Guide: Smuggling Your Boat Out Of Jail". *Lifestyle II* was a documented boat and it would be on the move for the next year and we didn't want to pay Florida the sales tax when it was not required, so we stayed on schedule to have the boat out of the state within 90 days. Our home port was Grand Rivers, Kentucky which is only about 90 miles from our Tennessee home. Kentucky is one of the states that does not collect sales tax on documented boats.

Two other time issues for us were a family reunion in July and a wedding in October. We hoped to be near Canada by the time we had to return to Tennessee for the reunion but we wanted to move along as fast as we could and have the boat in Tennessee for the wedding.

Log book: Tuesday, May 10, 2011: St. Augustine Municipal Marina. Up at 0630, away from dock at 0715, made bridge without having to ask for an opening. The height board on the bridge fender showed a 21 ft clearance.

The engine was running great with the new oil, and the air free fuel lines. It was one of those beautiful mornings in the sunshine state. There was very little boat traffic and the dolphins had come out to say good morning. Maggie was on the bow of the boat barking and running from side to side trying to figure out what these strange creatures were doing swimming at the bow of the boat. I was watching with amusement from my position at the upper helm. The plexiglas windows were all rolled up, the breeze was warm and we were once again under way. "How perfect is this day", I thought. It was at that very moment that Maggie decided to chase the dolphins! She jumped with full force off the starboard bow of the boat. Landing about 10 yards to the starboard of the boat and just about the place where a pod of dolphins had been swimming. I screamed "Man Overboard". Denniese had been on the aft deck tending to some lines and looked up at me, thinking maybe I had picked a strange time and place to practice our man over board drill. She looked at me and calmly said "what?" I said, "Maggie just jumped in the water". This was our little mixed breed beagle land dog that hated water.

During our sailing classes back home, we always practiced man over board drills and even in the "Suddenly in Command" class we practiced the established procedures for the occasion when a crew member would fall overboard. But this was our dog, our baby. What were we going to do? Could she swim? Of course she can swim, she is a dog. I yelled for Denniese to take the helm while I launched the dinghy. All the time I was thinking, "Do I know how to give a dog CPR? What if an alligator gets her before I can launch the dinghy? Are the oars still in the dinghy?" Denniese took the helm as the boat slowed to idle. By the time I got to the swim platform and started bringing in the dinghy, I could see the incoming tide and Maggie's forceful swimming was bringing her closer to the dinghy. I left the dinghy tethered to *Lifestyle II* and climbed into it. Maggie swam to me with all her strength. By the time she reached me, she was showing signs of exhaustion. Her big brown eyes were now twice as big as they usually are. The sweet little face was looking for me to save her. I reached down with my left hand while holding on to the dinghy with my right hand and grabbed her by the nape of the neck. I lifted the 40lb (dry) dolphin chaser out of the water, like a mother dog would grab a puppy, and brought her aboard the dinghy. She rewarded me by shaking a couple gallons of sea water off her coat and onto me. She was fine, but we were nervous wrecks. Back on board, we dried her off and attached her to the docking leash that we had established on the sun deck. There was no need to scold her. She disliked water and she had mixed feelings about dolphins. She wanted no part of either, ever again.

The morning was starting off as usual, hours of unique beauty mixed with a few minutes of stark terror. Maggie calmed down within a few minutes. Denniese and I managed to get our heart rate down to normal soon thereafter. That portion of the intracostal is wide and shallow. The channel is well marked but, as always, attention must be paid to the placement of the navigation aids. Denniese was at the helm and I looked up and saw we were out of the channel. At the same time I mentioned it to her, the boat slowed to a stop. We had run aground! Denniese quickly put the engine in neutral as we assessed our situation. We were out of the channel by 50 yards and it seemed we had run aground on a sand bar, a soft grounding. Our deep keel protected our prop and the engine was in neutral so we had time to find a solution to our grounding. The raw water intake for the engine cooling is a concern when you run aground. If the water pump picks up a lot of sand, the raw water filter may get clogged or damage the impeller and overheat the engine. Even if we did pick up a lot of sand, it would take a while to clog up the water filter. The good part was we were on an incoming tide. Hopefully, if we just sat still, we would float off in a few minutes. But on the other hand, we were far outside the channel and I was not sure which way the deep water would be. Most times the deep water is behind you but, without a sounding of the water I could not be sure. Some boaters think that they can power through to deep water. That usually just drives the boat further up on the sandbar and can cause damage to the boat. It is better to stop and consider your options. Handheld depth finders are available and should be considered for a Loop boater. Most handheld depth finders look like a flashlight and are held in the water and pointed toward the bottom. The readout on the side of the unit gives the depth of the water. If you don't own a portable unit, a line and a weight can be used. In the old sailing days this line was called a lead line and a very important part of the boat inventory. A good lead line has a weight with a hole in the end that could collect soil from the bottom to determine the type of bottom you had. Markings on the line such as shreds of leather or linen would tell the depth of the water. Another way to determine the depth of the water is to use a boat pole or even have a crew member go for a swim to find out how deep the water is. Our way of finding deep water came in the form of a working oysterman. He was working an oyster bank nearby and motored over to ask if he could assist. I asked if he could use his depth finder to find us some deep water. He asked how much water we needed and with that information he motored off to plot us a course to get off the sandbar. Within a few minutes we were off the sand and back in the channel. A quick look at the raw water filter showed it was clear of sand so we were good to continue.

BOAT RULE #5: Wine should be served by 1600. By wine time we were tied to a mooring ball at Fernandina Beach, only a mile from the Florida-Georgia state line. It looked like we were going to make our deadline of being out of the state within 90 days and save us nearly ten percent Florida sales tax. After wine, we motored ashore to pay for our mooring ball and give Maggie her time on shore. Before we left home, we had set up a blog through Blogspot.com. Our family and friends were following our daily activities. Each evening after the dishes had been cleaned and the maintenance work done for the day, we would sit down to the computer and send out our blog. Sometimes we were in such remote locations that we did not have a signal on our cell phone which meant our air card would not have a signal. I would do the blog in a rough form and Denniese would correct the spelling errors that the laptop could not recognize and my terrible grammar which can only be attributed to public education. Fernandina Beach had a weak signal leaving only one bar on our cell phone, but we were still able to send out our daily blog. We did not have a way of receiving TV except when we were in a marina that had cable at the docks, so we seldom watched TV. Besides, we rarely had time to watch TV. In addition to boat duties, we had to keep Maggie groomed. If not, dog hair would build up to the point where a person could trip over it. How could one dog produce so much hair? Denniese said it was because Maggie was nervous.

Maggie was a pound dog. She was on death row when I rescued her. I was single at the time and didn't own a pet. I needed a friend, so I went to the local dog pound. Maggie was about one year old and had never had a home. She was captured by the pound living under a house trailer in a neighboring community. She had turned over too many garbage cans looking for scraps of food and was reported to the county dog catcher as a nuisance. Her time for adoption had expired. She was sick and no one wanted her. I walked to her cage in the pound and she looked up at me and tears came to my eyes. There were so many dogs in the pound and I knew not all would be adopted. I also knew Maggie's chances were less than most. She was fully grown, she had a lot of long hair, and her heritage was questionable. She was not a house dog and that was OK because I lived in a rural area. I made up my mind; she was coming to live with me. After signing the adoption papers and paying the fee, the next stop was the veterinarian for spaying and a check up. By the time she came home, she was mostly over the kennel cough and on the road to recovery. She was my friend. At that time Denniese and I were dating and she had trained and bred dogs in another life. She would be a lot of help with Maggie. They soon became inseparable. Maggie was her running partner and my dog to enjoy in between. So when the boat came along, we thought it wouldn't change anything. We just needed to train Maggie for the boat and allow for her needs. We had no idea the challenges that faced us with Maggie while on the boat. Besides her need to hunt she liked to chew anything that carried our scent. She could eat a pair of deck shoes, including the brass eyelets. She slowed down her chewing only when she chewed down to the rubber sole. Her barking and howling were indescribable, but she was ours. She was our official boat dog.

The boat was not her first choice for a home but she was happy anywhere we were. At the end of the day she would crawl into her bed beside our bed. She was aware of boat sounds and became curious of strange sounds on the boat. She loved everyone. One serious problem we had was with her hearing. Once her nose hit the ground she would lose her hearing. She would run and bark and never answer to our calling. She was, of course, part beagle and tracking was in her DNA.

Our next stop was St. Simon Island and we pulled into the transit dock assigned to us at 1600. We were adjusting the dock lines and settling *Lifestyle II* into the slip when Maggie jumped off the boat onto the dock and took off. We had not attached her to the docking leash because the dock was an old style wooden dock that was so low we needed a ladder to get on and off the boat. Not Maggie. She could smell grass, land and maybe rabbits. She ran straight down the dock, out the gate, around the corner, down the road and across a four lane busy highway. She was out of sight in seconds. We chased after her and just knew we would find a dead Maggie lying on the side of the road or even worse, a crippled and dying Maggie. We both prayed that our little pet would be safe as we ran down the road to the highway. Denniese had the leash in her hand when a man pulled over and said, "Are you looking for a brown dog?" He gave us a ride to the spot where he had last seen her. There she was hopping up and down in the swamp beside the highway, looking for a rabbit. She was safe but we were spent. How could she have crossed that highway with all that five o'clock traffic without either getting hit by a car or causing a major wreck? We put the leash on her and walked her back to the boat. What were we going to do? Maybe we would have to face the reality that a rabbit dog does not belong on a boat. A decision would soon have to be made.

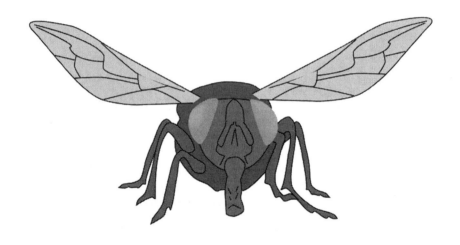

Chapter 10

Greenhead Flies

Charlie Allnut (Humphrey Bogart) and Rose Sayer (Katharine Hepburn) experienced many hardships and overcame all kinds of obstacles in the movie *"African Queen"*. Some were manmade and some were natural. One scene toward the end of their epic journey occurred when they pulled to the bank to drop anchor and rest. Within seconds insects attacked them with such force that they had to relocate the boat to deeper water. All the time they were slapping at the bugs and waving their arms to prevent them from attacking. Such swarms of insects have driven animals mad and even caused herds of cattle to stampede. That movie scene was replayed in my mind during our second day in Georgia. We had just departed St. Simon Island where we had enjoyed a day of rest and exploring. We had unloaded our bikes and found a little BBQ restaurant next to the airport named Southern Souls. I love BBQ and they served some of the best I had ever tasted. With good thoughts of St. Simon Island, we departed the marina at 0830 on May 13, 2011. A few minutes after entering the ICW the creatures appeared. They are known as "Greenhead Flies". The insect is about the size of small honeybee and has a bite that will draw blood. Maggie was going crazy, snapping and chasing the unwanted intruders. Denniese was on guard with a plastic fly swatter. I was trying to drive the boat and keep us in the channel. I looked down and saw blood running down my legs. The Greenhead Flies did not sting, but rather had a bite similar to the bite of a horsefly.

The inside of the canvas bimini was covered with the bugs. As soon as you killed one, another would take his place. The fly swatter broke after about a hundred kills. We were later told that an extra fly swatter is as important as an extra fire extinguisher and should be considered a requirement by the Coast Guard. But just then we were doing all we could to keep the swarm from over taking us. We had located the "Skin so Soft" that had been effective keeping other insects off but it had marginal effect on Greenhead flies. Maggie was doing her part and eating the ones that fell to the deck. A newspaper was located and rolled up to continue the eradication effort. The attack lasted until noon when a breeze came up and blew them away. At the end of our day, we found our anchor spot and went below only to find another swarm of Greenhead Flies trapped in the salon. Denniese came to the rescue by bringing out the shop-vac and sucking up all the remaining creatures. Maggie threw up green goo, but overcame her upset stomach when I started loading the gear into the dinghy for the evening dog walk.

Port and starboard, red and green, so simple how could you ever get the two mixed up. Those buoys even have different shapes and numbers to identify them. Red buoys are cone shaped and have even numbers while Green buoys are can shaped and have odd numbers, yet half the time when I would pull out into the channel I would turn the wrong way. To my defense, I'm not the only captain who has gotten the channel markers mixed up. Everyone has heard "red right returning". That means when returning to port the red buoys will be on your right. "Chapman's Piloting" in the Aids to Navigation section describes the buoyage system like this: "The U.S. Aids to Navigation system for buoyage is uniformly used in all federal-jurisdiction areas and on many other bodies of water where it can be applied. In the lateral system, the shape, coloring, numbering and light characteristics of buoys are determined by their position with respect to the navigable channel, natural or dredged; as such channels are entered and followed from seaward toward the head of navigation. They follow the traditional three-R rule of "red, right, returning." Returning from seaward and proceeding toward the head of navigation is generally considered as moving southerly along the Atlantic Coast, northerly then westerly along the Gulf Coast and northerly along the Pacific Coast. In the Great Lakes, the conventional direction of buoyage is considered westerly and northerly, except on Lake Michigan, where southerly movement is considered as returning from sea".

That's easy enough, Right? Well not for me, so I used an old trick that captains have used for ages – clothespins! I taped the ends of two clothespins with electrical tape, one red and one green. I placed each clothespin on the window in front of the helm. Each time I had doubt about which channel marker I was looking for I could check the clothespin. If I changed direction, I could reverse the clothespin. That system works very well except when you get into a side channel or marina markings. The intracostal waterway (ICW) has a small yellow square located on the navigational aid to help identify the ICW system. The red and green clothespins are a simple and a dependable way of keeping the correct buoy in front of you and only a glance away. Each morning we would compare the clothespins and the chart with the channel markers to make sure we had it correct.

By Sunday May 15, we had made it out of Georgia and the swarms of Greenhead Flies. Occasionally, we would get attacked by a few stragglers but not like the first days attack. That's good because we had not stopped to get a new flyswatter and our supply of newspaper was almost depleted. The Greenhead flies could have been minimized if we would have had screens on the windows of the bimini top and had it fully enclosed. Our top is about 90% enclosed but when an isinglass window is rolled up without screens a bug has full access. I heard other boaters say they would not travel through Georgia without screens for their bimini top.

We stopped at Beaufort, S.C. city marina at the end of the day and took on 80 gallons of fuel. That figured out to be about 1.8 gallons per hour and that included the running of the generator. We were doing well with our budget for fuel and dock fees. We had planned on only coming into the dock about once per week during the trip. After traveling a couple hundred miles, we saw that once per week was too long to be out and just took it as it came with good anchor spots and good marinas and of course when we needed supplies or we ran out of underwear.

Beaufort, S.C. is a very friendly boat spot and even offered a courtesy car to transits, such as ourselves. Many marinas offer courtesy cars and most of their cars are worn and look like hand me downs. This car was no exception, but it ran and that was all we cared about. In addition to the grocery list, this stop had to include a trip to the dentist. Denniese lost a crown the day before and needed to have a dentist re-glue it. All marinas have rules regarding the use of their courtesy car and Beaufort is no exception. The difference here was the administrator of the keys. She appeared to me to have been a grammar school teacher in a former life. Maybe she had retired and needed something to keep her busy and she found a job working in the dock masters office handing out keys to the courtesy car. I don't know, but when she told me I had one hour use of the car and not a minute more, I believed her. I didn't ask what the consequences were for returning the car late, I was afraid to ask. I just knew I would not want that to happen. I think I had a flashback to my second grade teacher, Mrs. Gorie, at Roosevelt Elementary school in Tampa, Florida taking a ruler to my knuckles when I got caught pulling Emily Sullivan's pigtails. The dock master lady had the same way of emanating fear as that second grade teacher. I dared not challenge her rule. We named her the "Courtesy Car Nazi" in honor of the Soup Nazi of the Seinfeld show. Denniese found a dentist just around the corner, so our plan was for me to drop her off and then I would get the groceries and return to pick up Denniese with the re-glued crown and return the car with time to spare. I invoked the seven P's. (Prior Proper Planning Prevents Pretty Poor Performance). On this occasion it was a good plan, but poor performance. We drove to the dentist and found she didn't really open for another hour. We asked for directions to another dentist and drove to that office. It was busy and couldn't take her but the third one would do. I dropped Denniese off and rushed to the grocery store. By now almost 20 minutes had passed. We could still do this, I thought. We were the King and Queen of getting things done in a hurry and on time. The grocery store was more of a problem than I anticipated. I could not find many of the necessary items on the list. This grocery stop needed to last us for a week, so I searched until my list was filled. By the time I exited the grocery store, I had only seven minutes left. I pressed the accelerator down on the car until it amazingly reached a top speed of 40mph. I slid to a stop in the spot reserved for the courtesy car and dashed to the office and dropped the keys on the counter only a minute late and under the glare of the Courtesy Car Nazi. I took the groceries to the boat and remembered that I had not picked up the admiral from the dentist office. Well, life is about choices and Denniese is a much nicer person and not nearly as scary as the CCN, so I was OK with my decision to leave Denniese at the dentist office. I just hoped she would understand.

Denniese arrived back at the boat about 30 minutes later after walking back to the marina. She had a firm look and her jaw was set tight as she boarded the boat, but I soon found out it was because the dentist told her to keep a firm bite on the tooth for a while until the glue set. All was good on *Lifestyle II*.

We walked the dock and met fellow Loopers Chuck and Claria Gorgen aboard *Odyssee*, a 43 foot Hatteras. They are great supporters of the loop and were always helping other Loopers in whatever way possible. They still have a blog of their travels with distance, time and good anchor spots. It can be viewed at www.Gorgensodyssee.blogspot.com. We concluded our visit with them just in time to get ready for dinner ashore. Our friends Nancy and Earl Keese were joining us for supper at a neat little restaurant Earl knew of. They have been retired in the area for a few years and it was good to visit with them again. We had been partners in some real estate ventures some years past. Earl had also been my racquet ball partner for some time and now he stayed active playing golf. They both looked great and were enjoying their retirement. The food was great and the fellowship was even better. Earl and Nancy drove us back to the boat where we enjoyed coffee and more talk.

Tuesday morning, with all our major maintenance items done and our stores replenished, we departed the Beaufort City Marina at 0845 with temps in the mid 60s. By Wednesday evening we were anchored in a narrow creek of the ICW beside a place called Wappoo Creek Island. The tide was strong there and the range was about four feet. Because of the fast current and the closeness of the land on both sides, our swing room was limited. I decided to set a bow and stern anchor. A stern anchor requires some thought when setting it and when retrieving it. This narrow creek had a mud island on the port side and houses with docks and boats behind them on the starboard side. To add to the mix, we were not the only boat anchored in the narrow creek. A sailing cat was the first boat in and he had a bow and stern anchor. His swing would be reduced by his anchor choice and I had to follow the protocol he had established. The best way to set a stern anchor is to set the bow anchor first and lay out twice as much rode as you normally would and then drop the stern anchor and bring in the bow anchor rode by half. I chose to take the stern anchor out in the dinghy leaving the end attached to the stern cleat and drop it at about the same distance from the boat as the bow anchor. Later I found out that in this case, just a small scope on a smaller anchor off the stern would have prevented the stern from swinging. The best way to prevent a boat from over running an anchor in a strong tidal stream and limited swing room is to anchor two anchors from the bow at 180 degrees of one another. That allows the bow of the boat to pivot with the changing current. My method was effective but would cause major difficulty in recovering the anchors, as I would see the next morning. With the boat secured with a bow and stern anchor, we loaded Maggie up and off to shore we went. Supper was a nice little seafood restaurant at the end of the creek. We were able to sit outside with Maggie at our side. She actually behaved. Maybe the promise of shrimp tails was the motivation for her good behavior or maybe it was just being happy to be on land for awhile. The next morning everything was going good until I tried to retrieve the stern anchor. Both anchors had done their job. We had not moved a boat length from where we were the previous night. The 45lb CQR anchor at the bow was holding tight and the 35lb Danforth anchor at the stern was in just as good. I didn't have enough rode on the stern anchor to allow the boat to go forward and pick up the bow anchor with the windlass and I couldn't raise the stern anchor without the windlass. Denniese and I talked it over while drinking a second and third cup of coffee. We came up with a plan. We decided to drop the stern anchor with a float attached to the rode, use the windlass to pick up the bow anchor, then motor around to the float and use the drum on the windlass to pick up the stern anchor at the bow of the boat. The plan worked great and we saw the reason for our difficulty. Both anchors had about 20lbs of mud on them. By the time we were underway, the bow of the boat was covered in mud. Thank goodness for a good anchor wash down system. During the process of retrieving the two anchors and rodes there were no yelling or anxious moments. We had a plan and executed the plan. All was good on *Lifestyle II* for a while longer. We had a short run over to Charleston City marina and arrived at 1000 hours. A friend had recommended a bottom cleaning service and, luckily, they were in the same marina cleaning another boat and said ours could be next. The bottom required only a light cleaning and then they checked the zincs and the prop and the rudder, all checked out good. I paid the charges in cash which made them a little happier.

Charleston has a large boating community. This was a time to catch up on the maintenance items I had been putting off. I had discovered the port water tank leak and had taken off the wood around the tank so I could access the leak. I applied the first coat of Marine-Tex to the aluminum tank after lunch. I would let that dry and apply another coat the following day. Next, I stretched out the anchor chain on the dock and reapplied paint at 60 feet, 100 feet and 160 feet intervals. I wrote down my code and entered it into the log book so I could refer to it later when I anchored. Denniese found a neighbor who was going to the Wal-Mart and she hitched a ride while I did the laundry. She returned later with a hand full of fly swatters and new blinds for the boat. The next day we stayed in place, tied to the end of the "T" dock, replacing the blinds and enjoying the mild weather.

Two days later, we dropped the anchor in a place that had been recommended to us, by a fellow boater, at Thoroughfare Creek near Belin, South Carolina. It is one of the best anchor spots we had found since leaving Florida. It was even better than Florida gunkholing because it is almost always deserted at night and during the week. No city lights or traffic. It had, at one time, been designed for summer homes and a marina development but a road to the area was never developed and now it is a wildlife reserve. Deep water and plenty of swing room allows room for a couple of boats up to 40'. When we first got there some local boaters had driven their ski boats up on the beach and were enjoying the sandy hills. It was all families with kids and dogs but by sundown we were alone. Maggie enjoyed the sand but still would not have much to do with the water. We walked the woods and found what appeared to be one of the only cabins that the developers actually built. We spent the next day at anchor in the creek and did nothing but small boat projects and enjoyed the beauty of the area. Netting was our next project. We put netting below the hand rail by the sundeck. That was Maggie's favorite place to stand and we feared she would fall or more likely jump overboard from that location.

We were not able to keep up with our own blog (www.lifestyleii.blogspot.com) when we couldn't get cell service so as soon as cell service was available we would send our post. By now we had several friends following our adventure and they worried if we didn't post a report. Thoroughfare Creek was a place where we had no service. A couple of days later, Denniese made this report on our relaxed afternoon in Thoroughfare Creek.

"In the afternoon, Mike was able to pick up a radio station that carried Rush Limbaugh. That kept him busy for a couple hours and me looking for earplugs! We took the opportunity to discuss such important issues as which should come first – flossing or brushing. Mike contends that flossing should come first, while I say brushing. The discussion must continue as we both firmly stand our positions."

We also celebrated our three month anniversary since purchasing our boat. We had made great progress along the Loop since the purchase and more importantly we had the proof of our location, in the way of fuel bills and marina charges. That was to prove that *Lifestyle II* was out of Florida within 90 days. Later, that paper trail would be needed for proof that we were traveling, not by Florida, but Tennessee who demanded payment of sales tax. We had to prove that we were not in Tennessee waters. Most states work together to force all boaters to pay sales tax. Documented boats need to keep good records to avoid paying unnecessary tax.

Log Book: Wednesday May 25, 2011, 0800, At dock at Ocean Isle Marina. Slept in because of long day yesterday. Warm day low 70 High 90.

We could not find a good anchor spot the night before and had motored beyond our normal anchor time. I spotted a Tow Boat US boat and hailed him on the VHF and ask if he could recommend a good spot to stop. He told us the closest marina was closed but he knew the owner and would make a call. The Tow Boat operator relayed to us that the owner of Ocean Isle Marina would allow us to tie up to his dock and settle up with us the next day. We docked the boat and walked the dog. We found a local man and ask for a restaurant because we were both tired and didn't feel like cooking. He said a good Italian restaurant was on the main road about a mile from the marina. We rigged the boat for "Maggie Alone". The procedure included removing anything breakable from the counters because she would climb on the counters. Secure the computer and put it away. Raise the blinds so they could not be destroyed. The last thing was to close all the windows and doors in the boat so her barking would not disturb the neighborhood. We started out walking and after about 20 minutes we could just then see the highway. We love to walk but not at the end of the day when we were overdue nourishment. We arrived at the Italian restaurant almost an hour later and were some of the last to get served. After dinner we called a cab to return us to the boat. We deserved to sleep in.

Our next port was Carolina State Park Marina. We had made reservations there because it is just off the ICW and cheap. The marina was new and very nice. The only problem was I think the designer was thinking canoes would dock there. They said 40 foot boats could get in there, but for me it was a challenge. Several turns we required getting inside the marina and then the space between the docks was very narrow. The good thing was there were no other boats in our way. Of the 50 or so slips, only a couple were occupied. I managed to fit *Lifestyle II* in a slip and we started our dock procedures. I tied the boat off, Denniese and I got the electric hooked up and then she walked Maggie. While she found the dog walk area, I checked in with the dock master. After that came repair items for the boat. The Auto Helm was not working; the engine kill switch solenoid was only working half the time and the aft head still did not work. The good news was the patched water tank was holding water. I cleaned the electrical connections on the solenoid, checked out the mark on the water tank and called it a day.

The next day we unloaded the bikes and rode off to the grocery store. The return trip was difficult with a week's worth of groceries hanging off the two bikes. The park was really pretty and had lots of paths for Maggie to explore. While waiting for my load of clothes to dry, I talked to the local Tow Boat US operator who was sitting on the veranda watching a boat that had run aground not far from the marina. It looked to be a go fast boat about 30 feet in length. The captain had run aground on a falling tide and damaged his props trying to get off. The Tow Boat captain was waiting for the next high tide to lift the boat enough so he could tow him to a repair facility. It made me think how wise I had been in choosing a boat where the prop was protected by a deep keel. Little did I know at the time, that before the trip was over my bungling would challenge even that design.

Memorial Day weekend is the first day of boating season in many areas. This Memorial Day weekend was beautiful and the people of the North Carolina coast were out in force. It looked like every boat registered in the state was on the water on Bogue Sound. We watched from the fly bridge as jet skis jumped our wake, crisscrossed in front of us and were amazed by all the crazy boaters out on the water. We saw one boater lose a dog overboard and then just in front of us a kid fell off a tube being towed by a ski boat. Even though we were going slowly, we had to turn to avoid the child in the water. By the time we got to the marina I was ready for a drink.

The AGLCA recognizes local members who volunteer to help other Loopers. These volunteers are called Harbor Hosts. The Harbor Hosts for our next port were Diane and Louis Wade. I had contacted Louis and ask for advice for a marina in the area since this was such a busy boating weekend. We had originally planned to dock at Beaufort Docks in the city, only to find them full. Louis recommended we stay across the river at Morehead City. He reserved a dock space for us and even left a car for us to use. The only thing he knew about us was that we were members of the AGLCA and we were working on the Great Loop. The vehicle he left was a Chevy Tahoe in pretty good shape. It would be needed for our next trip to West Marine. "I love this place," I said as I rested on the aft deck. The city dock is controlled by the city library. The library was closed so boaters left phone messages as to the slip they were in and the arrival time. The Chamber of Commerce was open and gave us coupons for local restaurants and a concert was planned for the park next to our boat. What's not to love? The trip to West Marine included purchasing a VHF antenna to replace the one I broke in Florida, the repair with PVC pipe did not hold. We also needed three fenders, we had lost one in Charleston and we were going to need lots of fenders for the locks that were in our future. In addition, we needed oil, oil filters, fuel filters and additional dock lines, plus a new raw water strainer. By the time we left West Marine, our credit card had been maxed out, but that was OK, we had a free concert in our front yard tonight.

Across the inlet, Beaufort was celebrating its most famous resident, Edward Teach, aka Blackbeard. Blackbeard was one of the boldest and most notorious pirates of his era. These were his waters and his refuge. It is said that Beaufort was his home and the people of the area protected him and profited by his pirating. He controlled these waters and the seafaring communities of the new colonies in the early 1700s. His end came in a series of mistakes. He blockaded the Charleston harbor and held the citizens ransom, taking not only the wealth of the community but also demanding medical supplies for his crew. Legend has it that many of the crew suffered from venereal disease. The plundering actions so enraged the local governor that he called for the Royal Navy to eliminate Blackbeard and his navy. Blackbeard's flag ship *Queen Ann's' Revenge* ran aground, which some say was deliberate in order to hide his booty. Blackbeard was captured by Lt. Maynard of the Royal Navy in 1718. His head was cut off, mounted on the bowsprit of the Royal Navy ship and Lt. Maynard sailed around the harbors with his prize, thus ending the career of Edward Teach or Blackbeard the pirate.

The North Carolina Maritime Museum in Beaufort is the depository of many items from that time and from Blackbeard's ships. The ship

Queen Ann's Revenge was located and salvage began in 1996 in Beaufort Inlet. Many items have been recovered from *Queen Ann's Revenge* including cannons, anchors, cannon balls and shot which are now on display. Beaufort is a good tourist stop in the summer and has lots of attractions dealing with that era.

After dealing with our purchases from West Marine, it was time once again to change the oil and the fuel filters. As the band started playing, I was still in the engine compartment trying to vent the air from the fuel lines. A fellow Looper came aboard and helped and within a few minutes we had the engine running. Oh how I dreaded changing those fuel filters. The oil change I had down to a science but it would be a long time before I gained that level of confidence with the fuel filters. We celebrated the completed maintenance work by going to supper with Diane, Louis and several other Loopers. Louis directed us to Luigi's Pizza for some of the best pizza we had eaten in a long time.

Tuesday ended the Memorial weekend and hopefully it would end the crazy boaters for a while. During my maintenance work, I broke a plastic bleed screw. Denniese spent an hour driving around to the various marine stores trying to find a screw with the same threads. After all her work and time she could not find a replacement screw. As a last resort, I put some duck tape over the screw hole and continued on. Great idea but diesel fuel dissolves duct tape so we had the potential for air to get in the fuel system. I used the transfer valve to shut off that filter and we were able to have air tight system but now only one primary filter. When duct tape does not work, try super glue. I glued the broken plastic screw and while it dried we could continue on the single filter. The engine was on at 0700 after I bled it one more time. The next couple of days we enjoyed the mild days and scenic waterways. By Thursday evening we had made it to our next fuel stop. This is one of the most unique fuel stops we have had. The Alligator Marina is a Shell Service Station. The front of the station services highway traffic and the rear services the marine traffic. We took on 60 gallons of fuel and visited with Jerry and Joan Muhme aboard Motor Vessel *N 2 Wishing*. They were on the back half of the loop and both were looking forward to completing the loop and getting home to Michigan. They owned a nice

1983 Defever trawler with a newly painted black hull. It looked sharp and had been a good home for them during the Loop.

Skipper Bob publications are a must for all Loopers. The cruising guide is divided into sections and gives a mile reference for the boater with anchor spots, marinas and advice for the trip. Since leaving Stuart, Florida we had mostly been on the inside or behind barrier islands or even inland on the intracostal waterway. In front of us was the Albemarle Sound and *Skipper Bob* advised to watch the weather before crossing. The Albemarle Sound is a stretch of open water about 20 plus miles wide and is known for its rough seas. The wind was blowing from the Northeast at 15 to 20 knots and had kicked up a fuss on the water. Sailors say that most times your boat is better than the crew. This old Marine Trader had proved itself many times over; this crew was green as a spring onion. We had been warned that wind from the north was not to be tested on this stretch of water, yet here we were. The wind on the water will provide information for the sailor. In the tall sailing ship days of old, a system was devised to read the water as to how the wind affects it. French Admiral Beaufort developed a system that measured the effects of the wind on the water and concluded that it was a consistent force that could be relied upon. The Beaufort scale is still used today by sailors and boaters. On this body of water, I estimated that the Beaufort scale was five or the wind was blowing at 16 to 21 knots, which caused us to experience a bumpy and rough ride.

I developed my own system that would be used often during our trip. When the wind and water were rough, but we could still steer the boat from the upper helm, and we had to hold onto something, we called that "Tie the dog down". If the weather decreased and the waves got worse, we would move to the lower helm and we called that "Let's go below". When the weather decreased further, we called that weather, "What the hell were we thinking".

We tied the dog down and held on. At six miles per hour, it takes a long time for a bouncing boat to cover 20 miles but we did it and the boat did a better job than we did. Maggie had that look in her eyes like she wanted to abandon ship, Denniese and I were a little green, but we made it to calm waters and soon we found the town of Elizabeth City,

North Carolina. I called on the VHF and was assigned a slip only to find the slip was too small and had to back out and relocate. The next slip was reserved for a boat race the next day but the third was just right. Half way through this "musical slips" the heat alarm for the engine went off. There we were with the VHF sounding off, the heat alarm buzzing, people on shore shouting directions, other boaters worried about this green captain, Maggie barking and me trying to maneuver this 40' single screw no thruster boat, and all that commotion happening at once. To the credit of Denniese and her calm approach, which helped calm me, we were able to finally dock the boat and shut off the alarm. We tied the boat, hooked up the electrical and walked the dog.

That night a concert was scheduled for the grassy area beside the boat and the only maintenance item was to find out why the high temperature buzzer went off. While we waited for the engine to cool, we toured the town and talked to fellow boaters and locals. We cooked supper on the barbe and sat on the aft deck talking to folks who walked past the boat. We listened to the music from the band and just enjoyed the evening. I soon forgot about the high temp buzzer and chalked it up to the slow maneuvering needed to dock the boat.

Log Book: Saturday June 4, 2011, Elizabeth City, NC. Mile Marker 51 engine on at 0700, away from dock at 0715, Outside temp. 59 degrees

We were going to pass through our first lock today. I had locked through several locks but this would be a first for Denniese and Maggie. We put out the extra fenders and lines. Maggie was put on her docking leash which secured her to the post on the sun deck. There she could watch what we were doing, see other people but not jump overboard or get in the way. The lock was a scheduled lock and we were early so we parked and talked to the crew of the other boat that was waiting. The high temp alarm sounded again so, after locking through, we parked the boat under a tree and had lunch while the engine cooled down. After lunch I added water to the cooling system and we continued on our way.

The lock is the entrance to the Dismal Swamp. Just the name was worthy of my attention. The authors of most articles and cruising books said the Dismal Swamp was a must for boaters. We had a choice of going around but we wanted to see it for ourselves, although we were apprehensive. The Great Dismal Swamp is a large swampy area on the coast of North Carolina and Virginia. The original swamp covered over a million acres but in 1973 congress established the Great Dismal Swamp Wildlife Refuge which is about 112,000 acres. The Swamp canal was authorized in 1787 and construction began in 1793. George Washington is credited with being one of the first investors. The canal connected Elizabeth City with Norfolk and eliminated the need for commerce to go out into the Atlantic to service these two important ports. The wood was harvested from the forest and the finished canal was soon a great success.

Today it is the oldest operating artificial waterway in the country. The canal is narrow, shallow and in some parts the trees connect over the canal creating a canopy. Deadheads, (submerged logs) tree trunks and wild life of a wide variety are a part of every mile in The Great Dismal Swamp. Half way through the swamp canal is a visitor's center which allows boaters to tie up and spend the night. It is operated by the state of North Carolina. Not to be outdone, the Federal Government operates a welcome center on the opposite side of the canal but does not offer dockage. The small dock has room for about four boats but since the canal is controlled by the scheduled locks at each end, boats are allowed to raft up to each other and spend the night. We tied up to the dock and checked in with the visitor's center office. Maggie loved the place. To her there is nothing better than a place where lots of rabbits live. In addition, the center is open to land access so there were lots of people to pet Maggie. A walking/bike trail allowed Denniese and Maggie to go for a walk until Denniese reached a point where she could not hear people, see any signs of humans and felt an encounter with black bear was a real possibility. She quickly returned to the boat where we tied Maggie to the sun deck and took off on our own. A small lift bridge allows people to cross the canal to the other visitor center. Inside the Federal visitor center, we could still hear Maggie's continuous barking. She was so loud we were afraid she would disturb the eco system and we were going to be asked to leave the canal. We returned to the boat and comforted our brave boat dog.

Log Book: Sunday June 4, 2011 - At dock Dismal Swamp Canal welcome center. Up at 0630 – cool and light rain temperature 68 degrees. Away from dock at 0800

We took our time getting under way. This morning I had a breaker on the AC electrical panel that kept tripping and a light switch that did not work at all and the two were not related; just something else to add to the maintenance list. As we putted down the canal enjoying the beauty and with the light rain, it felt spooky. We watched carefully as we passed under overhanging trees to make sure a snake did not fall into the boat. Of course we knew that Maggie the fearless guard dog would keep us safe, Right!! I calculated the distance to the next lock and determined that we were running out of time to reach the next scheduled opening. I pushed the throttle up and recalculated with the new speed and determined it was still going to be close. As we approached the lock, I saw that we were the only boat locking through so I felt the lock operator would lock us through.

The lock master was John and a very friendly person. He told us to enter the lock and tie up for the couple feet adjustment. Sometimes docking a boat or tying up to a lock is a beautiful thing, everything goes just right and the boat and captain act in harmony. Other times nothing goes right. Today was a day when nothing went right. I felt I could tie up to the port side wall but the boat wanted to tie up to the starboard wall. In the process of my confused and amateurish boat handling, the boat got turned 180 degrees in the lock. Years before when I was just learning to fly, my flying instructor would say, "Never try to make a good landing out of a bad one." This was one of those cases where I just needed to start over. John watched in amusement, offering suggestions from the bank. To add to the confusion, John raised beagles and had a half dozen barking beagles running up and down the length of the lock. Maggie was tied to the sun deck but added her greeting to her cousins. The dogs were baying and barking that loud and famous noise that beagles are known for. I'm sure Maggie was asking if she could come live with them. John took all this in stride and simply said "Go out and come back in". As we reentered the lock, he volunteered that this was the first time a boat had gotten turned around in his lock in five years. Well, that made me feel good! John offered a lot of information about the city of Norfolk that we were about to visit. He told us about places to eat and things to see. I told him he should get a stipend from the local Chamber for his knowledge. He neglected to tell us that the dock where we had reservations, was having a very special party, one we would have to see for ourselves to believe.

Stanley on aft deck

Chapter 11

"Stanley"

Norfolk is one of the busiest harbors in the U.S. It is home for Norfolk Naval Base which is the world's largest Navy base. Norfolk is also home to Maersk Line Limited who manages the world's largest fleet of U.S. flag vessels. Railroads and highways add to the commercial advantage this city offers shipping companies. This rainy Sunday morning, the harbor was only moderately busy. We weaved our way through the traffic and watched as our GPS directed us to our marina. Commercial traffic was generally courteous as we exchanged information of our course and destination. However, the U.S. Navy will not talk to you. You are expected to stay out of their way and to add to that expectation, they usually travel with escort vessels and all have deck mounted guns that are manned. We just gave them all a wide birth.

We motored into Waterside Marina at 1330 and Maggie was on her leash and ready to find some green grass by 1345. Our first clue to the events of the day was described by Denniese when she returned from walking Maggie. She said, "I saw the strangest thing. Two guys were walking two full size poodles and one had its hair dyed pink." The second clue was, a boat docked close to us had a man aboard wearing a two piece bikini. The best clue was the rainbow flag that several boats hoisted. We were in the middle of a gay pride celebration. I looked at Denniese and said "Dorothy, we're not in Kansas anymore". Our Middle Tennessee life had not prepared us for a gay pride celebration or the planned gay pride boat parade. I told her Norfolk had changed since I visited here while I was in the Navy. We didn't join the boat parade; not because I didn't' look good in a two piece bikini, but because "We had a lot to do and a short time to do it", to use a paraphrase from Jerry Reed.

The first chore was to locate a marine chart service so we could purchase a chart for the Chesapeake Bay, the next large body of water we had to cross. The chart we had was a good one except it lacked a full view of the bay and for planning, I needed a full view. Next we had to restock our pantry and visit a cousin who lived in the area.

My cousin Jim Smith had lived in the area since his retirement from the Navy. He had served during the Korean War and Viet Nam conflict as an engine mechanic and I enjoyed his real sea stories. I asked Jim if he wanted to go for a ride on our 40 foot Marine Trader? His reply was that he had spent enough time on the water to last a life time and declined my invitation with a few expletives favored by sailors.

We took time to walk over to Nauticus Maritime Center which displays the USS Wisconsin (BB64). She is the highest numbered battleship and the next to last battleship commissioned. She was launched on December 7, 1943 and served in the Pacific fleet where she won honors. Toward the end of WWII she shelled mainland Japan with her nine 16 inch guns and protected her flotilla, including aircraft carriers, with her other fire power. The 16 inch gun could hurl a 2,700 lb shell some 20 miles. The Wisconsin is 887 ft long with a beam of 108 ft and a draft of 28 feet. The propulsion system could take that hunk of steel up to 30 kts or 35 mph. Just to stand in front of this giant is breathtaking. I could only imagine how an enemy combatant felt as she came in sight. She was decommissioned for the second time in September 1991 and the city of Norfolk took ownership of the Wisconsin in April of 2010 for permanent display as a museum ship.

Two days after arriving, we took in our dock lines and motored out of our slip in downtown Norfolk and fell in behind US Warship Number 17; of course, not too close behind. The radio operator announced that Warship Number 17 was departing Norfolk. The ship was in my way so I called them on the radio. I didn't know at the time they would not answer. After several hailing attempts, my good judgment told me to just stay out of the way. Warship Number 17 is the USS San Antonio (LPD-17) an amphibious transport dock or landing platform dock. The ship is designed to deliver up to 800 marines ashore by landing craft and helicopters. She is 684 feet long and has a beam of 105 feet with a draft of 23 feet. Her 25,000 tons can travel at a speed of 22 kts. But it is her stealth design you notice first. Instead of a ship, she looks more like something out of a Star Wars movie. By 1000 we were in Chesapeake Bay with a heading of 08 degrees. At 1530 we dropped our anchor in Hills Bay, South of Deltaville. We were doing well maintaining Boat Rule #5 "In dock or anchor down by 1530 and a glass of wine in hand by 1600". We determined that we needed a glass of wine prior to taking Maggie for her evening walk.

Log book: At anchor in Hills Bay, Thursday June 9, 2011 Wind light and from West. Temperature 72 degrees and humid. Up at 0630, engine on at 0730, anchor up at 0745

Thursday we traveled up the Chesapeake on the west side. The day was work with limited visibility but little wave action to slow our trip. Anchor spots are limited on the west side of the Chesapeake and our first spot offered limited protection and a rock outcropping near, so I pulled up the anchor and continued north. We were not sure we could make the last bridge opening that allowed us into Annapolis. If we could not get into Annapolis, we would be forced to anchor out in the bay. All the marinas were full and protected anchor spots were few and a weather front was on the way.

We pushed hard and at 1645 we had the bridge in sight. I called the bridge tender and ask for an opening. The wind had picked up and the next 15 minutes needed to get to the bridge was a bouncy one, but we made it. The bridge lifted as we motored to it. We had been to Annapolis just the summer before by land. We had been in the area looking for a Loop boat. We saw the crowds of people and the large number of boats that made their way to this city in the summer. If you have a boat on the Chesapeake, then Annapolis is the place to be. We saw every kind of boat you can imagine with some owners names you would recognize from celebrity magazines. They were all tucked in here at docks that seem to cover every square inch of land and then mooring balls that dot the water. All are available for an inflated summer rate. Very few anchor spots remain outside the channel but our budget didn't allow for this high priced tourist spot so as soon as we passed Spa Creek Bridge, I started looking for a spot to drop the anchor. All the mooring balls were set in the bottom and the pennants didn't allow for much swing room. If I was going to anchor, I had to allow for limited swing room. I spotted a spot between two large sailboats. Sailboats swing at anchor somewhat differently than trawlers but with this crowded anchorage, my choices were limited. I pulled between the two boats as Denniese questioned the location. I said, "What choice do we have?" I put the boat transmission in neutral, Denniese took the helm and I went forward to drop the anchor.

As I approached the bow of the boat, I spotted an official looking craft motoring our way. I stiffened as the harbor patrol came within a few feet of the bow. I felt sure a confrontation was going to ensue as my rights as a boater conflicted with the local authority's right to maintain a safe harbor. But to my genuine surprise, another angel appeared in the form of "Stanley". Instead of saying, "You can't anchor here", which would have developed into a debate, Stanley asked, "How can I help?" I confessed to him that I needed a place to drop anchor for the night. He said, "Follow me, I have just the spot." We motored to the back of Spa Creek where Stanley showed us a spot in 10 feet of water with lots of swing room. Then Stanley pointed to a well kept sloop, two boats in front of us, and told us that sailboat was his boat and if we needed anything to let him know.

By the time we got the anchor set, it was 1830, well past our "wine time", supper and Maggie's walk. Annapolis residences love boats and the city provides for the boating community by creating a dinghy dock at the end of each street that dead ends at the water. Within an easy dinghy ride, we had three choices for walking Maggie. Each dock had a small park with trees, benches and manicured landscaping. Added to each park were a trash can and a post with a dispenser of doggie bags.

These people did as much for pet owners as they did for boat owners. I warmed up the barbe on the aft deck for an overdue burger as I loaded the dinghy for the short trip to shore.

After supper and dishes were put away, we relaxed for a few minutes. It had been a long and stressful day but we were in a great place, thanks to Stanley.

BOAT RULE #6: When the opportunity allows put out extra anchor rode.

Before turning in I went forward and let out another 10 feet of anchor rode and secured the snubber to the Samson post to take the stress off the windless. Now we could sleep well, at least for a while. At 2345 the first of three squall lines pasted over us. I climbed out of bed to check the anchor as the wind picked up, as the first of the three came upon us. *Lifestyle II*'s anchor held as the wind would swing us one way and then the other. But the distance between *Lifestyle II* and the next boat decreased with each wind guest. The wooden boat between *Lifestyle II* and Stanley's boat was drifting down on us. Her anchor was dragging! The boat was unmanned and appeared to be abandoned. I woke Denniese and told her of the dilemma. The boat drifting down on us was unmanned so it would be up to us to protect ourselves and keep the wooden boat from damaging our Loop boat. The good thing was she was dragging very slow and swinging much the same as *Lifestyle II*. We laid out all our fenders on the starboard side, expecting her to crash into our starboard side with her port side. She had no fenders out and the rode appeared to be just a three strand half inch rope. If I had to guess, her rode was most likely tied to a cinderblock instead of a quality anchor. The wooden boat had no anchor light and the flashes of lightening reflected off her wet decks in a ghostly fashion. We continued to watch as the wind controlled our destiny. We were safe in the dry salon of our home for now. Maggie could feel our anxiety and watched as her brown eyes focused on our every move. Our spotlight was trained on the swinging offender as she approached our steadfast anchor rode. If she tangled in our rode she might pull our anchor free and then both boats would be washed up on the shore. The third and final squall line passed and the sky cleared as the wooden boat stopped dragging her anchor about 20 feet from *Lifestyle II*. The front had passed and we had escaped the possible tragedy. We dried off and climbed back into bed to Maggie's delight.

Log Book: Friday June 10, 2011, Up at 0730 – Long night with 3 storms passing, wooden boat dragged anchor, everything wet but OK. 0900 Stanley came over for coffee.

Stanley was not scheduled to work until that evening so he was able to dinghy over and spent some time with us. We thanked him for finding such a good anchor spot for us. I confessed that the spot I picked out would have resulted in real trouble as the storms passed over us. He said he helped us because of the size anchor we had hanging off the bow roller. In tight anchorages like these, size does matter. Stanley told us that Annapolis Harbor Patrol was his summer job. Each spring he would sail his boat to this spot and then in the fall would return home. He had retired a few years before and this was something he looked forward too. He took us under his wing and told us of all the places we should see while we were in Annapolis. He had a car parked close by and said we were welcome to use it if needed. He also knew the owner of the wooden sailboat and would contact him about his timid anchor. It was getting time for him to report for work and he climbed into his dinghy to depart. Stanley had recently purchased a new dinghy motor. Each time he tried to start the motor; he would get frustrated to the point of calling it names because it just would not start. He had even resorted to giving it a proper name. He called it "Henry" and said it was after his first wife who had also been very difficult.

Annapolis is so boat oriented that most everything is only a short dinghy ride away. Well, almost, we needed to visit West Marine and always a grocery. The Harbor Patrol boat stopped by before noon and told us we needed to check in with their office in town and told us they offered a holding tank pump out service that would come to our boat if we called them on the VHF. We dinghyed into town and saw the town offered a harbor officer at the dinghy dock to look after the dinghies and encourage safety by all the folks motoring around the harbor. We were on a mission; we needed to do a load or two of laundry, get lunch and visit the Naval Academy. I added a stop at the hardware store located across the street from the dinghy dock. I can never pass up a hardware store. This one was special because of its age and location. The families who owned and operated it were the third generation owners. The Navy Academy can't be seen in one day and certainly not in the time of a drying cycle of our clothes, so we put that visit off a day. We stopped at the same sandwich shop we had stopped at the year before and took time to consider our options. "We just need to stay here longer".

With the clothes cleaned, dried and folded we slowly motored back to *Lifestyle II*. We took our time looking at all the nice boats stuffed into every inch of shoreline, dock slips and on mooring balls. We arrived back with a welcoming bark and howl from the guard dog Maggie. It was a hot day and all the homes were closed up to keep the air conditioning in so we hoped Maggie's voice would not disturb the surrounding residences. Supper was next on our list. A friend asks, "What do you eat while on your boat." *Lifestyle II* has a full size refrigerator, three burner electric stove with oven and a microwave oven. In addition, we have a butane camp stove and a LP Bar-B-Q grill mounted on the aft rail. We can cook the same food on the boat as we could at home. The difference would be if we were at dock, under way, at anchor or running the generator. Not everything worked when you want it to. The refrigerator had a mind of its own. When we were not using dock power the refrigerator received its power from the 12volt DC battery bank through the inverter which converted the battery voltage into 120 AC household current. Sometimes the inverter would not deliver enough amps to start the compressor in the frig, so food in it would start to thaw. That would result in a short prayer for the refrigerator and our quantity of food it stored. The refrigerator thawing became such a common problem that when we found it running we would shout "Thank you Lord". The microwave required so many amps that it only worked when we were at dock and had a good energy supply. The stove required dock power or the running of the generator. The camp stove used a bottle of fuel about the size of a hair spray can, so we just used it when needed. The most dependable cooking source was the Bar-B-Q grill. The standard size LP bottle was located on the aft deck just below the grill and was only changed twice on the entire trip, even though we used the grill almost every day. So, what did we eat? Tonight we cooked blackened salmon on the grill and yellow rice on the camp stove with a fresh green salad from the refrigerator. We love our coffee and could use the electric coffee maker, the electric stove top or camp stove using the percolator pot. We enjoyed coffee with some pastry we purchased at the sandwich shop for desert. Maggie had her usual bowl of dry food and we found a way to slip her the cooked skin from the salmon. Just don't tell her vet, he thinks she needs to lose weight. We all eat good.

Our Standard Horizon 1000C GPS chartplotter had served us well. The 7 X 10 inch screen was visible from the captain's chair and could be operated by Denniese the navigator with ease. Denniese had studied the manual and knew the systems far better than I did. She would chart our path with ease. She put in waypoints and knew the distance to the next anchor spot or marina when queried. The chartplotter shows a line where the ICW is in relation to the boat and keeps me in-between the markers with a bright colored picture of the chart. The manufacture programmed the chartplotter to use chips or cards for the information of a specific area. The prior owner of the boat used it mostly on the east coast of the U.S., so we had a good chip up to this point. Now it was time to purchase a chip that would take us further up the east coast and across the bottom of Canada and then down Lake Michigan to the river system and then across the Gulf to the West coast of Florida. I had not purchased the chip until now because, frankly, I was not sure we would get this far. Now that we were actually making progress on the Loop trip, I was fairly sure the money would not be wasted. I had contacted the West Marine at Annapolis a couple of days before and talked to the electronics expert who assured me the chip could be purchased at that site. With two chips my Standard Horizon 1000 GPS chartplotter would be equipped to provide information of the entire Loop.

Saturday was Stanley's day off and he wanted to show us around. We started off with coffee and breakfast on board and then a ride into town. Maggie was so calm here in Spa Creek that we didn't fear leaving her on the outside deck without her tie down leash. After all, she hated water so she was on her own island and that allowed us to go into town with piece of mind that she would be OK without us for a while. Our first stop would be West Marine for the chip and other supplies. Stanley was at home there. It seemed that everyone at West Marine called him by name. His kindness was genuine but it made me wonder how often he made this trip. By the time we finished our shopping, Stanley decided it was time for lunch and he had the perfect place. Davis' Pub at the corner of Fourth and Chester has been a local attraction since the 20s. Not much more that a shotgun shack, it is credited with having great food and a reputation for attracting boaters of every pedigree. Their slogan is "Where there are no strangers, only friends you haven't met." The only problem is parking. The pub is tucked into a residential neighborhood that fronts the marina area on Back Creek. We found a parking place up the street and had about a half block walk down the narrow street. Like the slogan said, as soon as I walked through the door a guy at the bar spotted my Tampa Bay tee-shirt and wanted to know about it. We talked for a few minutes and found we had graduated from the same high school and knew some of the same people. By the time I disengaged from him, my crab pretzel and tall draft had been served. What a great place and such good food. I told Denniese," I love this place, let's move here".

Back aboard the boat, we watched as the marine taxi delivered people to several of the docks nearby. A tour boat came by with its speaker blaring out significant facts of the area. I wondered if *Lifestyle II* had now become part of the historic significance of the area. Maggie barked at the canoes and I sat on the aft deck with my feet propped up and enjoyed the mild weather. For once I had no major maintenance projects to do and I could just take it easy. After a couple hours of doing nothing, I felt guilty for my lack of accomplishment, so I called the harbor master and ask if they could send the poop boat to *Lifestyle II* for a pump out. Within a few minutes they pulled up alongside and passed me the black hose to pump my holding tank. After the pump out, I paid the $5.00 and they motored off. As Captain, I then initiated **"Boat Rule #5", "Wine on the aft deck at 1600".**

Sunday, Stanley invited us to attend services at his church. We attended the early service at St. Martins Lutheran Church. It was the first time either Denniese or I had attended a Lutheran service. I found it agreeable and some similarities to the Catholic services. The members of St. Martin's were very gracious and inviting to us as visitors. After church the three of us ventured downtown to find another of Stanley's favorite eating places. After a fabulous brunch, we returned to the boat and spent some time with Maggie. I ran the generator for an hour to top off the batteries and did some minor boat projects.

Monday we had reserved as a tourist day. We took the dinghy into town hoping the tourist would be back home on a Monday. Some of the tourist had stayed away but most places still had waiting lines. We visited the Naval Academy and found an interesting display in the chapel to a famous Tennessean, David Farragut. David Farragut had been born in Tennessee but his parents gave him over to a family friend in the Navy at a young age. David Farragut started as a cabin boy and rose to the rank of Admiral. At the beginning of the American Civil War his allegiance to the U.S. came under question only because he had been born in Tennessee, a Rebel state. He convinced the officers that his allegiance was true and later became the hero of the battles of New Orleans and Mobile. In the battle of Mobile he is remembered for his famous saying, "Damn the torpedoes, full speed ahead". Winning the ports of New Orleans and Mobile virtually cut off the South from their foreign suppliers and the South's ship building industry and hastened the end of the Civil War. Back onboard *Lifestyle II*, we were pleasantly enjoying this lovely spot, when we remembered that we had a family reunion and a wedding to attend in Tennessee. If we were going to continue this Loop adventure, then we needed to get under way.

Tuesday, June 14, 2011, at 0715 we reluctantly pulled up the anchor and motored out of our little inlet and made the opening of the Spa Bridge at 0730. Before we departed, we stopped at Annapolis Marina and purchased 75 gallons of fuel and topped off our water tanks. Spa Creek was a perfect anchor and saved enough money on docking fees that we could afford the fuel to take us to New Jersey or beyond. Thank you Stanley.

Mike and Denniese at Delaware City

Chapter 12

"Jersey"

By the end of the day, we were anchored in Turner Creek only 18 miles from the C&D canal. Wikipedia says this about the Chesapeake and Delaware Canal: "The C & D Canal is a 14 mile long, 450 foot wide, and 40 foot deep ship canal that connects the waters of the Delaware River with those of the Chesapeake Bay and the port of Baltimore. In 1829 it was opened for operations after many unsuccessful starts. The canal connected two of the most popular ports of the time, Philadelphia and Baltimore, and saved almost 300 miles as compared to the trip around the Delaware peninsula. When first constructed, the canal had many locks and bridges which were sources for accidents. One notable accident occurred in January 1862 when a train could not stop for the open drawbridge at the canal and plummeted into the canal. The current between the two bays and the swift tide are still a problem today even with all the modern day engineering upgrades. The commercial traffic was a concern for us. The canal, even at 450 feet wide, seems very narrow when you share it with an oncoming freighter. Fortunately, we only encountered a sightseeing boat which did not take up much room and we were safely tied to the Delaware City marina dock by 1300. Which was at one time a major commercial port before a short cut in the original canal was dredged which bypassed the quaint city, and now it is more oriented toward tourism.

The harbormaster took a special interest in boats that stopped at his dock. His experience was appreciated when it came to venturing down the Delaware Bay. This bay has its share of obstacles but, for us, it was the lack of a place to anchor or dock and the substantial commercial traffic to be encountered. Our *Skipper Bob's* book suggested the trip to Cape May was attainable and should be considered in one day. With that trip in mind we conferred with the dockmaster and he told us to wait one day for a better weather window for the trip. Since we would be on the open bay for eight or nine hours we wanted a mild day and took his advice. I had not equalized the house bank of batteries since their installation in February. A day off from our moving about, and while hooked up to shore power would give me time to do that. Equalizing the batteries is an over charging method that boils the accumulated oxidation off the plates of the batteries and is necessary for a battery's long life. The process takes about eight hours and it is best to ventilate the battery storage area during the process. That was an excuse to stay off the boat for most of the day. Since we had a free day, we toured the town, I got a haircut and we enjoyed a good meal at Crabby Dick's. Maggie enjoyed the town park with us in tow. The dockmaster had offered good advice, for the weather on the bay was choppy at best. The following morning, the weather had improved and he helped turn us around at our slip. The waterway was narrow, the tide swift and without a thruster we needed help turning the boat to the outbound direction. We ran lines across the boat to the outside cleats and then let the inside dock lines loose. With the engine running at idle, the transmission in forward and with the dockmasters help from shore, the boat turned 180 degrees in its own length. Proud of our efforts, we took up our south heading to Cape May, New Jersey.

Nine and a half hours later we were at anchor beside the Cape May Coastguard station. Maggie was looking fondly at a grassy area on shore within a short dinghy ride. Denniese and I, were however, looking at a sign that said, "U.S. Government Property NO TRESPASSING". We discussed out options while Maggie looked on. We finally decided our little brown furry friend was worth taking a chance of trespassing. After all, do you really think they would shoot a man, his wife and their dog.

Beyond that, we could handle most anything. The east coast of New Jersey was not what I expected. I thought it would be a pleasant sandy beach with large manicured estates similar to what we saw in Florida. It was more like the southeast cost of Georgia; swampland with a narrow and not very deep trench cut into it known as the intracostal waterway. Unlike southeast Georgia which was devoid of people, this area of New Jersey was occupied with structures old and new, splendor and squalor. The coast line had the beauty but the intracostal was bleak and sad in most places. At least it felt that way to us. We had been advised to take the outside route up the coast as opposed to the intracostal, if the weather permitted. *Skipper Bob*'s book explained that the ocean route was more desirable. The weather was not as good as we would like, so we took the inside route. To add to the lack of beauty on this course, we found that we had to contend with the most inconsiderate boating community we had experienced to date. Most of the boaters acted like the boating season is only one day long and this was it. It seemed as though we were among the worse combination of boaters that could be gathered; fast boats, uninformed captains and a short boating season.

The most disagreeable boat was the style known as the "Sport Fisherman" and, advertised as a fishing machine. These boats were identified by the large aft deck with a fighting chair located in the center of the deck. The hull was designed to go fast and powered by massive twins or more, capable of carrying them in excess of 50 mph. A quality used 40 foot Sports Fisherman can easily sell for over $600,000. They are built to go fast and catch fish and usually the owner or captain has only those two things on his mind. They were not built to travel slow and made a large wake when they went slow, which we had to contend with. Their goal was to get to the ocean and find that large fish. In addition to the go fast boats and the Sport Fisherman boats we had a high number of wave runners and cabin cruisers. The channel was narrow and outside the channel the water was shallow. *Lifestyle II* draws four feet, she is slow and sometimes difficult to maneuver which makes for a stressful day when dealing with all the other factors of New Jersey.

By the second day on the water in New Jersey, I was at my wits end. My stress level increased as the temperature did. The VHF radio was no help. My training as a pilot and as a U.S. Coast Guard rated captain taught me certain etiquette was required when talking on the radio. The FAA and the Coast Guard require certain language, procedures and etiquette. Channel 16 is designated by the Coast Guard as the "Hailing Channel". It is reserved to hail or call another radio operator; at which time the two radio operators are required to switch to a working channel for further communication. The state of New Jersey must be exempt from that law because no one respects it. Boaters would talk to one another on channel 16 at length about everything from a baseball game to how much fish they caught. The radio chatter, the wake from the discourteous boats and the sheer number of boaters anchored in the channel finally brought me to a boiling point. We were passing under a bridge and, just on the other side, a 30 foot cruiser sat anchored in mid-channel. The captain of the boat, appeared to be alone, and was resting in a chair on the aft deck. He was sitting with a fishing pole in one hand and a beer in the other. As I slowly motored past him, trying to stay in the channel, trying to avoid hitting his boat or hitting the bridge and not running aground, I looked down from my flybridge and exclaimed, "HEY, you're anchored in the channel". He looked up causally, smiled and said, "Yea, that's where the fish are." I motored on past, wanting to board his boat and choke him, but then I thought, that made sense. It was hot and the fish liked the deep cool water of the channel. Now I know why *Skipper Bob* said "Go outside".

Log Book June 18, 2013: South of Atlantic City, South New Jersey is not attractive, not friendly and not a good place for trawlers like *Lifestyle II.*

By 1600 we had tossed the anchor out in a little cove off the ICW and next to a little mud island where Maggie could hunt rabbits for a few minutes. The view wasn't pretty but it was a well protected area and free from boat traffic and that made it nice.

The last time I was in this area, I was just out of the Navy and in my second year of college. I was working on my commercial pilot license and at the same time taking the required courses to gain my BS degree. As a low hour pilot, I would do anything to log a few hours in the air. I was flying for a radio station in the afternoon that did a live drive time traffic report, when I heard of an aviation company next door that needed a pilot and mechanic. At the time I had an FAA private pilot license and an FAA Airframe Mechanics license and a lot of fortitude. I was building hours for the other half of the mechanic license known as a power plant license and the flying hours required for the commercial ticket. I contacted the chief pilot Joe who was the head mechanic and also the only full time employee of Fromhagen Aviation. My main qualification was that I would do most anything and I would work cheap. The company was owned by a local physician who had visions of becoming another American Airlines. He owned two airplanes. A Beach 18 and a DC-3. Both planes were old even in the 60s, but both were solid airplanes and could make him money if he could keep his expenses down. I was a perfect fit for the job. Each time one of the planes started up, I wanted to be aboard. His company had two specialties that paid the bills. He would fly golfers to the Bahamas for weekend outings and he also had a license as a "hospital carrier" that was needed if you were flying sick people under a doctors' care. He maintained his doctor practice during the week and did most of the flying on the weekend. That worked for me since I was in school during the week. After my classes during the week, I would work on the planes and on the weekend I was part of the flight crew.

One weekend we had a flight scheduled on the DC-3 to take a patient, his wife and an assortment of prize winning orchids to his hometown of Pittsburg, PA. Doctor Fromhagen was the pilot in charge, Joe was the co-pilot and mechanic and I was left to load the orchids, luggage and fly third seat. The DC-3 does not have a third pilot seat so when we were in the air, I usually stood between the left seat and the right seat. In addition, we had a nurse on board to help the patient.

The development of the DC-3 changed aviation in the world. It was such a success that over 10,000 planes were produced for the military during WWII. The plane could carry 25 troops plus aircrew and all the gear that could be packed in the plane. It was not pressurized and cruised at about 170kts. Our DC-3 had two Pratt and Whitney

1830 radial 14 cylinder engines that produced 1200hp each. Earlier versions had smaller engines but this old bird had been produced for the military for use in WWII and had the bigger engine. I would learn the significance of the larger engines before that trip was over.

Our flight from St. Petersburg to Pittsburg had been mostly uneventful, except I could not locate the valve that turned on the heat in the cabin. We had not had an occasion to use the heat since most of the flights had been to the Bahamas and back. The nurse piled a couple of blankets on the patient and I searched the maintenance books for the valve. I finally located the valve about an hour outside of Pittsburg. We landed, off loaded the patient, his stinking pots of orchids and the crew went for coffee and a bathroom break, except me. I had to oversee the refueling. After refueling, I made a dash for the bathroom and the restaurant. The doctor filed his flight plan and I checked the fuel and oil with Joe watching closely. We departed Pittsburg and called the FAA communication center for instructions. Our flight plan would take us east and then down the east coast. The nurse had cleaning and reconfiguring duties in the cabin and I took up my position in between the pilot and copilot in the cockpit. We were about an hour and a half into the return flight and I was standing between the seats scanning the gages when my eyes locked on the oil pressure gage. I watched in horror as the oil pressure on the starboard engine steadily dropped to ZERO. I pointed to the oil pressure gauge with my left hand as I looked out the right cockpit window and saw a large oil slick over the wing and pointed to it with my right hand. Had I forgotten to replace the oil cap? Had I done something wrong? Were we all going to die? By this time we were possibly over New Jersey and piloting by dead reckoning, a method of navigation based on speed and time. This was before a GPS system told your exact location and before large screen displays showed the nearest airport. What were we going to do? I couldn't even make a phone call to say goodbye to loved ones. The doctor/pilot took charge. He cut the engine, feathered the prop and yelled to me, "Find me the nearest airport." Find the nearest airport? I wasn't even sure what state we were in. Joe yelled out our approximate position while I pulled out all the Jepp charts we carried behind the seats that showed all the airports in

North America. Maybe I could narrow it down some. Ninety minutes at approximately 150 mph possibly 200 miles east of Pittsburg, maybe middle or northern New Jersey.

There were a couple of good things about our situation. First, the remaining Pratt and Whitney 1830 engine is powerful enough to fly this airplane on a single engine and, second, we had a light load and, more importantly, the radios still worked. The doc and Joe finally gave up on me finding an airport and decided to declare an emergency. Once the call to the FAA is made declaring an emergency, the FAA takes over. The FAA Center routes you to an airport, clears all traffic from your path and stays in constant communication with you. We were directed to Lakehurst Naval Air Station. Suddenly I had a flashback and remembered the history of this area. That's the place where the HINDENBURG CRASHED! Oh No! What a bad omen to be directed to the same airport that is famous for a fiery crash. My thoughts were interrupted by Joe telling me to go into the cabin and inform the nurse of our predicament and tell her to strap in. I went aft and informed the nurse that we were going to crash, well not exactly. I just told her we were making an unscheduled landing, to take a seat and put on her seat belt. The landing a few minutes later was uneventful but the taxi down the runway past every piece of firefighting equipment on the base was somewhat unnerving.

The Navy was nice to us and allowed us to park the plane on the tarmac for a few days. Joe and I examined the engine and, to my relief, the oil cap was on. It seemed the engine had blown a jug. That's mechanics language for "It just broke". We flew on a commercial airline home and I rented a truck and drove back to Lakehurst, NJ with a new engine. Joe met me at the motel I had rented and three days later we had swapped the engine. The doc flew up to meet us and check out his new engine. They asked if I wanted to fly back in the DC-3 and I declined saying, I had to return the truck. I worked for Fromhagen Aviation for a couple months after that event but I never flew in the DC-3 again.

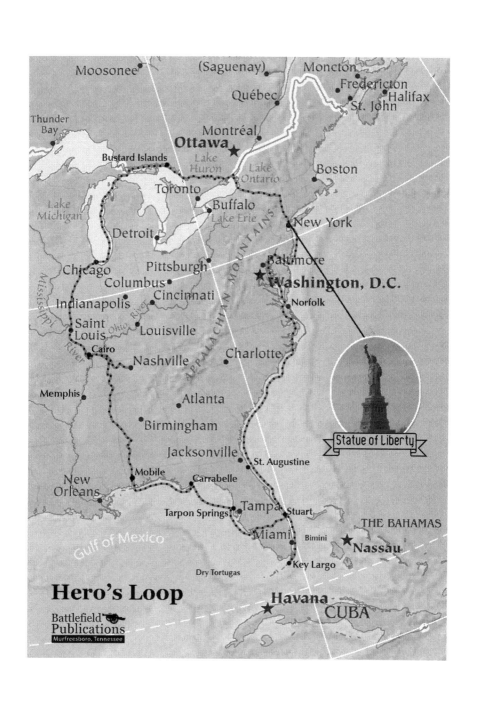

Moosonee

(Saguenay)

Moncton

Fredericton

Québec

Halifax

St. John

Thunder
Bay

Montréal

Ottawa

Lake
Huron

Boston

Bustard Islands

Lake
Ontario

Toronto

Lake
Michigan

Buffalo

Lake Erie

New York

Detroit

Chicago

Pittsburgh

Baltimore

Columbus

Cincinnati

Washington, D.C.

Indianapolis

Norfolk

Saint
Louis

Ohio River

Louisville

Cairo

Nashville

Charlotte

Memphis

Atlanta

Birmingham

Mississippi River

APPALACHIAN MOUNTAINS

Jacksonville

Mobile

Carrabelle

St. Augustine

New
Orleans

Tarpon Springs

Tampa

Stuart

THE BAHAMAS

Miami

Bimini

Nassau

Gulf of Mexico

Dry Tortugas

Key Largo

Hero's Loop

Havana

CUBA

Battlefield
Publications
Murfreesboro, Tennessee

Statue of Liberty

Chapter 13

Turn left at the Statue of Liberty

By noon on Sunday *Lifestyle II* and crew were docked at Hoffman's Marina at the Manasquan Inlet. We soon would be out of New Jersey. One more day to Sandy Hook or, if the weather was good, we would cruise the Lower Bay to Staten Island. It was time to do maintenance on the engine, wash the clothes and buy groceries. The owner of Hoffman's took us to the grocery, picked us up and located three gallons of oil for us. He did all that running around without asking a penny for his trouble. He was so nice that I almost wanted to take back all the bad things I had said about New Jersey, well almost. A couple of days later with clean clothes, a fully stocked pantry and new oil and fuel filters we crossed the Lower Bay and picked up a mooring ball at the Richmond County Yacht Club in Staten Island, New York. We had made it to New York. Another milestone accomplished for *Lifestyle II* and crew. Staten Island is the only borough that is not connected to the subway system. A free ferry service travels between Manhattan and Staten Island which keeps the harbor water churned up while the Verrazano-Narrows Bridge is busy overhead.

I looked across the inlet and spotted *In 2 Wishin* and Jerry and Joan whom we had met at the Shell Service station dock. We took the dinghy over for a visit. We told them that we were getting close to our time for docking the boat for a while and driving back to Tennessee for the family reunion. The only problem was that dock space or even mooring balls are all New York prices, very expensive. In the book *"Honey, Let's Get a Boat"* a cruising adventure of America's Great Loop, Ron and Eva Stob tell of a yacht club up the Hudson River that was favored by Loopers. It was the Poughkeepsie Yacht Club. We decided we would go on to Poughkeepsie and make it the respite spot. Poughkeepsie was only two or three days away, depending on the weather and the tides. The next challenge before us would be the rounding of Staten Island, running the narrows of New York and the traffic of the Hudson River at Manhattan. The stories we had heard about the next 20 miles terrified us. Our little boat and green crew were going to drive through the busiest boating area in the country. In addition to the boat traffic of every conceivable type, we would have to overcome the current of the Narrows. Stories have been told of old shipping masters who would sit outside the Narrows for days waiting for the right wind and tide to take them into New York Harbor. Jerry and Joan had the same concerns that we had so we decided to buddy boat through the New York harbor. His boat was faster so he would take the lead. We would wait for the right time and weather to make the race past Manhattan.

Log book: Wednesday June 22, 2011 On ball at RCYC up at 0600. 0900 in the Narrows, tide out going, making 4.5 kts.

My navigation techniques had proved correct. When I told people that I would travel up the east coast and turn left at the Statue of Liberty I had been joking but now it was a reality. There she was on the port side. We were there at the Statue of Liberty. What a grand experience. I felt as if I would cry at the sight or at least stand at attention. Even Maggie seemed mesmerized by the view of the grand lady. Maggie stood on the port side with her feet on the rail staring at the statue. Denniese and I stood and watched as the island seemed to float by at 4.5kts. Maybe it was a blessing that we had an outgoing tide. It gave us time to enjoy the moment and give thanks for our safety and the opportunity to be in this place.

The spell was broken by the scene that unfolded in front of us. It seemed as if a thousand commercial vessels had been turned loose and were all headed in different directions; ferries to Jersey City, ferries to Manhattan, ferries to the Statue of Liberty, ferries to Brooklyn. There were so many ferries that they were color coded so people could tell the different lines and destinations. Next were the water taxis darting in and out. Then mix in a pleasure craft or two, one loan fisherman at anchor in the middle of it all, add in a few containerships, military ships and harbor patrol boats and you have the picture. What could I do to get through this mess? Just then I remembered the advice Capt. Ron (Kurt Russell) gave Martin Harvey (Martin Short) in the movie "Captain Ron". When the crew was worried about the boat traffic, Capt. Ron stated, "They'll get out of our way." I could only hope.

I saw *In 2 Wishin* ahead of us about a mile. Even with all the traffic, they seemed to be safely maneuvering through the maze of boats. If Jerry and Joan could do It, I felt confident that we could do it. The significance of the water we were in was almost overwhelming. This port has been so important to the U.S. and to the world. The location of the childhood home of Cornelius Vanderbilt was only 200 feet from the shore of this river at the Narrows. I was floating across the route where young Vanderbilt sailed his many boats as he laid the foundation for his transportation empire. Across the bay at the bottom of Brooklyn at Cropsey Ave. at one time had been the home of Wheeler Shipyard Inc. That shipyard built the special motor craft ordered by Ernest Hemmingway which he christened *Pila*r. Next to Liberty Island is the famous Ellis Island, the gateway for millions of immigrants between the years1892-1924. To my right was the Governors Island, which at one time housed the largest U.S. Coast Guard station and now is known as the, "Playground for the Artsy." Past Governors Island is the entrance to the East River and just within sight is the historic Brooklyn Bridge.

Battery Park came into view and brought back memories of a time when my oldest son Jay and I traveled to New York and stood on the sea wall at the Battery, looking out over the bay and wishing we could be on the water. We had walked through the Twin Towers and then down to Battery Park to get to that spot. Of course the Twin Towers are no longer there. Several marinas are located along this part of Manhattan, but with our tight time schedule and limited budget, we continued on. Within a short time we saw the commercial docks and spotted the pier from which Denniese and I took a dinner cruise only a few years before. By that time the crew of *Lifestyle II* had relaxed some and we were even able to hastily sing a few bars of "New York-New York", just like the dinner cruise had played that night as we pulled into the pier. We both smiled at the thought of that quick trip where we had taken in a Broadway show, gone to the top of the Empire State building, gone for a bike ride in Central Park and ended the day with the dinner cruise.

The George Washington Bridge seemed to be the dividing line between mayhem and the normal pandemonium of Manhattan. By that time the tide had turned and we were able to throttle down and still make over 6kts. At 1430 we passed Sing-Sing prison. The prison is now a maximum security prison that houses some 2000 inmates and occupies some valuable real estate along the banks of the Hudson River. The prison dates back to the first quarter of the 19th century and among its more notorious inmates were Julius and Ethel Rosenberg who were executed at Sing-Sing in June of 1953.

We tied our dock lines to the dock at Haverstraw Marina at 1515 or 3:15PM. The wind had been picking up and finally developed into a full summer thunderstorm by 1915. We were dry and Maggie had spent some quality time on the dog path, so we just enjoyed the rain. I checked the log and saw that we had put nine hours on the engine this day. It had been a long day but the trip today was a memorable one. The rain continued the next day so we used that day to catch up on planning and maintenance. I worked on the genset and changed the oil and filter. The generator had worked well and I wanted to show it some love. I phoned the Poughkeepsie Yacht Club and they reserved us a mooring ball for the next day. We still had not confirmed plans for our trip to Tennessee. We had an idea of how our trip should work, but no idea of the specifics. We had to see if PYC would allow us to leave the boat for about 10 days then find a way to get to the car rental agency and rent a car. That was just the outline. Making it all happen would be a bit more of a challenge.

Log Book: Friday June 24, 2011 Haverstraw Marina. Rain last night-Front has settled over this area, cool 68 degrees and high today expected 78 degrees-cloudy and foggy. Up at 0700 engine on at 0845.

By 1130 we had West Point in view. The landscape had changed from the low coastal area to the valley of the Hudson River. The roll of the land and green hills reminded us of the rich vegetated hills of the Tennessee River. The main difference was the history that this river held over almost any other river in the world. West Point, the United States Military Academy is distinctive sitting on the hill above the Hudson at an "S" curve in the river. The gray and black granite of the castle looking structure extends down to the water's edge. They even have a dock for boats to tie up and visit the facility. Since 911 permission and a reservation are required to dock, which we didn't have. The original fort was fist occupied in 1778 and has been part of the Army since. The graduating classes of the early 1860s supplied the general officer ranks of both the Union and Confederate ranks for the Civil War. Around the corner we passed the location where in 1778 a chain was strung across the Hudson by the Continental Army to keep the British out of the lower Hudson. The Academy extends along the west bank of the Hudson for nearly two miles.

By 1530 we passed Poughkeepsie, NY and were surprised by the size of the city. The city has a population of over 30,000 and is known as the "Queen of the Hudson". It has good curb appeal from the river and boasts the longest walking bridge in the world. The Poughkeepsie Bridge is a former rail bridge that was converted into a walking bridge and park in 2009. It is a nice walk of over a mile and over 200 feet above the water at its center span. North of the city and almost a half hour up the Hudson was the Yacht Club. I was able to raise them on the VHF and they told me, "Just tie up to a ball and come in to the clubhouse."

As the PYC came into view, it reminded us of the clubhouse where we had taught sailing classes in Nashville. It was a large two story wooden building facing the Hudson with a backdrop of woods and solitude behind, windows facing the river, and a veranda made it inviting. Floating docks and mooring balls were mostly occupied by sailboats with a few trawlers and powerboats scattered about. A courtesy dock for dinghies and a launching ramp made it accessible to most all boaters. It was a very appealing yacht club where just the appearance made us feel welcome. The club is a cooperative club, meaning that all the members are required to work at the club as part of their membership. The docks and the boats are all pulled out of the water for the winter and stored on land. Electric and water lines are all rolled up and stored till spring. The season is short here but the enthusiasm overcomes the short summer. We checked into the clubhouse and were told that we were invited to a party that evening at the club house. It was Friday and it was warm, so a party was in order. The club and its membership are a world apart from the metropolitan city of New York just 60 miles to the south. We were welcomed by everyone we met and we enjoyed the Bar-B-Q and fellowship. Most of the members guessed that we were not from New York. They said we talked "funny". That was OK because we felt the same about them. They all wanted to know how we were able to get by water from Tennessee to Poughkeepsie. They all loved boats and water and were entertained by our water stories. Friendships were made and help for our needs were extended by all. Maggie even found some barky dogs to make friends with. Later we climbed into our bed with full tummies and smiling faces. We pulled the blanket up over us and snuggled up close to ward off the cool night. It was late June and our friends in Tennessee were experiencing a hot summer but here it was a cool spring night.

The next couple of days were spent working on boat projects and getting to know the people at PYC. The members had adopted us as guest members and we enjoyed their friendship.

Sunday we were offered a car so we could attend services at the local Baptist church. We had first thought of riding our bikes but after talking to some folks, we found it would be too long ride. Pete and Cheryl Carr said, "Take our car, we have two cars here." Actually, it was Cheryl's car, a new Lexus LX with all the bells and whistles. I was afraid we would be late for church because I wanted to try all the extras the car was equipped with. We made the church on time with help of the factory equipped GPS and enjoyed the service. When we returned, Pete told us to keep the keys they would not need the car till Monday. We took the opportunity to check out the area and see some of the sights. Back on board *Lifestyle II*, I decided I would take on a project I had been putting off for a while. *Lifestyle II* had a "mustache". A mustache develops on a boat because of the bow wave that going through the water at slow speeds creates. The waters of the south are brown from the decaying trees and plants which produce a brown substance called tannins. The tannins makes the water brown and the brown water stains the bow of the boat in the form of a mustache. Those brown streams were mostly behind us for a while, so it was time to clean the mustache off our pretty boat. Boaters always have a solution for every problem. The recommended method for removing a mustache is to use concentrated lemon juice on the stain. The application of the lemon juice was a joke to this stain. After all, by this time we had traveled a couple thousand miles in those tannins waters which had deposited a stain with an impenetrable barrier. After several attempts with applications of mixed compounds which were all were applied from the dinghy that was tied to the bow of the boat, I gave up. Fighting the current from the tide of the Hudson added to my frustration. Finally I took the advice of a PYC member who had been watching my efforts from shore. He said use "toilet bowl cleaner". Suddenly a project that I thought would take a commercial buffing wheel and a couple of day's labor turned into a couple hours of wiping on and wiping off. At the end of the day we had a white hull again. The toilet bowl cleaner removed the brown stain but also removed the wax on the hull. As soon as possible I would add a couple coats of wax. The new wax should keep the tannins from adhering to the hull.

Monday arrived and we had designated it as the day to rent a car and make final preparations for our departure of *Lifestyle II* and our trip to Tennessee for the annual family July 4th golf scramble, picnic and get together. Pete and Cheryl our PYC angels had offered to keep an eye on *Lifestyle II* and also take us to the rental car agency. They were such great folks, we were truly blessed by their acquaintance. We were planning our departure for the next day so were took the opportunity to blitz some of the sites of Poughkeepsie. Our tour was just as impressive close up as it was from the water. We walked the River Walk Bridge, making it the third way we had crossed the Hudson. We had flown over it, boated over it and walked over the Hudson River. Next to Poughkeepsie is the world famous CIA headquarters. No, not the Central Intelligence Agency, but the Culinary Institute of America. The CIA started in 1946 to further educate cooks returning from the various branches of the service after WWII. It is now located on the banks of the Hudson in Hyde Park in a former Jesuit monastery. It offers a four year degree and is recognized as the world's premier culinary college. The CIA offers five award winning student staffed restaurants which are quite popular to visitors. Reservations are suggested but with our blitz technique, we seldom made reservations to anything. This time it would affect our choices. This Monday was presentation day. Presentation day is the day when the students show off their work to their professors. All the restaurants were closed to visitors but we quickly found a student run cafeteria which offered a choice of a lunch menu which surpassed many New York City restaurants.

Our next stop was the Vanderbilt mansion located down the street. The 54 room mansion was built by Frederick William Vanderbilt, the grandson of the famous Commodore and director of the New York Central Railroad for 61 years. A tour of the grounds and the bookstore was all that time allowed. Even with our limited tour, we witnessed a snap shot of the grandeur and wealth the Vanderbilt family experienced. The home of Franklin D. Roosevelt was just down the road but our time line did not allow a visit. Maggie was greatly disappointed that we didn't make it to FDR's home because she was working on a record for leaving her scent at "Mansions on the Hudson". Instead we went to our floating home and prepared for our departure the following day. We made several trips to the dock to load the car for our trip home. For me, a checklist is always necessary. The departure list went as follows:

1. Close all threw hulls
2. Turn off all breakers (except sump pump)
3. Empty trash
4. Clean and close toilets

5. Remove clothes
6. Remove previously used charts
7. Remove files box and laptop
8. Store outside items
9. Secure dinghy at dock
10. Put plants outside.

After all the trips to the dock and preparations, we were ready for an early departure.

Logbook: Tuesday June 28,2011 On mooring ball at Poughkeepsie Yacht Club. Departed by car @ 0700 arrived in Murfreesboro, Tennessee @ 2200. 945 mile drive.

Our return trip to Poughkeepsie on July 7 was smooth and even faster than our trip home. We made it back to Poughkeepsie in 14 1/2 hours. We felt good after our visit home and everyone wanted to know about our trip and the places we had visited. Denniese posted the following blog about our return to *Lifestyle II*.

"We made the whirlwind trip home, driving 16 hours on the first leg but the trip back did not take as long, about 14/12 hours. It was great to be among family and friends, and we were sorry we did not get to see everyone we wanted to see. We arrived in Poughkeepsie around 8:00pm and stopped at the Subway, got a foot-long and headed for the boat. The sun was just setting as we arrived, so we ate our sandwich on the porch of the yacht club while Maggie ate her dinner. We loaded the dinghy with most important stuff (cooler, clean clothes, dog, captain, admiral, ect) and decided to get the rest in the morning. No problem. I got on the boat first, then we got Maggie on board, (it was pretty much dark by then) next the travel bags with the clothes, and last, but certainly not least, the cooler, which was full and awkward and very heavy. Mike lost his grip on the cooler and it went in the Hudson River and of course it came open. There was a ziplock bag in the very top of the cooler filled with fresh blueberries, a half carton of eggs, little Debbie Swiss rolls (one of Mike's favorite snacks) a carton of orange juice, milk, bacon and cheese all floating in different directions toward Manhattan. The current was swift and the night was dark. My first thought was there goes breakfast, Too Bad! Not to worry, Mike hollered for me to untie the dinghy from the boat and he went after the groceries like a rodeo champion. After a few minutes of motoring the dinghy around in ever increasing circles, he had rounded up all the food and even the wayward cooler. My hero saved our food. Thank you Lord. What a mighty God we serve."

Log book: Wednesday July 6, 2011 On mooring ball at PYC. Up at 0700. Glad to back on our floating home. Even Maggie seems to be happy to back on board.

After we made another run to the grocery store and unloaded the car, it was time to return the rental and start our planning for the next leg of the Great Loop. One major concern was the air height of our boat. Air height or bridge height is the height from the water to the top of the highest object on the boat. So far, if we were in doubt about a bridge we would ask for an opening. Chicago bridges are the exception. They don't open!! Many years ago, in order to save on the operating expenses of the bridges and with the increased pedestrian and vehicle traffic flow over the bridges, the city decided to limit the opening of the 18 bridges. Sailboats transit the bridges in the spring and again in the fall. Boats with an air height of 17 feet or less do not need to wait until spring or fall for an opening. They can go under the bridges. But if a captain does not want to wait or cannot reduce his air height to 17 feet, then he must use the Calumet canal and go around the city.

We wanted to go under the bridges and see the city from the river. We had visited Chicago and even taken the river tour. Now we wanted to captain our own boat through downtown Chicago. The height had to be under 17 feet. Our bridge height was approximately 21 feet. Before we purchased the boat we were assured the boat could get down to 16 feet without removing the bimini or the radar arch. Now while we were in a friendly spot we had to test that measurement. But just how to do that remained a mystery to me. I had never had to measure a boat height before and really didn't know where to start. I did know that working from a dock would be easier than the mooring ball. We moved the boat over to the courtesy dock and there I met a young couple, Robert and Lori Dahl, who were members of the club. After several tries, I came up with the idea of winding a weighted string around the boat hook and standing on the top deck with the boat hook resting horizontally on the radar arch and the end of the hook extending over the water. I unrolled the line and weight as Robert, Lori and Denniese watched. Denniese was on the dock and called out when the weight touched the water. At her command, I marked the line with a felt tip pen. The radar arch became my reference point and from there I could tell we had work to do. After measuring the string, I determined the radar arch was 16 feet off the water, but mounted on the arch were the radar unit and the anchor light. Mounted on the top deck and extending above the arch was a three inch steel pipe crane with a winch and cable for lifting the dinghy and a satellite dish that we had not used. Removing the dish, the light and the radar unit would not be a problem but the crane would be. I estimated it weighed close to two hundred pounds and power wires were running down the center of the pipe, needed to power the winch, added to the problem. Ask and thou shall receive. "Hey, Robert do you think we can take this crane down?" I asked. Robert looked like he could bench press a Volkswagen and was eager to meet the challenge. Denniese fed the wires from the bottom as Robert and I lifted the crane. After a few tries the crane was safely lowered and resting on the top deck. Even with the two of us lifting and Robert's superior strength, I don't think we had another try left in us. Another angel had appeared, this time in the form of a weight lifter.

Logbook: Thursday July 7, 2011 At courtesy dock at PYC, up at 0720 rested and ready to continue our voyage.

We pulled away from the dock at 0900 after a wonderful stay at Poughkeepsie Yacht Club. We regretted our departure but we knew we had a long way to go and a short time to get there. After all we had a wedding to attend in Tennessee in October. By Friday afternoon we were tied up to the free dock at Waterford. The town of Waterford offers free docking and electricity to boaters. We took the bicycles into town and shopped at the Ace Hardware. We bought tee shirts from the dockmaster and, on Saturday morning, we had breakfast downtown. Then we said goodbye to Waterford and started our trip on the first lock of the Erie Canal, lock number two at Waterford, New York. There is no lock number one, go figure. The Erie Canal is such a significant water way. It connects the great lakes to the Atlantic and made New York the great port that it is. The canal is 363 miles long and the 36 locks lift a boat a total of 565 feet. The man- made and manually dug canal opened in 1825 and is said to have paid for itself in two years. Railroads and other canals have now reduced its use to just pleasure craft but the significance of the Erie cannot be overstated. In 2000 Congress designated it the "Erie Canalway National Heritage Corridor" in order to recognize it as the most successful and influential human-built waterway and one of the most important works of civil engineering and construction efforts in North America.

BOAT RULE #7: If you are going to hit something, hit it softly or when in doubt go slowly.

The rain the day before and during the night had created a lot of fast water and trash in the canal. Each lock has spillways at the side that regulate the water height and keep the water from overflowing the lock. As I approached lock number nine I saw all the spillways were open and dumping thousands of gallons of water into the canal. The turbulence created by all this rushing water was bad and had created eddies of swirling fast water. Our single engine was pulling us left and right as much as forward. Logs in the water bumped against our boat and, then at the entrance of the lock, a rented pontoon boat cut in front of me and stopped. I could not stop so I veered to the left to avoid the pontoon boat and a large log and hit the stone lock wall. Wood shattered from the port teak rail and splinters flew up and onto the deck. From my station I could see a once beautifully varnished six foot piece of teak rail had now been reduced to splinters. I had hurt our beautiful boat, my heart sank. I could not see if the fiberglass bow was caved in or if the boat was taking on water. Denniese confessed later that she felt the trip was over. We tied to the starboard side of the lock and the pontoon operator apologized, saying he was trying to push the same log out of the way.

An inspection of *Lifestyle II* showed only six feet of the teak rail was damaged. It was only cosmetic damage but a heartbreaker just the same. A lesser built boat would have been taken to the scrap yard after such a collision. Our grand lady had survived once again and would live to carry us on.

By wine time we were parked at Amsterdam, NY at the free dock wall the city provides. Tied up behind us were fellow Loopers from *EricaLynn* and *Little Latitudes*. Both boats are Mainships and are very nice Loop boats. Leo and Marion Carey were aboard *Little Latitudes* and behind us when I hit the lock wall. Sympathies were given by all as the fellow boaters surveyed the damage. As I thanked them for their concern, I was already calculating how I could fix it and how much it would cost. We agreed to meet across the street at Russo's Italian grill for supper. We toured the lock house that has been part of the system since it was built and has been a residence, a tavern and now a museum.

Within six months of our visit, storms would cause the locks to overflow, almost destroying the locks and the spillways, flooding Russo's and knocking the museum off its foundation. But our visit was tranquil and relaxing. Sunday morning we had located a Baptist church on the internet and we locked Maggie in the boat and Maggie proofed it. As we walked from the boat across the park and toward the main road, a car approached us and the driver asked if we needed a ride. We told him our destination and he offered to take us there. We agreed to the offer and introduced ourselves. Richard Conti was a retired accountant and was our next angel. Richard took us to the church and after services took us on a tour of the area. He was not only knowledgeable of the area but an interesting person to talk with. He enjoyed our stories of the Loop and we enjoyed his knowledge of the area. We visited some of the old Erie that was in the original design. It was far narrower than you would expect. Special boats were built to transit the goods. Mules were bought to pull the craft at one end and sold at the other only to be purchased by another group heading back with a load of goods. Houses along the way were turned into stopping points to supply the needs of the traveler. From that, towns sprung up and commerce grew. The Erie Canal like the Interstate highways today was a boom to the local community. By the end of the day, I was in a much better frame of mind and even made a temporary repair to the port rail. A few screws and several layers of duct tape would hold us until I could arrange a professional repair.

Monday morning we had a big breakfast on the aft deck and walked Maggie. We weren't ready to leave this quiet town and nice park but we knew we had to. By 0830 we were tied up to the wall of lock number 12. The next town was Canajoharie, NY and it offered some amenities according to *Skipper Bob*. After walking Maggie we unloaded the bikes and got directions to the laundry mat. Of course I got the directions wrong and so we got lost. That was bad enough but a record heat wave was settling down on the area and the temps were in the 90s. The bikes were loaded down with the clothes, detergent and softener and after we got the correct directions, we had to peddle uphill for about a mile. The reward came on our return because it was all downhill to the boat and there was an ice cream shop on the way. We stopped at the soda shop and celebrated our clean clothes and this hot day with a banana split which made it all worthwhile. Rejuvenated, we peddled back to the boat. Later I found the post office on the first try and mailed a radio back to Jay that had been a problem from the start. That evening we turned the air-conditioner on for the first time. It worked until about 0530 the next morning when it started making noise. I investigated and found it had a block of ice on the coil. That usually means the refrigerant is low so I just turned it off and hoped the heat wave would pass.

After breakfast Hank Evans helped us off the dock and on our way. We had passed them and they had passed us along the way ever since our first time to meet at Morehead City, NC. Hank and Ann are always good to talk with and lots of fun. He is a retired Navy officer and she is from Jackson, TN, so we can understand each other's dialect. The next free dock was Herkimer, NY and is the back of a restaurant next to the Interstate. The restaurant was undergoing some renovations and the work crew found these two Tennesseans and a brown beagle dog a source of entertainment. We were happy that they found us interesting and we talked with them as they continued to hammer at their work. Soon wine time came and the work crews headed home while we dressed for dinner, that meant putting on our shoes.

We stepped off the boat, walked around to the front of the building and we were seated for a delicious pasta dish. The next day at wine time, we were at Sylvan Beach free dock. They don't provide electricity so it was necessary to run the generator for an hour. After the batteries were charged, we walked into town. Sylvan Beach is now a resort community for people wanting to get away from the city and the heat in the summer months (July and August). At one time it had been an important destination point for the Erie Canal but now it depends on the tourist trade. It sits on the shore of Oneida Lake which is now the major attraction. We enjoyed our walk but could not find a place to mail a letter and were told the only drop box was at the post office which we had passed a mile or so back without noticing. Not wanting to walk any longer, we saved the letter till our next stop. We did find a good restaurant for breakfast the next day. Back on board, we planned for our crossing of Lake Oneida. The lake was about 30 miles across and a north wind would make for an uncomfortable trip. We listened to the NOAA weather reports to decide our departure would be the next day.

Log book: Thursday July 14, 2011 Tied to wall at Sylvan Beach up at 0615 temp. 60 degrees. 0700 breakfast at Flashback Café. Engine on at 0730 on lake by 0800

The lake was kind to us this day and the waves were small and not so bumpy. We didn't even reach "level one" of the weather preparedness system: "Tie the dog down." The wind was blowing from the north but our morning start did not give time for the waves to build. Most of the marinas were full because of the summer boat traffic. Just past Brewerton we found a marina that had space. Winter Park marina was very nice. They sold us 45 gallons of fuel, pumped the holding tank and gave Denniese a coupon for 20% off any clothing item in the shop. It was the end of summer sale. After all, it was mid July so for these folks summer was ending. The marina was a full service marina and even had a wood shop. I ask the foreman if he would give me a ball park price on the little boo-boo on the nose of our boat. A few of us ventured out in the courtesy car to the local West Marine for supplies. When we returned, the foreman had a proposal ready for me; $2000 and two weeks, which did not include the dock fee which would be another $100 per day. "Don't ya just love these New York prices?" I thanked him and told him it could wait till we returned to Tennessee. Besides, in two weeks this place would be shutting down for the winter. There are strange people here in upstate New York. The nice thing about the Loop adventure is the people you meet, the things you see and the experiences you have. The people were great and if they didn't have a thing called winter, we would have stayed longer.

We finally arrive in Canada

Chapter 14

Canada

We purchased another flip chart with the Canadian route we were going to travel before leaving Winter Park and started planning our trip into a foreign country. Just a few miles past Winter Park we had to decide if we were going to go left to Buffalo or right to Lake Ontario. We would love to see Buffalo but time and boat height were the determining factors, so we were going right. Besides, at this point we had two more locks left on this side of the US, and that way we would stop transiting the water elevators for a while. We entered the Oswego Canal at 1000 hours on Friday and by 1500 we were tied to the wall between lock seven and lock eight for the evening. Saturday we left the city dock and locked through the last lock on this portion of the New York Canal system. By 0830 we were officially out of the canals and into Lake Ontario. Our first impression was how big the lake was and our second was how clear the water was. It looked like we could see the bottom when our depth sounder showed 30 feet. The weather was great with highs in the mid 80s. You gotta love this. Here we are from Middle Tennessee, sitting on a boat we purchased in Key Largo and we are on Lake Ontario. We were awestruck! But, we also remembered that the conditions on this lake can change quickly and, being the chickens we were, we headed for the next stop.

At 1400 we were tied up to Henderson Yacht Club and enjoying a glass of red. Harbor master Chuck showed us around and treated us like family. Denniese and I went for a swim in the Great Lake Ontario. It was so clear that I was able to check the prop, the zink and the bottom paint all without a divers light. Later we sat on the grass and talked to members of the club who gave us advice about crossing the lake and even clearing customs in Canada. We were also told that the little cove where we were now docked would have three feet of ice in the winter. Fish houses would be taken onto the ice and streets with names would be established on the ice. They said the winter wind chill would be as low as minus 40 degrees. I said, "Well, I'm sorry we are going to miss that." RIGHT!!

Sunday, we decided to make the jump across the lake to the Canadian side. We heard on the radio that Bob and Lynda aboard *ErikaLynn* and Leo and Marion aboard *Little Latitudes* were about an hour ahead of us with the same idea. We were hoping for a smooth crossing and for the first few miles, it seemed that would be the case. The further out on the lake we ventured, the more the wind increased and the more it came on our nose. We heard Leo talking to Bob on the VHF and said he was turning back. We passed them about 30 minutes later and we considered going back with them but by that time we were approaching the halfway point and decided to continue. Shortly after that, the weather and waves reached Level One, "Tie the dog down". Poor Maggie, she was trying so hard to be the good boat dog but she would slide from the port side to the starboard side and then back again. We took her leash and hooked it on a grab bar and put her between the seat and the dash compartment. She was stationary but not too happy. I think our little scent, land dog was getting seasick. We might have also, but didn't have time. I was driving the boat trying to hit the waves just right and Denniese was navigating and giving me ETAs on getting out of the mess. We finally got behind an island and turned into the North Channel which offered protection.

We tied up to Loyalist Cove Marina at 1455. I ran up the Q flag and asked the dock master if he could help me locate the customs office. I'm not sure he had ever seen a Q flag before and to clear customs, all I needed to do was make a phone call. With that done, Maggie and Denniese were able to leave the boat and head for the sweet smell of

Canadian grass and maybe a Canadian rabbit. After our stomachs settled, we had a late lunch and ask some of the folks gathered at the dock house if a washer and dryer were close by. We were given instructions on the location and ask if we had any "loonies". Loonies are the Canadian dollar, a coin so named because it bears the image of a loon.The lady was nice enough to offer what she had. Four loonies were equal to about four US dollars at the time and we made the exchange. Denniese was not watching as I made the exchange and so when I handed her the loonies I said, "These are for the washer and dryer." Thinking they were the same as a quarter and there were two loads of clothes, she knew it would take four quarters for each load for washing and the same for drying, so she thought would need sixteen loonies. The lady offering the loonies said, "Sixteen loonies, how long has it been since you washed your clothes?" I explained to Denniese the loonie was equal to four quarters and she would only need four to do all the laundry. We all laughed and enjoyed the moment.

Monday morning brought thunderstorms and hard rain. The power was knocked out on the dock and the town for a while. The warm temps had brought a pattern of thunderstorms but it seemed they had passed by about 1000 hours so we departed our first stop in Canada at 1045. We had planned a run of approximately 30 miles for the day. The trip started out smooth with light winds and a warm day. The scenery was beautiful. Rolling hills and a wide freshwater bay that was protected from the south by a chain of islands was our picture of the day. The hills were a lush green and the trees were full. Development was sparse and the land seemed to be used for agricultural means. Herds of black and white or Holstein cows could be seen roving the hills. Holsteins are high producing dairy cows and beautiful cows that require a lot of attention. Milking is required twice a day every day and in some cases three time a day. These cows don't take a day off so the farmer that owns these walking milk producing machines has to love his work and his cows.

We celebrated Maggie's first poop on the boat at 1100. We had worked so hard with every conceivable form of encouragement to entice her to pee and poop on the boat and she finally did it. Only it was the result of an upset stomach from the trip the day before. We told her what a good dog she was and heaped high praise on her for leaving us the present. The upset stomach seemed to be over and she felt much better as I attended to the cleaning. From my sailboat days I have always kept a bucket with a rope attached so with a toss in the water, a bucket of water can be retrieved for a wash down. A couple of buckets of water and the poop washed down the scuppers. One more bucket load and I would be finished. Care must be taken when retrieving water in this fashion while underway. The force of a full bucket of water and the boat moving at six kts will be more that the bucket or rope can take and that was the case on that toss. Our only bucket was a sacrifice to the Canadian sea gods.

As I moved back to the helm I noticed a strong thunderstorm building over my shoulder. It was large and seemed to be moving in our direction. We had lots of room on the water and plenty of water under our keel. Just for precautions, Denniese moved the moveable gear to safe places and I turned on the radar. From our experience we knew what would turn over or fall or be damaged by this time on our trip. We didn't like rough weather and tried to avoid it but felt confident that our boat could take more than we could so we just prepared for the worse and prayed for the best. I saw the thunderstorm coming closer and announced level one of preparedness, "Tie the dog down". That also gave us time to prepare. When a storm is approaching on the water, you have few choices. You can't go to the storm cellar and wait it out, you can't dodge it left or right, you just have to get ready and hold on.

At 1500 we were at the south end of Big Bay and the storm hit. It reminded me of the terrible storm I encountered off the Yucatan Peninsula which damaged so many boats. Within a minute the wind was blowing close to 40 knots. Hail was pounding so hard that I fully expected the bimini top would be penetrated by the hail or blown off by the powerful wind. Our visibility was down to zero. I could barely see the pennant on the bow of the boat. The wind was swirling and I could not hold the boat into the wind. My GPS and radar were my only source for our position. I watched as the compass tried to keep up with our moves as the storm pushed us around. It was of little help. During my flying days, I would have declared this IFR weather. Meaning I was flying by instruments. I could not see land but my radar showed I was still in the middle of the bay. Buoys or navigational aids have radar reflectors on them and I found a buoy close by and used it as a reference point and source for my radar in order to keep me in the middle of the channel and being driven on to the land. My radar unit was seeing no other traffic so I did the best I could to keep the boat circling the buoy. The radar reflector gave me a good target.

Most boats show a good target on the radar screen, but sailboats don't. A sailboat must have a deflector hanging from the rigging. A radar deflector looks like a basketball made of metal and has right angle projections from its core. Sailboats are the original stealth vessel. They are low to the water, made of fiberglass and have very few pieces of right angle metal projecting from the vessel. The storm lasted about 30 minutes during which we were under level two of preparedness, "Get below". The only problem was I had to stay in the cockpit because the radar was needed to maintain our position. *Lifestyle II* did not have radar at the lower helm. Denniese and Maggie maintained their composure, although we were all scared. Our only option was to trust our boat and stay away from land.

The storm finally passed and to my amazement, sitting behind and maybe tied to the buoy was a 30 foot sailboat. How or when he got there I will never know. I tried to contact him on the VHF but he did not answer. We set our heading for our next anchorage and watched as the sailboat crew came on deck to start back on their course. Both boats survived a terrific storm with zero visibility. I could not see a radar dome on his boat so how he found the buoy and how we avoided each other is a mystery. I have heard that the Lord watches over sailors, fools and little children. Many times I have felt I was looked after and fell into two of those categories.

After the storm the sun came out and it was a beautiful day. The sky cleared and the temperature was pleasant. We motored to an inlet which had a small island guarding the entrance. Behind the island was a bay about a mile long. The area was still agriculture but a couple of homes could be seen along the shore and on the hills. We dropped the anchor in ten feet of clear water and, with the admiral's permission I announced double grog for the crew. We even gave Maggie some extra time on shore to recover from her upset stomach. We had survived another storm and *Lifestyle II* proved her mettle. We hoped this would be the last time we encountered such a storm but sadly we had more storms and greater challenges ahead. Had we known our future, we may have turned and joined Leo and Marion and headed back toward the Erie Canal. But we had come this far and since we were approaching the half way mark of the Great Loop Adventure we were determined to continue and earn our gold flag.

Log book: Tuesday July 19, 2011 Muscote Bay off Big Bay on anchor. Temps today low of 68 degrees and high of mid 80's. Some chance of thunderstorms. Up at 0630 Everything outside wet from storm yesterday. Everything inside still rearranged from the storm.

By noon we were tied to the dock at Trenton which is the last stop before we entered the Trent-Severn Waterway. The Trent-Severn is a series of canals, locks and streams that meander 210 miles through central Ontario. The system has 44 locks and one of the most unusual locks in the world. The Big Chute Lock is a railway system that carries the boat over a hill and from one lake to another. It is designed to carry boats up to 99 feet in length. The time required for the canal was four or five days of continuous travel. The Trent-Severn would take us to Georgian Bay which was the north part of Lake Huron. We purchased a Canadian pass for *Lifestyle II* and were surprised to find that we also needed a pass for our little gray dinghy. We gladly paid the fee for pulling the dinghy behind the boat because it is far less expensive than a set of davits to raise the dinghy up on the transom and we still would need the dinghy for trips ashore. The pass included tie ups at the lock wall for evening stops. We purchased fuel, had the holding tank pumped and purchased a Canadian flag to mount on our bow staff. That flag shows we are a guest of Canada and the aft mounted U.S. flag shows our boat is registered in the U.S.

The Canadian lock system is one the U.S. could take lessons from. The locks are run very efficiently; the lock masters take a lot of pride in the grounds and successful movement of boats through the locks is their goal. They give advice on the future locks as well of the towns that offer free tie ups or are having a special event. Many of the locks still have the gates and valves operated by hand. Most of the locks have a short distance to raise or lower the boat and a hand held rope is all that is necessary to control the boat. Most times the lockmaster or his helper will hand you the rope and go turn the turnstile for the operation of the lock. The grounds are always well kept and awards are given to lockmasters for their landscaping efforts. Most locks have interns or college students to help. All personnel wear the uniform of the Canadian Lock System. One requirement, even if it is a ten minute stay, requires the boat captain to shut off his engine. Diesel engines don't run off electricity as gas engines do so just turning off the ignition switch will not shut off the engine. A fuel shut off valve is required to kill the engine. The valve is controlled from a switch on the dash of the boat to a solenoid at the engine that closes the fuel valve and the engine stops. Pulling into lock # 7, the fuel solenoid would not kill the engine. The lock master would not shut the gates until I shut down the engine. I told Denniese to hold on and I raised the hatch to the engine compartment and climbed into the engine compartment and looked for the faulty solenoid valve. The engine was running, the lockmaster was waiting and so were several other boats in the lock. Within a couple of tries I found the manual shut off and successfully killed the engine and we locked through.

Lock #7 is at Campbellsford, Ontario. A small town half way between Toronto and Ottawa and is the home of three wonderful companies. Blommer Chocolate factory, Empire Cheese and Doohers Bakery. Denniese considers chocolate and cheese a substitute for any other food group and I was only able to persuade her away from a full out run to the chocolate factory by describing how Doohers Bakery makes all their products fresh daily and a promise to buy a dozen cream filled donuts. Doohers has been in business for over 60 years and started baking their goods by wood fires.

The engine now had 5201 hours on it and we had put over 400 hours on the engine since our purchase at Key Largo. The faulty solenoid was the first failure of a part since the purchase. Jim, the former owner, must have experienced the same problem since an extra solenoid was in our parts inventory and I replaced the faulty part before bed time. It was also time for another oil change. Three gallons of used oil and an oil filter were stored in the engine compartment until I could find a place to recycle them.

Log book; Thursday July 21, 2013 at the end of the day we are tied up to the wall on the low side of lock # 18. Record heat wave Today record high temp 37 degrees Celsius. (whatever that means) Everyone complains about the heat. Walked into town and had some great fish and chips in a restaurant that had a faulty air-conditioning unit. Food was good but we were hot.

Friday morning we woke to milder temps. Seventy-five degrees at 0630 with a light wind felt better than we had experienced in a while. We had a nice talk with a Canadian police officer who was on vacation and traveling along the Trent-Severn for his two week vacation. Doug owned a 21 foot runabout and carried a tent that he would pitch each evening. We cast off at 0900 and ended the day past lock # 20 at Peterborough on Little Lake in 10 feet of water. Peterborough is a large town and we were able to restock the boat. I found a mop that was lost in one of the storms and found a grocery across the lake and a short walk. Milk was a thought provoking problem. It only was available in plastic bags. It would be a week before we discovered a holder for the plastic bag which allowed the milk to take shape and be poured from the container. Wine was a bigger problem. We were accustomed to buying a five liter box of reasonably good merlot for about $17.00 per box. Here we found the lowest priced three liter box of merlot selling for $31.00. Pumpout for the holding tank is free at most places you purchase fuel. Not here!.. We paid $35.00 for a pumpout of the holding tank and at the same time paying the highest price for fuel we had ever paid.

We had a great anchorage and loved our spot even though a marina was only about 100 yards away, we stayed on anchor. We did motor over to the marina and use their dinghy dock and walk upstairs to the restaurant to enjoy a good meal while overlooking the lake and our boat sitting at anchor. Maggie loved Peterborough also. She loved all the people that showed her some attention.

A large water fountain was located at the far end of the lake and each evening it had a color water display. A park was located near our boat and we could watch kids playing and swimming in the warm lake waters. A group of boys had built a ramp at the end of the dock at the park and used it to launch a bicycle in the air as the rider jumped off and into the water. They would then pull the bike out of the water and start over again. I enjoyed watching their game as much as the boys did playing it. We enjoyed the evening light show and we especially enjoyed watching the birds sitting around the fountain as the show began. Ducks and water birds seemed to think the fountain was built as a perch for them, that is until the water started shooting from all directions and scattering the birds. Sitting at anchor is fun but the batteries still need charging and the generator must run. The generator had been working well but **"BOAT RULE #8: "If it can break, it will"**. The generator cut off on high temperature after about 15 minutes of charging. The batteries would have to do with that charge until we could reach a marina or repair the generator.

A couple of days later it was time to get underway again. The next lock was the Peterborough Lift Lock, one of the more interesting ones we would encounter. It was a "pan lock". I had no idea what to expect. It had been described as a big swimming pool where the boat is driven into and then water is added, which adds weight to the other balanced swimming pool and a see-saw effect takes place. The upper pool lowers and raises the lower pool. Thus a boat is raised to the higher waterway or lowered to the lower waterway. It is simple and very effective. Because the pans are side by side, this type of lock takes a lot less real estate than the conventional horizontal lock that sometimes takes a fourth mile of property to execute the change and can be effective in a populated area.

Log Book: Sunday July 24, 2011 up @ 0630-Some clouds, wind from N lite. At anchor on Little Lake at Peterborough. Engine on @ 0740, anchor up @ 0800. Out of first Pan lock at 0945 GREAT!

The next couple of days were spent in some of the most beautiful parts of the Trent-Severn Waterway. We spent nights on secluded lakes with few people and days passing small towns with the summer tourist going from shop to shop. As we passed through the locks, people would crowd the rail watching the boats locking through. Conversation was started and ended as the boat lifted up and up until we would be standing onboard our boat looking down at our new friends. Most of the conversationalists were Canadians but occasionally we would find a US citizen that recognized the hailing port on the stern. The question was always, "How did you get that boat from Kentucky to this place?" Our answer would always be, "By water."

Wednesday July 27, 2011 was a memorable day because we had finally reached the top of the Loop. We were docked at the Pride of Balsam Marina at lock # 36 on the Trent – Severn Waterway. We were 840 feet above sea level and had gained that elevation by traversing the many locks since the Hudson River. My work on the generator had continued with the replacement of the impeller but the pump was still not pushing enough water to cool the engine and it would shut down after a few minutes of running. We needed an hour of running to generate enough power to recharge the batteries. Without batteries we could not run the refrigerator and other household items. The boat and the boat electronics would run off the boat alternator so we could continue our trip but we needed the house batteries for the fridge and our food. If I could not fix the generator, we would have to hire a mechanic to repair it. This type of mechanic was very specialized and was usually only located in the larger cities and not in remote Canada. Even if we could find a mechanic, it would require down time and possibly a large expense. Our options were limited but I had a few other possible repairs before a mechanic was called. We had completed almost half of our trip and we took the time to reflect on this experience.

We had started our adventure less than six months before without a boat and with little else than the desire to accomplish this thing known as the LOOP. We did have two major elements beyond just a driven desire. We had the time and some money. Boat handling experience is important but I think without the first two, time and money, the later would not be needed. I lacked boat handling experience on a boat of this type and size and I overcame that lack of experience with a few costly bumps along the way. Time and money can make up for the lack of experience but without the time and money this trip could not be made. We all know people that say, "As soon as I have time I'm going to.." or "If we just had the money we could..." and it never happens because of a long list of excuses. This trip does take time but the money can be just a little above the expenses a couple would normally incur by staying at home. Generally speaking, people will spend money at the level of comfort they are accustomed to. That means if you budget 100K for this trip, that is the level of spending you are accustomed to and you will spend it. However, a person could have just as good a trip if they stayed out on the hook and cooked on board and only budgeted half that amount. When we started putting a budget together, gas prices were soaring. I told a friend this trip is going to cost a fortune with diesel priced at $4.00 a gallon. My friend said, "Don't worry, fuel is going to be one of your least expenses". When I look back he was correct. The boat purchase was first and food and docking expenses were far ahead of the fuel bill.

Time is the most important element and can't be compromised. I have heard of people who have done the Loop in three months. But you have to ask "Why?" Allow a year for the Loop and enjoy it. If you want to go fast, take a plane to a remote place and sit on a boat and call it an adventure. The Loop is a boating traveling experience that is to be enjoyed. At our time of reflection we gave a title to our trip: "An Intense Adventurous Challenge", which in a few short words best describes the undertaking known as the Great Loop. Without an adventurous spirit and the confidence to accept the challenges of this trip it would be difficult if not impossible to complete. Other elements worthy of mention are faith that God is in control, physical condition of you and your partner, intelligence, experience, mechanical abilities, ingenuity, agility, a margin of insanity and a large dose of a sense of humor. The bottom line is just do it, and all the elements will fall in place if given the chance.

Wednesday evening we pulled into the Beverton Yacht Club on Lake Simcoe. The clubhouse and grounds were among the prettiest we had seen while in Canada. I was admiring a well kept sailboat to our stern when the owner came on deck and we started talking. Within a few minutes I had begun to explain the generator problems and another angel appeared in the person of Vince Arsenault who, without inspecting the generator, felt sure the problem would be solved if I cleaned the cooling element with a straightened clothes hanger. He then offered new zincs for the cooling element. The cooling element is a radiator using outside water to cool the genset water. It is a cylinder with tubes inside for the two fluids to pass. It made sense that the cooling tubes were stopped up. Back on board, I climbed into the engine compartment with my specialized tool (straightened clothes hanger) and within an hour the genset was purring like a kitten. It seemed the radiator or cooling element had been stopped up by the old impeller pieces and the disintegrated zinc. With the problem now solved, we planned our trip for the following day with renewed assurance that we would not have to toss overboard all our refrigerated stores.

Thursday morning, we departed Beverton Yacht Club and started our 12 mile open water crossing of Lake Simcoe. The wind was above the comfort level but since it was from the stern it was not necessary to tie the dog down. We were rewarded by stopping at The Waubic. The Waubic is a unique restaurant which is located on an island in-between two locks. It is known far and wide for the fish and chips and unique atmosphere. The dock is old and worn but since it is located between two hills on an island and between two locks, wind and water are not a problem. We tied up to the dock which left little room for any other boats. Each time we locked through, we would ask the dock master where to dock and where to eat. For the past couple of days we had been told to stop at The Waubic. The stop was worth it. As soon as *Lifestyle II* was tied to the dock, George Fleet came on board to celebrate the day with us. George and his family own and run the restaurant. We talked about his place and how he came to be running a restaurant on an island. We loved talking to him and discovered that he had run a restaurant in Knoxville and said he loved Tennessee and would still be there if he didn't have this place. Maggie loved it there also. George had two dogs that had the run of the place. Winston and Tanner were mixed breed dogs that had much to say to Maggie. We didn't even try to keep Maggie quiet since we were the only guest and George didn't seem to mind the dogs running and barking. George took our order for supper and departed. I ask if he wanted me to pay and he said we would settle up tomorrow. The supper was so good that we decided to start the next day off with a Waubic breakfast. By 0930 the next day we had finished our breakfast and paid our tab for the stay and the meals. The bill was about what a dock space only would have cost at other marinas. I ask George if anyone had run off without paying their bill. He said, "Where would they go, we are between two locks and the lock masters eat here."

We had two more locks to traverse before we would complete the 45 locks of the Trent-Severn Waterway. Lock # 44 is the jewel of the waterway. The Big Shute is a railroad track system where the boat drives up on a large travel lift and is carried over a hill by this mechanism to the next body of water. Ahead of us, the fun begins. We didn't know what to expect but the wild stories we had heard about the180 mile body of water known as the Georgian Bay would get any captains attention. The Georgian Bay and the North Channel are the northern part of Lake Huron.

We docked *Lifestyle II* at the staging dock for the Big Chute as instructed by the lift/lock master. We took the time to walk Maggie and just look in amazement at this engineering marvel. This huge railed travel lift could carry a 100 foot boat over the hill and into the glacier bay on the other side. It could carry as many as a dozen boats our size. As we looked around we could only see two other boats other than our boat. Not wanting to be left behind, I queried the other captains and discovered that they just came down to watch the operation and would not be locking through. On the hill beside the lift was a museum for the locks and a viewing area to watch the boats being moved from one side to the other.

Denniese is always looking for opportunities to take care of boat duties and soon found a row of trash cans to drop our trash into from the past few days. The trip for the day almost ended as Denniese, with a full bag of trash and Maggie on her leash, raised the lid of the middle trash can to drop the bag in, only to interrupt a fat raccoon from chewing on a chicken bone. As the startled raccoon jumped straight up from the bottom of the trash can into the bright sunlight, a screaming woman and a barking dog were its welcoming committee. The raccoon scurried off into the brush but Maggie was at full speed and only a few feet behind. Maggie was close to capturing her first Canadian raccoon when the flex leash ran out and jerked Denniese's arm almost to the point of dislocating her shoulder. All was calmed within a short time when Maggie lost sight of the raccoon and was confused by all the other animal smells. By the time Denniese arrived back at the boat, she could laugh at the event but still needed time for her arm to rest before we continued.

At 1130 we drove *Lifestyle II* onto the lift. We were the only boat. We felt special. People were on the viewing platform pointing and looking our way. The lift operators made several adjustments as the belts started taking up the slack. Soon we were high and dry. The operators walked forward and aft on their cat walks making sure all was good. Prior to driving on lift, we had marked the boat with blue painters tape to mark the proper lift points. The giant lift raised us out of the water and slowly started the climb up the hill. We were on the sun deck and could talk to the operators as our travel proceeded. We asked the operators the same silly questions that all boaters ask. "How does the bottom look, or can you check my zincs while we are in the air?" The lift operators take it all in stride because they have heard it all before. Even Maggie seemed to enjoy the ride. She ran from side to side barking at the operators as we rode slowly over the hill. It was a coordinated effort by about half a dozen people that was done with precision and perfection. About 15 minutes later we were lowered into the water with just as much care.

We exited the Chute at 1215 as the sun came out and the temperature soared to a mild 85 degrees. This was the time of the year when Canadians came out and enjoyed the great weather. The boat owners were out, the kids were swimming and for a few days this time each year, this was the best place in the world to be. We were near the top of the Loop and the next lock would be our last until we were back in the

States. The last lock of the Trent Severn,# 45, was just ahead. After that, we would be dumped out into the southeast end of Georgian Bay. What lay ahead was a long stretch of open water broken up by what is called the small boat channel. A larger boat or a braver captain could take the most direct route across the open water, which would mean 120 miles of open water. The small boat channel is not direct by any stretch of the imagination but it is scenic. This bay was created by glaciers at the end of the last ice age or about 11,000 years ago. Eastern Georgian Bay is part of the southern edge of the Canadian Shield, granite bedrock with tens of thousands of islands exposed throughout the bay. The small boat channel meanders through the islands and the cuts are sometimes so narrow that only one boat can pass at a time.

At 1530 we dropped anchor in Honey Harbor, a tourist destination favorite by many during the few days of summer. We were anchored about a quarter mile from the marina and away from the channel. We favored the anchor spot because we were told a transit slip at the marina would cost us about $130.00 per night US. WOW, that would be higher than a Miami dock fee in winter months. The anchor spot was better than being tied to a dock anyway. We were in about 15 feet of crystal clear water and away from the boat traffic. The marina was just a short dinghy ride away. The granite rock and large evergreen trees made for a sharp contrast. It was a beautiful place to be. We started the generator and it hummed along as it charged the batteries and ran the refrigerator. All was well aboard *Lifestyle II*. After supper we still had daylight enough to dinghy to the marina to let Maggie visit with some other four legged friends and spend some quality time on grass. While walking around the marina, I saw many boat props of varied size and shape used as decoration at the foundation of the building, hanging from nails on the side of the building and even used as door stops. All the boat props had similar damage. They all had come in contact with a solid object at a high speed. I causally made the observation that, "That's a lot of props." A mechanic near smiled and said, "Yeh, they hit Miami rock." I replied, "That's an interesting name for a rock in the middle of Canada." The mechanic looked at me and raised a brow and tilted his head as he reported, "There is a rock near the channel that boaters run up on quite often. It's called Miami rock because each year the owner of this shop spends the winter in Miami from the money he makes on replacing props that hit that rock". I thought, I will have to remind Denniese to help me stay in the channel when leaving this area. Unfortunately, there were so many "Miami rocks" in this part of Canada that we would both be nervous until we got to Lake Michigan.

The next morning after breakfast we reviewed our course for the next few days and found we would need some fuel. I motored to the fuel dock and ask the attendant to pump the diesel until I called out from the engine room for him to stop. Denniese had the good sense to stop the pump before we ran out of money. At $1.38 per liter and $35.00 for a pump out, I had found the most expensive place to buy fuel in the northern hemisphere. The 200 liters of fuel and a pump out totaled $321.78. The only thing worse would be to hit Miami rock on the way out.

At the end of the day, we dropped anchor in a small bay that looked truly inviting. It was not on our chart as a designated anchor spot but it was for us. We were in about 15 feet of water and it was so clear I could see the anchor sitting on the bottom some 80 feet away. I had only experienced water that clear once before and that was in White Bay off Jost Van Dyke in the BVI and then only on a calm day. In Canada it was summer and all the kids were on the water, while the adults supervised from shore. We dinghyed over and introduced ourselves to some people we saw on a pier. It seemed they were camping on the shore of the lake and had a couple of families in the group. They invited us to come ashore and have a cup of tea. That was too much for Denniese to turn down since she is the daughter of a full English lady and tea was never denied. Besides, we had been out of tea for a couple of days and even I agreed to the invitation. We sat in lawn chairs with the group and sipped our warm tea as kids and dogs played. They had purchased the lot for building several years back but had never received a permit to build on it. So each summer they would come to the lake lot and camp on it for a couple of weeks. It was good to talk to some real people for a change and as most Canadians are, these people were very gracious and interesting to talk with. Of course, they wanted to hear all about our trip and the motivation for a 6000 mile journey in a boat. It was fun talking with the family and we barely made it back to *Lifestyle II* before dark.

We pulled the anchor up at 0900 Sunday and were starting to head out of the bay when we saw Pam, the lady we had visited the evening before, paddling out in her kayak. She waved us down and I went to the starboard rail to meet her. She said how much she enjoyed our visit and she wished us well on our voyage. Then she handed us a ziplock filled with teabags. That gift was just another example of the attitude most of the Canadian people had toward their neighbors to the South. The remainder of the day was a challenge with narrow passageways, approaching thunderstorms and then the chartplotter and the chart did not agree. All the stress and bouncing gave Denniese a headache and me a churning stomach. Maggie slept through it all.

By 1645 we had found our destined marina and pulled into a slip behind a new Beneteau 365 that had a new dinghy hanging off davits on the stern of the shiny sailboat. The dock worker took our lines and pulled us within six inches of the suspended dinghy. Our 45lb CQR anchor with clumps of black mud hung over the dinghy and looked like an arrow pointed toward a balloon. The sailboat owner quickly came out of his boat and onto the dock. He stood looking at the arrangement and contemplating his forthcoming statement. I moved from the helm to the foredeck and looked at the precarious arrangement as if to convey my concern. Wrights Marina is a small marina and in a very remote area. We almost bypassed it in favor of another marina on down the stream. Fortunately, we didn't because later we drove past the other marina and saw it was even smaller. Wrights Marina, although small, did have everything we needed and the people running it were very nice. The time of the year required double docking for all the boats and everyone had to squeeze into their slips. The sailboat owner was rightly concerned because if a boat passed and caused a wake, his dinghy could bounce up and hit my anchor. I doubted if the inflatable could possibly damage the anchor, so I assured him I would reposition my boat so as to eliminate the possible damage to his dinghy. This was my first occasion to meet a French-Canadian. They are a special breed and not nearly as friendly as other Canadians. First, they require that you speak French. Now living most of life in Tennessee, I have fallen into the unique colloquialisms of the South and maybe even my lack of ability to speak other languages has limited my understanding and verbalization of any language except Southern English. Secondly, French-Canadians have an attitude of stuffiness toward US citizens and lastly, I don't think he liked stinkpots (motorboats). About the best I could do was just move my boat back and leave him and his wife alone. Later the great peacemaker Denniese, would warm them to us by stopping and talking about the impending visit of their grandchildren.

Wrights had a nice shower and laundry room and a courtesy car for our use. The day's trip had been so stressful that we decided to stay for an extra day and rest. The following day, we used the car to find a small store which offered a few items to restock our pantry, but could not find any Beanee Weenees. Van Camp's Beanee Weenees are the original MRE (meals ready to eat); a can of beans, sliced hot dogs in a tomato sauce, all cooked and spiced, ready for a spoon. After a hard day or a bouncing trip, a can could serve as a ready source of energy till a proper meal can be prepared. We had consumed our last can and felt sure our travels would be limited if we did not have a proper store of Beanee Weenees. On the way back to the marina, we stopped by the Britt Inn and made reservations for the evening meal. Reservations were recommended, not because of the expected crowd, but because the Britt Inn only employed one cook and one server. Jim the owner was the server while the cook stayed busy in the kitchen. The meal was very good and Jim added to the ambiance by telling stories of the community of Britt, Ontario.

Don't hit that rock!

Chapter 15

"We're Draggin"

Log book: Tuesday August 2, 2011 Wrights Marina Britt. Up at 0600 study charts, cool morning high expected 85 degrees. Destination today Bustard Islands.

The Bustard Islands are a popular destination by Loopers because they are one of the few sheltered and accessible group of islands in the Eastern part of Georgian Bay. The rugged beauty of the granite archipelago is a striking contrast to what we were accustomed to. The few trees that have grown over the smooth rock are wind worn and tested by extreme winter temperatures. Access by the marked channel is not to be deviated from because of the rock outcropping in every direction. Once inside the bay, it is recommended that boats anchor bow and stern to the bank. The clear water is deep up to the bank. Boats drop their anchor and back to the preferred spot, then tie the stern line to a tree or rock and take in the anchor rode. A prudent boater anchoring by this method should be safe from the frequent summer storms. If all the preferred spots are taken, maybe a dozen, then a boat can anchor in the open bay. The difficulty with anchoring in the open bay is the bottom has only a shallow depth of holding ground for the anchor to dig into over the granite rock. We found a spot in the open bay along with a couple other boats and dropped the anchor in 15 feet of clear water. We had a late lunch and an early glass of wine and we enjoyed the scenery and the beauty of this spot. The rocks have become the summer home for several families. Rocks or islands can be purchased and homes can be built. No power or water lines would distract from your view. Also no highway, walkway or bike trail would take away from the site. More precisely, you have a rock in the water and that is about all. The waterfront lot would be a big rock, possibly with a few trees and little else. Having built houses in the past, I can only imagine the obstacles that must be overcome to build a house in the Bustards. Everything would have to arrive by boat or maybe float plane. Heavy equipment could be driven out to the building site in the winter months but would quickly depart before the spring thaw. Sewage would be another problem that I do not know how would be handled without contaminating the water. Many problems would have to be overcome to live on the Bustards, but in spite of the problems a couple of nice houses were within view. One smaller summer home close to us was being rebuilt by a couple of hard working folks. We watched as a new roof was being added to the refurbished summer cabin. Beyond the house footprint, a wrong step could result in a twenty feet fall to the water below. During the building process, a need for an extra 2X4 or a box of nails would mean a boat ride of an hour in each direction and then a drive from the boat ramp to the hardware store. Once you return, you might encounter a dead drill battery or a generator without fuel. The problems building on a small island would be never ending. The activity was entertaining and the clear skies made for a good afternoon, but storms were forecast.

We loaded the dinghy and with Admiral and crew we set off to visit our boat neighbors. One was a gold Looper and we were able to get some advice on what lay ahead in our trip. Maggie had a hard time finding a grassy spot to poop and finally settled on a mossy rock. The next day we woke to gray skies and cooler temperatures. After all, it was August and summer was officially over for this part of the world. It looked like it would rain most of the day, so we decided to stay put for the day. Killarney was our next stop and it could wait for a day. This was a good day to sit back and enjoy a good book. The wind started blowing with force about 0900 and we watched as a sailboat to our port started dragging their anchor. The boat was anchored in the inlet and there was little danger of running up on a rock with the general direction they were moving. We watched and tried to attract the attention of the crew but they were tucked in below and out of the weather. A half an hour later the captain stuck his head out to check his location and discovered he was about 100 yards closer to the inlet than where he had dropped the anchor. Denniese and I watched as other boats added scope to the anchor rode or dropped a second anchor just to be cautious. Other boats were dragging anchor but we held steady. I fully expected the admiral to congratulate me for my anchoring skills. We closed the hatch and I opened my book and began my reading of a Clive Cussler book that I had been working on for about a week. Clive Cussler is a real hero that not only writes with authority about boats but puts his money toward searches for historic sunken ships. As I adjusted my cushion, I heard some hollering from the outside. I asked Denniese what all the hollering was about. I casually raised from the comfortable worn green chair and stuck my head out of the hatch. My eyes widened as I grasp the situation. We were dragging our anchor at an alarming rate toward a huge rock. The yelling we heard was from people on boats and on shore trying to warn us of the pending doom. The stern of our boat, the swim platform, and more importantly, the prop or rudder would be the first things to hit. Damage or destruction was inevitable if we could not stop the boat. I jumped from the ladder and ran toward the lower helm as I shouted for Denniese to prepare for the crash. The trusty Ford Lehman started on the first turn. As I took the helm, Denniese instructed me on the proper heading. I always leave the key in the ignition and the fuel system on while at anchor and am glad I had developed that good habit. I engaged the transmission and waited to hear the crushing of the prop blades against the solid granite rocks to our stern. Seconds passed as the wind continued to push us toward a piece of granite the size of a barn that had not moved since the last ice age. The prop sliced through the water and ever so gently overcame the force that the wind had established. We were seconds from crashing into the rock and only the yelling and noise from our neighbors averted the disaster. Out of danger, Denniese took the helm and I reeled in the anchor. I looked for another good anchor spot but all were taken and eventually we anchored back at the same spot only with additional scope. Next we loaded the dingy and went around to the people rebuilding the summer home and thanked them for getting our attention. Then we went to each boater who had blown an air horn, yelled or broke out the dinghy and were on the way that helped with the accident avoidance and thanked them. What was it that Denniese called this trip, "An Intense Adventurous Challenge"? Maybe we should add dangerous somewhere in that statement.

That afternoon *The Cooper* pulled in to the cove. I had communicated with Rusty and Betty Hughes through the AGLCA because we were both planning our trip at the same time but had never met them. They had started out before us so we had passed them somewhere along the way. We would continue to leap-frog until we both passed our starting point back in Florida. We talked for a while and shared stories of our trip. We warned them against getting too comfortable here in the bay as the holding ground was minimal. Back on board *Lifestyle II*, we watched the sun set and prepared to turn in. That was our schedule while making our runs, like chickens, up at sun up and in bed at sun down.

Thursday August 4 - happy birthday Denniese. Her present this day would be a gift of a cool, clear and calm morning. We started the engine at 0700 and departed the Bustards at 0730. We had a smooth trip across the open water to Killarney. On the way over we were able to listen in to the cruisers net. A radio program of sorts broadcast on VHF channel 71 as a safety net for the cruisers in Georgian Bay. It was started and run by ham operator Roy Eaton as a service to the boating community in the area. Modeled after cruising net programs in the Caribbean, Roy has developed a loyal following of boaters and friends. His broadcasts originate from the Anchor Bar and Grill in Little Current, with the antenna on the top of the hotel where the bar and grill is located. The three story building is the tallest in Little Current and with the antenna on top he is able to broadcast over much of the Georgian Bay and the North Channel.

Each morning at 0900 during the months of July and August, Roy will open the program with, "Are there any emergencies, medical or priority traffic?" After Roy gives a news report and activity report of Little Current the boaters will take turns calling in and announcing the name of their boat, location and any help they may need. Since VHF is a line of sight transmission, many times boaters will relay to Roy the transmission of the boaters on the fringe of their transmission range. All of this works amazingly well and the system continues. Roy's first year, in 2005, he received just over a thousand calls during the season. Now he receives over six times that during the season. The Canadian Coast Guard and the U.S. Coast Guard depend on him with help keeping track of missing or overdue boats. He has been awarded for his service to boaters by many organizations and has had several articles written about his volunteer service. Cruising World Magazine has featured him on several occasions. When it came my turn, I reported that *Lifestyle II* with a hailing port of Grand Harbor, Kentucky was on the Loop and north of Bustard Islands and I had a special announcement. "Today is the Admiral's birthday". After the transmission was received, Roy congratulated Denniese and wished her a happy birthday. That mostly got me off the hook for not having a birthday present.

We docked at the Sportsman Marina in Killarney next to another couple of Loopers aboard *Merluza*. Patty and Eric were fun to talk with and we were able to share stories of our trip to this point. Patty won Denniese's favor when she shared some sort of hair product that seemed to work well aboard boats. Killarney is part of a wilderness park and get most of its income from tourist dollars. The Red Bus is the main attraction for all that find them in this small remote community. The Red Bus is just that, a red bus that has been adapted to cook and serve fish and chips. It sits on the waterfront next to the fishery that delivers fresh trout, perch and other white fish for the famous fish and chips. Any time the open sign is displayed, a line will form. There is no inside seating but a couple of picnic benches are on the concrete pad in front of the red bus. I picked up a couple orders of the famous product and delivered them back to the boat which was about a block away. We had arrived early and, as we sat on the aft deck enjoying our dinner, we watched as the marina became not just crowded but overcrowded. A new cigarette boat (a boat with a long nose designed to go fast and offers little else) parked behind us. The captain and boat fluff crew (boat fluff is necessary for owners of cigarette boats) possessed little boating skills but they were very proud that he was able to jockey the 35 foot 600 hp boat behind *Lifestyle II* on a Tee dock. We watched as he put out his two three inch fenders and tied his new 1/4 inch nylon dock lines. The boat was a beauty, even if I don't like that type of boat. The black hull glistened in the warm Canadian sun. The new chrome cleats and the few tiny stainless-steel rub rails accented the black gel coat. The boat fluff looked young enough to be his daughter but, in her bikini, she seemed to fit all the requirements for boat fluff. About the time he and his mate were starting off to the marina bar, I ask if he was going to be staying the evening. He said they were staying the night. I said, "The reason I ask is we are leaving early in the morning and I just have a single screw and no thruster and I would hate to get any of that black paint on my white hull." I could see the blood drain from his face. I thought for a moment he was going to pass out but, to his credit, he regained his composure and said "Let me know when you're getting ready to leave and I will help".

A band played at the marina bar until near one AM. I was almost sure my friend in the black hull speed boat would want to sleep in but, to my surprise, when I started the engine he and the young woman appeared on the dock. I jockeyed *Lifestyle II* out of the tight enclosure and, to everyone's amazement I didn't hit a single boat. The young woman had taken my warning and prepared the boyfriend's new boat by laying a beach towel over the starboard bow like that would magically keep my 40 foot trawler from crushing the fiberglass toy. I know they were glad when we departed and set a course for Little Current which was about 20 miles away.

Little Current is one of the bigger cities along the way and it has a grocery store that will deliver your groceries. Getting to a grocery store is not a problem. Getting the groceries back to the boat is always a challenge. A folding cart is used when the distance is short. The bikes have saddlebags and baskets but, if all else fails we call a taxi or use a courtesy car. Little Current has a free wall to tie up to for a couple of hours but if you want to stay the night you have to pay a dock fee. We felt we could see the town, buy the groceries and be gone in a couple of hours. Denniese took off for the grocery while I started my painting duties. *Lifestyle II* has lots of teak all of which has been painted with Sikkens Cetol product which gives it a high gloss but still must be maintained. In addition, each time we passed through a lock the teak would take a scratch or ding. Varnish requires seven coats but the Cetol product required only a couple of coats. I was working on the aft rail and talking with the people on the boat to my stern when the owner said he was mixing up some epoxy glue for his inflatable dinghy and ask if I had a need for any. Thinking of the ore lock that came off in Miami bay, I quickly seized upon the offer and went scurrying off the find the broken ore lock. He had mixed enough that he made his repair, then, I re-glued the ore lock and re-glued several frayed places on our dinghy. Just another example of how nice the Canadians are. By the time I completed the gluing and painting, Denniese returned with the groceries, carrying all six bags herself because the delivery guy was busy elsewhere. She could not call me because we had turned our cell phones off, not wanting to pay the Canadian connection charge and the inflated price for per minute. So she grabbed all six bags and walked the one mile back to the boat. What a great admiral I have. After restocking the boat, we returned the favor of the glue by holding on to our parking space until a boating friend of our neighbor could position his boat to slide in on the dock as we departed.

By the time we departed, boats were waiting in the harbor for spots along the wall. Some were just stopping for supplies, as we did, while others were planning on spending the night. A big concert was planned for the evening and the star attraction was a big draw for the area. We anchored in the bay behind Little Current in about 15 feet of water with a muddy bottom. Thank you Lord for a muddy bottom and not a rock bottom because the wind had picked up to about 15kts. Also, a nice quiet anchorage was much desired after the band music the night before. We were now in the bigger part of the north lake known as the North Channel. Our trip across the North Channel would be over some open water and some island hopping. The weather patterns were changing and violent thunderstorms were more prevalent this time of year, so the weather, more than ever, would dictate our travels.

Saturday morning we took our time getting under way and first motored Maggie over to shore for her morning walk. Last night was a good night to sleep with the low around 69 and the high today should be in the mid 80s. We pulled up the anchor and headed out into the North Channel at 0830 and were listening to the cruisers report on the VHF at 0900. We had ahead of us about 30 miles of mostly open water to our next anchorage at Sturgeon Bay behind Barrie Island. Denniese had done another great job of finding us a place to drop anchor. Sturgeon Bay was a scenic and remote sheltered bay. We could only see one house and only a couple kids out playing close by. I had trouble setting the anchor, and only after the second try, did I feel it would be secure for the night. For the last several evenings we had been plagued by swarms of gnats and they seemed worse this day. The gnats are not as bad as greenhead flies because they don't sting or bite, but when they come in by the swarm, they are just as irritating. We had to duck inside and take shelter to avoid the cloud of tiny insects.

Log Book: Sunday August 7, 2011 Anchor in Sturgeon Bay. Up at 0615 Engine on at 0630 Anchor up at 0650

A low pressure front had been predicted to pass and the morning felt like a storm was on the way. Maggie had issues during the night and I was up several times checking to see if the anchor was dragging or what Maggie's concerns were. The anchor held but when I raised the anchor it had very little mud on it, indicating it was sitting on rock. Our choices were to sit here and wait out the storm with minimal shelter and holding ground or try to beat the storm and dash over to Cockburn Island. The Government wall at Tolmsville on the island was our next stop and it was about four hours away. We both agreed that sitting in this dead end bay with possible strong winds was not a good option. We headed out and set a course for Cockburn Island. All was good until about 0900 when the first of many squall lines passed. The wind was so strong that it rocked the boat one way and then the other. We quickly decided this was a level three storm. We had experienced several level one storms (Tie the dog down) and a couple of level two (Lets go below) but this was the first "level three" (What the hell were we thinking). We moved to the lower helm but the wind and rain were so bad that we could not see an object to take a bearing. We were once again boating by instruments. We were out in the middle of the North Channel and away from land, so we felt if we could keep the boat on course we could find our destination. *Lifestyle II* was being tossed around like we were in a commercial washing machine. Maggie could not find a spot to keep from being tossed from side to side even though we were at the lower helm. We first put her in our bedroom but she fell and hurt her tail. We then moved her to the forward Vee berth where she could wedge herself in the smaller birth. She was scared and hurt and Denniese was trying to give her aid while I drove the boat in the worse storm I had been in since the one off the coast of Mexico. Waves were breaking over the bow and spray was covering the upper helm. The rain was so intense that the windshield wipers were useless.

My only instrument at the lower helm was the compass and I could not hold the boat on the required heading. We finally settled on just trying to maintain a heading between 240 and 270 degrees. Every fifteen minutes Denniese would take the helm and I would go to the upper helm and check our location on the chartplotter. By 1100 the rain had let up but the wind was stronger. We were still on course and headed toward Cockburn Island, but if we drifted up to over 270 degrees, the wind would heal us and the waves would bounce us to the point where we felt our boat may not recover if a rogue wave hit us at that moment. At 1130 I spotted the island but could not make out the entrance to the harbor. The spray off the seawall was about twenty feet in the air. I could not tell if we were to tie up to the wall or enter a harbor. I called on the VHF for information but got no response. I made one last dash for the upper helm to check our position. The chartplotter now showed we were on course for the Government dock. Leaving the upper helm meant hanging on to a rocking, bucking boat on a wet deck with slippery hand holds. Consideration was given to each step or grip. One slip and a fall could be disastrous in a storm like this. All the extra equipment that was tied down seemed to be holding in place and the dinghy was bucking and jumping but still following behind us. I worked my way down to the lower helm and asked Denniese if we had received a call from the dock master at Tolmsville. Her replay was negative.

We had no choice, we had to continue and if the tie up was on the outside, we would just have to try it. At 1200 we spotted the cut into the harbor. It was narrow and we had a strong east wind pushing us at the narrow rocky channel much faster than I desired. I pulled the power back and aimed the boat like I was threading a fast approaching needle. Waves were inches from topping the sea wall as we made the small cut. Just inside the harbor, we saw several boats but none our size. I hoped we had enough depth, but at this point, I was willing to park the boat on land and walk home if necessary. The inside was much calmer and we were able to make a 180 degree turn and pull up to the concrete dock behind the sea wall. We were getting some spray but we were sheltered. Thank you Lord.

BOAT RULE #8: Any port in a storm is a good port.

That statement was never truer than this port. We had been beaten, bounced and rained on for the past three hours and we showed the signs of the stress and discomfort. We tied the boat down and rested for about 10 minutes. The inside of the boat was a mess. Things had been moved from places where they had weathered other storms. Maggie was hurt and could not move her tail. She trusted us and we had let her get hurt. We felt bad about that. Other than the hurt tail, she seemed OK. When she tried to wag her tail, she would let out a little cry. *Lifestyle II* proved she was better than the crew and she seemed to have a little extra bounce at the dock after weathering the storm. We were the only boat tied to the wall and the marina looked to have about a dozen boats tied to the random pilings. A couple of people were out checking dock lines in their sturdy foul weather gear.

Before long, the dock master appeared and introduced himself. He looked as rugged and windblown as the island and marina did. The island claimed to have about 300 residents but only one full time resident and he was standing before us. We could only imagine what a winter would be like on Cockburn Island. It would take a rugged individual to stay here during those long lonely and cold months. His black lab said hi to Maggie, but Maggie only had a limited response. By the time the boat was tied down and details had been taken care of with the dock master, the rain had let up and the storm had moved off. We decided we need to get off the boat and walk on terra firma to settle our stomachs and nerves. Even Maggie seemed to cheer up when we took the flex leash out of the drawer.

We walked past the shed that seemed to be the city garage which held an old tractor with a road scraper attached to the front. The shed looked as if it had a small office attached to it and possibly the dock masters office. The little town had two or three paved streets with a short row of houses on each street. A few of the residents were starting to appear to check and see what damage the storm had done. A few cars were parked beside some of the homes, although I could not imagine where they went. Most of the homes were closed for the winter and it seemed this was mostly a summer resort community for the working class. One building was marked church but when we tried the door we found it locked. We spotted some people loading their car and stopped to talk to them. They had spent a month at their summer home and were loading the car to take things to the ferry dock and return home. The car would stay on the island and wait for them to return in the spring. By the time we returned to the boat, the sun had come out and the afternoon looked to be nice. Everything was drying out and the warm afternoon made us feel better. We started the generator since the government dock did not offer electricity, which made me think, I don't think this island has electricity. Anyway, our generator was working well and we were able to charge the batteries and cook supper within an hour. A good hot ham and cheese sandwich with a cup of soup topped off the day. After supper we sat on the sun deck and watched a beautiful sunset while we sipped a glass of merlot. We had survived the storm without any real damage and Maggie was on the road to recovery, so this day was turning out to be a good day after all.

Denniese at helm

Chapter 16

Back in the USA and Lake Michigan

Monday was a day we had been looking forward to since July 17. That was the day we left US waters and entered Canadian waters. This day we hoped to dock at Drummond Island Yacht Haven our entry port to the US.

LogBook August 8, 2011 @ 1000hrs Half way between Cockburn Island (Canadian) and Drummond Island (United States) wind calming and moving to the NE as predicted. Maggie still nervous from yesterday. She is holding her tail at an angle and we think she broke her tail bone in a fall. She can't wag her tail but does not whimper so we feel she is improving. Heading 300 degrees speed 6.1kts at 1800 rpms depth 155 ft. LAT 46.05.16 - LON 83.28.54 approximately 7 miles from the US border. 1115hrs *Lifestyle II* entered US waters with Admiral Denniese Liles at the helm.

As we approached Drummond Island Yacht Haven, we heard a call on the VHF from the motor vessel *Coconuts*. She was in the same storm that we were caught in yesterday and, like *Lifestyle II*, she had made a run for a port. Upon entering the cut, she had struck rocks first on the port prop and then the starboard prop. She was limping in with assistance from another boat. *Coconuts* was able to make way but only at about four knots. She was a beautiful 1996 Krogen 49 Express. The shiny black hull looked like new. Sandy and Bill Brubaker were the owners and both had retired and were on the Loop. I could hear the despair in their voice as they spoke to the marina. Instead of asking for a slip, they said they needed to drive straight to the travel lift and pull the boat out of the water. Bill was reconciled to the fact that he had some serious damage to his running gear. The boat had two 420hp Caterpillar engines capable of taking the semi-displacement hull to a speed of 21kts. But today four kts was her max speed.

At 1315 we tied to the dock at Drummond Island Yacht Haven and by 1330 we had cleared customs and once again were able to walk on US soil. The custom officials were nice and efficient. We laughed when they ask if we had brought any alcohol beverages from Canada. "At their prices we couldn't afford any", I said. Our slip was next to the travel lift and within a few minutes *Coconuts* came limping in and drove into the travel lift space. They raised her out of the water and the problem was immediately noticeable. The port side prop had a ding in it that would make it run out of balance but the starboard prop was curled over like a wilted flower. Both props would need to go to a shop for repairs but upon further examination the mechanics discovered the starboard prop shaft was bent. A replacement shaft would be needed and something not easy to find. Sandy and Bill were sitting on a bench beside the seawall considering their options and the look of dejection was evident on their faces. They decided to continue on the Loop but I'm sure the thought of selling the boat and renting a car and driving home crossed their mind.

By 1800 we had finished the laundry and reserved the courtesy car to drive into town to the only grocery store. After the grocery run, we grilled a steak on the grill and sat on the aft deck watching the sun set and thankful for good days and single screw boats. The next couple of days, the wind blew like a hurricane was on the North Channel. No one came into the harbor and no one departed. We all just stayed aboard and played cards or caught up on maintenance. We had a neighbor in a sailboat and we overheard him announce that he never found anyone who knew the character his boat was named for. The name of his 46 foot Jefferson sloop was *Passepartout*. The name was familiar but I could not remember anything about the name. Denniese, not to be outsmarted, went to the Internet and quickly brought up the name. It was the little character from the movie "Around The World In 80 Days". Later in the day, we set a trap for the sailor on the sloop. We walked up to his boat and knocked on the hull. The owner came up and we started the conversation. Soon the conversation came to the name of the boat and Ron made the statement we had been waiting for. "I have never found anyone who knows that name", Ron stated. Without missing a beat Denniese said "Oh yes, that is the valet for Phileas Fogg, played by David Nevins in the movie "Around The World In 80 Days". Ron was blown away. He could not believe that this woman had called his bluff and held the key to his secret. He thought she was possibly the most knowledgeable person whom he had met in his entire sailing career. Ron and his wife Mavis were fun to talk with and he turned the tables on us when he announced that our boat looked familiar. He asked how long we had owned the boat and then said, "Was it ever named" *Sue-Me?* Now it was our turn to be blown away. It seemed he had looked at the boat to purchase while in Key Largo. We all had lots of laughs before the days end but we never told him of our Internet search.

Another boat was pulled out with bent props. It had been in the same storm as we had, and had hit rocks trying to escape the powerful winds. This time the props were just out of balance and the captain carried a spare set. We had drinks with Rick and Carol Nick aboard *Salt and Sand*, a 54 foot Sea Ray, and talked about the storm and the Loop.

Thursday, the wind finally abated and we made our way out of Drummond Island Yacht Club for our run to Government Bay about 30 miles away. We dropped the anchor in Government Bay which was a long narrow waterway to a big open bay at the end. It was a favorite anchorage and recreational spot for summer water lovers. The grassy bottom didn't want to hold our anchor and it took several tries to get the anchor to dig in. Just about the time we felt good about the anchor, we watched a sailboat drift out into the narrow waterway dragging its anchor. I jumped into the dinghy and caught up with the errant sailboat and rapped on the side of the boat until two sleepy people appeared on deck wondering what I was doing. They later thanked me after they estimated they had drifted about a half mile. The next morning we woke to a cool morning with temperatures still in the 50s. We would soon be on Lake Michigan and the stories we had heard did not help with the fears we already had about open water. The storms we had experienced in the past were child's play to the storms of Lake Michigan.

The Mackinac Bridge is the entrance to the big lake and it was already in sight. From the bridge to Chicago is almost 300 miles. The Mackinac Bridge is the third longest suspension bridge in the world and the longest in the Western Hemisphere. The center span is nearly 200 feet above the water and the navigation channel is 3000 feet wide. We didn't even have to lower the antennas to get under it. But while thinking of Chicago and our height, we still had one remaining obstacle on our boat that would keep us from having the needed clearance for the Chicago bridges. Somewhere along the boat's life, a satellite TV dish antenna had been added to the sun deck cover and it extended above the magic number of 17 feet we needed for the bridges of Chicago. When we made our calculations in Poughkeepsie, I had moved the crane to the cover over the sun deck. Now it was time to clean up a few other obstacles. The satellite dish found a new home as a fish sanctuary in 100 feet of water within sight of the Mackinac Bridge. The anchor light and the radar dome were the remaining two items but could be removed within a couple of minutes.

It would take us another three days until we motored under the bridge. From Government Bay we motored to St.Ingnance marina and took on 60 gallons of fuel. Minutes after refueling, the marina was closed and a hazmat team arrived. Nothing scares a boat owner more than the thought of a fuel tank leaking. Since we had just topped off our tank, the thought occurred to me that my tanks were leaking and all the events that would take place if that were the case. I may even have to file a report with the Coast Guard. The leak was located in the marina supply lines and not in my fuel tanks, much to my relief.

We met a fellow Looper who had just begun the Loop trip. Craig and Ginny Ryland were aboard *Brown Eyed Girl*. Craig confessed to me that he knew almost nothing about anchoring. I told him not to worry, by the end of the trip he would be an expert. The weather was not cooperating for a run thru the straights, so we moved over to Straight State Park Marina and waited for a window to start our run down Lake Michigan. At that time of year, a boater will have one good day and two bad days. Later in the season the ratio would change to one good day and three bad days. Loopers agree that it is best to be off Lake Michigan before Labor Day. It was now August 13 and Labor Day would be late this year, so maybe we had a chance. In any case, we had to pick our days and not get anxious on this big lake. We met Carlton and Becky Moore aboard *SeaMoore* a Mainship 40. We had heard them talking on the VHF on several occasions and had talked with them, saying that we finally found someone we could understand. Someone that talked Southern English. This would be our first time to meet them in person. It would be only a couple weeks later that we would hear that Becky had been taken to the emergency room and would spend a week in the hospital. While waiting for the weather to improve, we toured a retired Ice breaker and I did the usual engine maintenance. The engine fired on the first turn after I changed out the fuel filters. Maybe I was getting the hang of the fuel filter maintenance.

Monday, we decided we would make a run for Harbor Springs about 50 miles away. If possible, we were going to try to make 50 miles each day of travel to get down the lake as fast as possible. Later we would decide that was way too optimistic and on one bad day we only made ten miles. But Monday was a good day and we pulled into Harbor Springs behind another trawler that looked like he had been there before. We followed him to the end of the lake and watched as he dropped his anchor in 30 feet of water. We had never anchored in 30 feet of water, so I made some quick calculations. If I did a 7 to 1 ration, it would mean 210 feet of rode. I was not sure I had that much chain. So I opted for a 5 to 1 ratio and put out all the chain I had and hoped for the best. We were in a sheltered cove and I felt OK about the anchorage. Plus, it had a sandy bottom and would be good holding ground for the 45# CQR. Harbor Springs is an upscale resort community in the northern part of Michigan. Our guide book stated that slip fees would be among the highest on the lake which made our anchor spot even nicer. We were not far from the veranda of a country club and we watched as the dinner guests arrived and were seated by the white coat wait staff. It was time to walk Maggie. So, we loaded the dinghy and found a pier that bordered the country club. We tied the dinghy to the pier and walked Maggie on her long flex leash. I could tell she appreciated the soft, well manicured grass of the country club I'm sure she wanted to move here. While loading the dinghy, we forgot to replenish our stock of poop bags, so we pretended not to notice when Maggie found that certain spot and stopped to squat. On our return, we motored around the harbor in our worn gray dinghy and I saw more polished and varnished wooden boats in this harbor than I had seen in all other places combined. Back on board at wine time, we enjoyed the parade of wooden boats. They came rumbling by, barely making a wake as they smoothly drifted along. One boat came up to our starboard side and we started talking. The captain was driving a beautiful classic. The long teak and holly bow accented the mahogany hull. The signature chrome ChrisCraft logo was mounted on each side just in front of where the driver sat. A chrome incased auto style glass windshield protected the driver and passenger from the spray. The front seat and the back seat were separated by the engine nacelle. The owner complimented me on the varnished brightwork and asked about our home port. I told him about our trip and then ask about his craft. He said it was a 16 foot 1934 ChrisCraft Duluxe Model 52 with a duel cockpit and powered by a Chrysler flathead six. My mind drifted as he spoke. Suddenly I was back in the 60s and the driver was Frankie Avalon and sitting alone in the back seat was Annette Funicello. The dark haired beauty was wearing a two piece bikini that modestly covered her navel but provocatively exposed cleavage. She was looking at me with those beautiful dark eyes. She was motioning me to join her. Just then I felt a jolt to the ribs and I snapped back to reality as Denniese punched me in the ribs and said "You're spilling your wine." What a great place to be in the summer anyway.

The next morning we had to wait for the fog to lift before we could depart. We finally got underway at 0730 and could still see patches of fog sitting in the low places. Our next harbor was about 26 miles away and I had reserved a slip for us at Northport, Michigan. Michigan is the "Great Lakes State" and a state that appreciates boaters. The state in partnership with private marinas has developed a system of safe harbors along the lake to provide a level of safety for the boating community. Each harbor of refuge is no more than 15 shoreline miles from the next. The program has been underway since 1947 and has added to the safety and convenience of the boaters. A booklet is available to all boaters at each marina showing the location of each harbor. It is a great service that has saved many lives and many dollars of property that could have been lost without them. Before we completed the trip down Lake Michigan, we would utilize a couple of those harbors of refuge in less than safe conditions. The size of Lake Michigan makes conditions on the lake similar to those on an ocean or the Gulf of Mexico. The width of the lake varies from 50 to 100 miles east to west. Weather patterns move from west to east, so the wind pushes the water for that width. A ripple on the water at Milwaukee, Wisconsin can become a 6 foot roller at Holland, Michigan as a front passes. For that reason, every trip on Lake Michigan starts with a weather update. The next thing is, knowing where the ports of refuge are located.

We had a good run down to Northport and were safely in our slip by 1400. We only logged 6.3 hours on the engine but the first test of the open lake had been rewarding. The next day we stayed in port to wait for a frontal passage. We took the opportunity to do our usual maintenance items and shopping. It was good to be back in the states again. Prices were good and the selection was even better. Thursday morning we woke to 59 degrees and clear skies. By 0815 we were east of Cathead point turning 1900 rpm's and making 7.4mph in 223 feet of water with a heading of 55 degrees. The wind was coming from the southwest at 5 mph. We docked at the Leland Township Marina early to get a slip. Leland is a very popular place for boaters and local tourists. The fishing village is still a working fishing endeavor and fresh fish can be purchased at the dock. Plus, the community has lots of boutique shops. In addition to the inflated slip prices, we donated to the local economy by purchasing some local art work and trinkets at the shops. We happened upon a small shoe store and I attempted to purchase a new pair of Sebago Docksider boat shoes, but I could not find my size. Boat shoes are important to the serious boater. Paul Sperry is generally credited with developing the modern day deck shoe. It is said that he copied the sole pattern after the design on his cocker spaniel's foot. He made the boat shoe popular and available. A boat shoe must be able to grip in wet conditions and last under extreme conditions. Just importantly, they must not scuff or mark the deck. Docksiders by Sebago have been my favorite for decades. I feel they are superior to the Sperry brand in many ways. Disappointed by not finding my size of deck shoe, we set out to find an ice cream shop and enjoyed a couple of chocolate cones. Maggie enjoyed the outing because it seemed that most everyone had a dog on a leash. She also enjoyed the attention from everyone who stopped to pet her. Before heading back to the boat, we purchased some fresh local white fish for our grill.

As expected, the next day the weather was marginal and we stayed in Leland an extra day to allow the weather to calm. By Saturday it looked like we had a good window to make our next little village. By the end of the day we had made over 50 miles and had dropped anchor in Arcadia Lake in 12 feet of water. This was a very good anchorage. The rural community allowed for plenty of privacy and very few Sea Do's or skiers were around to break the tranquility. Then it happened! Every since Drummond Island a boat had been following us. Not just any boat but a homemade boat that looked like it just dropped out of the Jules Verne 20,000 Leagues under the Sea epic. I guessed he was heading down the lake also and was making about the same speed we were, but the mere presence of the boat offended me. First, it didn't look nautical. Being the traditionalist that I am, I like a boat to look like a boat. Now I'm not a snob but a boat must look like a boat. This one looked like something built either in a barn or a garage. It was made of flat sheet steel and had visible welded seams. The ports looked like they were purchased at Home Depot and even the 5/8 inch nylon line was not coiled, but still on the reel sitting on the deck. It was a sloop design and had two outboard motors for auxiliary power. The small craft had an elevated dog house that was too small to serve as a navigation station and a covered cockpit that also served as maybe outside sleeping quarters or fish cleaning station. Secondly, it was bright yellow. Now how nautical was that? But what offended me was he was some ten feet shorter than *Lifestyle II* but making the same speed I was. A planing sailboat, what a novel design. Oh well, I'm sure he was living his dream and that is the nice thing about the water, everyone can enjoy it.

Logbook: Sunday August 21, 2011 Anchored in Arcadia Lake. Great anchor spot, quite community temp 59 degrees, 0745 breakfast and wait for weather to improve.

By noon time I had had enough. The weather had improved only slightly but if we had to stay here all day looking at that yellow craft, I would lose it. We pulled up anchor and departed our quiet little harbor for the roaring Lake Michigan. Within five minutes of clearing the breakwater we were in level three conditions. Remember, that's "What the hell were we thinking". The wind was blowing about 20kts and worse than that, the waves were on our beam. Occasionally a large wave would hit our stern and lift the boat like a giant hand had picked it up and pushed it forward. Maggie needed no encouragement when we went to the lower nav station. She found her safe spot in the vee birth and Denniese and I held on to the bucking, bouncing wild thing we were driving. As I tried to control the direction of our mighty craft, Denniese looked on our paper chart for the next "harbor of refuge". Thank you Lord and the state of Michigan, we were only ten miles from the next harbor. Could we stand this misery for an hour? The wind was a steady 20 knots and the waves had built to eight feet. Within about 30 minutes we turned down wind and the ride eased somewhat. By 1345 we were inside the seawall once again and safely anchored in Portage Lake. I put out extra scope on the anchor rode as well as my 20lb weight to keep the chain horizontal. Everything downstairs was on the floor. The boat was a mess but we were swinging on the hook and holding, so we went to the chore of cleaning up the boat. By 1415 everything had been cleaned up and only a couple of items were found to be broken. Of course as always, most of Denniese's plants had been upended and it was necessary to replant the vegetation. Later, we watched as a group of sailboats attempted a race. We had logged 2.1 hours on the engine this day but it was some of the toughest hours this crew would experience. What was I thinking? That yellow boat was messing with my mind.

The bad days are sometimes necessary to get to the good days. The following day was beautiful on Lake Michigan. The cold front had passed, the seas had calmed and the sky was clear. We motored along enjoying the day from the flybridge.

Boat Rule # 9: Locate the Stink before you Sink.

Every couple of hours, or at least at noon, while under way I climb down into the engine compartment and check it out. Sometimes I will just open the engine room door and stick my head in. Whichever, I use all my senses to evaluate the mechanics of the engine room. I listen to make sure all the little squirrels are running on the tread mill in sync. I smell the air to sniff out anything getting hot and then I feel the cool pieces of metal to feel for elevated temperatures or excessive vibration. Sometimes, I just sit and look in amazement that it is all working so well. I call that inspection the S&S tour. I tell Denniese to take the wheel, "I'm going below for the S&S tour". S&S stands for Sound and Smell or Spray and Screech. Today was no different and everything checked out without a problem. Once, a while back I was on Mobile River, about a day's run above Mobile, and I opened the engine hatch on *Lifestyle* (1) and was greeted by an engine compartment full of smoke. Nothing is more frightening than a boat fire. That time, it was just a frozen water pump that had melted the drive belt which had smoked up the engine compartment, no fire. But it sure taught me the value of checking the belts, pulleys and pumps before starting the engine and to do the S&S inspection often while underway. We passed Big Sable Point at noon and continued the pleasant trip south.

Pentwater is a nice little tourist town with lots of little shops and restaurants. The town is clean and well kept and seems to cater to upscale visitors. We slipped into Snug Harbor Marina with the help of a good dock staff. After we settled into our slip Denniese noticed a couple of boats anchored across the bay. She is always interested in saving a dock fee if possible and we both enjoy swinging at anchor as opposed to being tied to a dock. She asked the dock hand, "Is anchoring in the bay permitted?" The dock hand was very positive and answered saying, "Oh yes but they request you move every week or so." Denniese chuckled and said, "Who would want to stay over a week." We met Peter and Maureen Mezei aboard *The Duddon Pilot* a Monk 36. We walked into town and had supper with them and told stories of our Loop adventure. Strong winds kept us in the slip the following day. The temperature was warm but the winds were strong. It was a good day to continue on the never ending maintenance list. Denniese made a great seven bean soup in the crock pot, and while we were in town Maggie ate the wooden spoon used to stir the beans. When we returned to the boat all that remained of the 12 inch spoon was about three inches of the handle. We just looked at each other and agreed she acts like a dog. When I first adopted Maggie from the shelter, she was grown and had developed some annoying habits, several of which I have already discussed. One which concerned me was her desire to eat grass. When I let her out to potty, she would spend most of the time searching for that certain brand of grass. I was so concerned I took her to the vet to see if she was deficient in her diet. I had always heard that a dog would eat grass if its stomach was upset. Not Maggie. She just loves to eat grass. The vet told me some dogs just like to eat grass. Maggie grazes like a goat. Sometimes we would kid that we think her mother was a goat.

Wednesday came and it was our third day at the dock. Dock fees can take a big part of the budget if not diluted by days spent on the hook. So with no improving weather in site, we relocated to the back part of the lake. The Pentwater Lake was wide and deep with a soft mud bottom. We found a spot in the back about a quarter mile from the end. Several nice homes were visible but we saw little activity among the homes because of the high winds. The anchor set without a problem but I added the 20lb weight or sentinel for the added assurance that we would not drag since the end of the lake was near. We dinghyed Maggie to shore for a walk and I started talking to a fisherman sitting on the bank with a pole and a bucket. After a few minutes of talking, we had developed a kinship because his sister lived in our little town in Tennessee.

Back on board we saw sailboats getting into position for a Wednesday afternoon beer can race. They looked like J-boats. A well recognized one design boat, meaning all the boats are alike and only the skill of the crew makes the difference. The J-boat is known worldwide for its speed and competiveness. The owners and crew are known for their extreme dedication to the sport. I remember crewing aboard a J/24 on Lake Pontchartrain one summer in a regatta, when a race boat fouled our course by passing in front of us. The owner of our boat, who was trimming sails, instead of hoisting a protest flag, yelled to the helmsman "Ram the son of a Bitch". We missed the offending boat but only by inches and it was the last time I sailed in a regatta aboard a J-boat. Here we were anchored at the back of the lake past one of the orange floating race course marks and we watched as the J/24's made their mark and were over powered and knocked down by the force of the new wind. Sails and spreader would come down onto the water as the crew held on. Not to be deterred these experienced sailors would flog their sails till the boat righted itself. Then the mainsheet would be tightened and the jib sheet brought in and off they would go on a new heading with just as much gusto.

Thursday came and went with no relief in the strong winds. Denniese thought back to what she had said about spending a week here. Now it seemed if we didn't get a break in the strong winds we would need to change our mailing address. Friday was our fifth day on this little lake and we finally got a break. We pulled up the anchor first thing and stopped by the fuel dock to top off the fuel and get a pump out of our holding tank. Of course we had to walk Maggie and it was then that she spotted a rabbit. It was 0630 and most of the world was still asleep when a constant loud, alarming, primal barking came from our little rabbit dog. We tried to shut her up but when Maggie gets on the trail of a rabbit, all her rational thinking is overcome by her instincts. It took both of us to load her on the boat and we quickly departed before someone decided to shoot the dog and its owners. Out on Lake Michigan we found what we had been waiting for, a very pleasant day.

The mild temperatures were complimented by a light wind. It was such a good day we extended our day until 1730 where we anchored in Lake Macatawa at Holland, Michigan. We had traveled 80 statute miles (statute will be used on the remaining portion of the trip) on that day and if we had the light, we would have gone another 20 miles. Saturday the weather was holding and we hurriedly made our way for our next destination. South Haven was about 40 miles away and I had made reservations at the Southside Municipal Marina which was only a block from town. We arrived at 1300 and enjoyed a late lunch and then a walk into town. We were even able to scarf up a few remaining items from the local farmers market. Back on board I changed the engine oil and we still had time to have supper with some fellow Loopers.

The wind had picked up and it was blowing rollers in the marina, but since we were on the inside and not on the wall by the channel, we were not disturbed and had a good night's sleep. The next day, as expected, we didn't dare go out on Lake Michigan. We stayed in the marina but took the opportunity to go grocery shopping and I found a NAPA store to replace the oil and filters I had used. They were also good about taking the used oil.

Monday proved to be a good day and we scooted down to New Buffalo Municipal Marina where we had planned a mail drop. It had been almost a month since we had received a package from home and we were excited to catch up on mail and business. We had also ordered a new navigation chart that we would need from Chicago to Mobile. We arrived at New Buffalo at 1430 and picked up our mail at the marina office. Unfortunately we did not find our chart. We needed the chart. We called the supplier and they assured us that the chart had been sent out and should be there. After lots of questioning and phone calls, we found the chart at City Hall where the marina office staff had sent it when they did not find a boat with our name in the marina. Upon looking at the marina reviews on Active Captain, we discovered several other boaters who had problems with the marina staff. Most complaints were similar. "They are just not attentive", is an example of the reports. It was the only Michigan Municipal Marina where we experienced a problem with the staff. This was our last stop on the Michigan side of the lake. Our next run would be to cross the bottom of the Great Lake to the windy city of Chicago. We had finally made it down the lake. What a relief it would be to get off the lake and get into the safe protected waters of the river system. Right!! Little did we know what was in store for *Lifestyle II* and crew.

Homeland Security says "Hove to"

Chapter 17

Chicago and
the Rivers Beyond

Log Book: Tuesday August 30, 2011 At dock at New Buffalo Municipal Marina. Up at 0630, engine on at 0730, away from dock at 0740 on Lake at 0745. Heading of 270 degrees to Chicago.

The mighty lake was giving us a present today, one foot waves and a gentle breeze. Maybe it was to make up for all those days when the wind blew 20kts and we experienced eight foot waves. By 1000 we could see the outline of Chicago. Everything was wonderful as we sat in the flybridge motoring across the bottom of the lake, watching the skyline of Chicago growing bigger as the minutes passed. Without warning I spotted something out of the corner of my eye. Something was behind us. I turned to see a large rigid inflated boat with a guard house structure, blue lights and machine guns. Several camo clad officers stood on deck with shoulder weapons and side arms as the pilot eased the official looking craft up to the starboard stern of *Lifestyle II*. One officer hailed me to "hove too" (that's sailor talk for pull over). I thought this can't be good. What did I do? Were we speeding? No that's not possible we only go eight mph. Did they find out about me traveling to Cuba? Maybe they thought Denniese was a child and I was guilty of the Mann Act. We are in Illinois by now. Maybe they want to inspect my "Y" valve. Oh no, what position did I leave the Y valve? I pulled back on the throttle and told Denniese to take the wheel. The senior officer who wore an American Flag shoulder patch, which was a relief, told me they were coming aboard. What could I say? This is not a time to debate the issue. Maggie on the other hand was not so sure she wanted people dressed like this aboard her boat. Her barking and snarling continued until I snapped her on her aft leash. There she would remain until I could find out what was going on. They identified themselves as Homeland Security agents. Two agents boarded our boat while an undisclosed number stayed in the dark glassed pilot house. (No one was manning the machine gun. That had to be a good sign.) We all gathered in the flybridge because they wanted me to maintain slow forward speed. They asked, where we were going and where we had been. By now all you could see out of the front window was Chicago, so the first question I could answer. Where had we been? That one was a little more difficult. They finally determined that we had been to Canada which opened a new set of questions, like did you bring back any wine (couldn't afford it), did you spend the night? (well yes, we were there almost a month) Did you bring anyone else back? Does Maggie count? After a few minutes they finally got around to asking for the boat papers. We are a "documented boat". That means it is registered with the US Coast Guard. I had to go below to retrieve the boat papers and passports. The two agents stayed on the bridge at first, then, one decided to join me below. I had left my reading glasses on the flybridge and was having a hard time reading the file folders in our boat file box. I finally found the correct papers and presented them to the agent.

Back on the flybridge, they had a couple of follow-up questions about when we checked back into customs and what our destinations would be. Denniese answered most of the questions, occasionally referring to the log book for an exact date. I suddenly had cotton mouth and had a hard time talking. After answering all of their questions they departed as quickly as they had appeared. Afterwards, Denniese and I sat and looked at each other saying "What was that?" Welcome to Chicago!

I had visited Columbia Yacht Club in the past during my sailing days but this was my first visit as captain of my own boat. The CYC is famous for producing great sailors who love to sail and enjoy the water. The clubhouse is a retired icebreaker affectionately known as Abby. The MV *Abegweit* retired from service first as a Canadian icebreaker then as a ferry for New Brunswick in 1977. She was purchased by the club to replace a smaller CYC club ship in 1983. The 372 foot boat could carry 950 passengers and 60 cars. The highlight of the present facility is the dining hall which is finished with heavy wood, formal trappings and a world class chef. An invitation to the dining hall is sure to be a special occasion. An evening meal on the bow has the best view of the city lights in Cook County.

By 1300 we tied *Lifestyle II* to the transit dock at CYC. We were docked about 50 yards down the wooden dock from the port side of the large ship Abby. The dock master was very gracious and accepted our little sailing club in Tennessee for our guest membership. From our aft deck we could see all the activity of downtown Chicago. We could also see the sailors ferrying back and forth to their boats as well as the busy Abby behind us.

Toward the end of the day, a brand new Mainship 40 pulled in behind us, between *Lifestyle II* and the CYC ship. The couple Kate and Greg Pfleger had recently purchased the vessel for the Loop. They had started the Loop on June 20 from Oriental, NC and although we had been close to each other on several occasions, this was the first time we had the opportunity to be introduced. They were nice folks and living the dream. They had a beautiful boat with a cream colored topside and black hull. It had a fully enclosed flybridge that was khaki in color. She was truly a beautiful boat and looked like it just rolled off the showroom floor. We talked about having dinner during the few days that we would spend in Chicago. We departed to our floating homes without setting any definite plans. Denniese and I fixed supper, cleaned dishes, and turned in early. Maggie had already christened the Chicago soil.

About 2200 I was awakened by the dinghy banging against our swim platform. CYC is a great place with a beautiful view and a truly unique clubhouse. The Achilles heel of the marina is they have no protection from a southeast wind. I went on deck to adjust the dinghy and discovered the wind had shifted and was blowing at more than 20kts from the southeast. The wind was driving waves into the marina and after the long run of open water, they were stopped by the port side of the Ice Breaker *Abegweig*. After bouncing off the hull of the ship the energy was displaced down the long transit dock. *Grianan*, the new 40 foot Mainship, was the first boat to receive the full effect of the waves. I watched in amazement as the craft rotated horizontally on its dock lines six to ten feet in each direction. The boat was caught in some strange wave energy that moved it as though it was possessed. Since I had gone on deck to adjust the dinghy, I had not put on my shoes. Luckily, I did have my pajama bottoms on. I looked to the dock and saw Greg and Kate trying in vain to adjust the dock lines to stop the gyrating motion. I hopped off *Lifestyle II* onto the wooden dock to help with the effort. As I ran toward them, I felt the wooden dock and hoped the splinters would not penetrate my feet.

The boat was out of control and no amount of adjusting was going to snatch it from the grasp this monster had on it. The boat rotated down to the level that the roof of the sun deck was parallel with the dock. I could not believe my eyes as I saw Kate jump from the dock to the sun roof, grab a stanchion and hold on. She was going to save her baby from this monster. Greg and I were trying to hold the boat off the dock, when a violent rotation forced the port rail under the dock and the counter righting motion ripped the 11/4 stainless steel rail, off the boat, from bow to stern. I felt the hull and deck would be the next structure to get caught under the dock. I hollered at Greg to "move the boat." He timed his jump and boarded *Grianan* safely. Both Greg and Kate retreated into the pilothouse and as soon as I heard the engines fire, I tossed the lines onboard. As soon as they were away from the dock, the gyrating action lessoned and *Grianan* gained her feet. By that time Denniese was out on the dock in her nightgown ready to help.

They moved *Grianan* to an empty slip at the end of the dock and a couple of sailors helped us put some extra lines on *Grianan* to lessen her movement. No one was injured and the boat railing could be replaced. The thought of the boat movement is alarming to this day. Strangely,

Lifestyle II docked just 50 feet from the spot of the reverberating motion, was calm by comparison. Our dinghy was bouncing and the boat was rocking but nothing like the forces that gripped *Grianan*. It would take a hydro engineer to properly evaluate all that went on that night but the location of the 40 foot Mainship in relation to the Icebreaker, and the hull design of the Mainship, as well as the weight of the Mainship all played a part in the dynamics of the accident. I also think those same dynamics were the reason our boat did not experience those same effects.

The next morning a worker from the yacht club came around checking to see if everyone was OK. We volunteered that we made it through the windstorm without adversity. We did take him up on the opportunity to move to a more remote dock. *Grianan*, however, elected to vacate the marina and motored over to a neighboring marina. We heard later that the boat had tilted so far that water flooded the exhaust riser of the generator and it had to be drained prior to starting. Denniese and I walked into town and enjoyed a famous Chicago pizza. Later, we biked into town and quickly came to understand that for Chicago drivers bicycles were considered moving speed bumps. We were both happy to get off the streets and back on the trail. We spent the rest of the day studying the bridges and locating special phone numbers necessary to communicate with the few bridges that would actually raise for us.

Log Book: Thursday September 1, 2011 CYC Chicago up at 0630, temp 72 degrees light wind from SW. Engine on at 0730, Lock #1 @ 0745

We motored outside the seawall of the CYC marina and spotted Navy Pier. As we approached the lock that would take us to the river system, we could see the large Ferris wheel on our right at the entrance to the pier. We remembered taking a ride on that Ferris wheel and then later a boat tour of the city. It was such a great trip which was the start of an Amtrak train trip that ended in Florida. We never dreamed at the time that one day we would be driving our own boat on that same river. We drove into the lock and the gates were shut and the water lowered about a foot. The doors were opened and then we were there, downtown Chicago. We were amazed at all the tall buildings; it made us feel tiny by comparison. The bridges were named after the famous street that they connected. There we were in our little boat on the Chicago River that weaves in-between all that history. The sun was reflecting off the windows of the skyscrapers, people were hurrying to work, cars were bumper to bumper. Even the water taxies, were doing their work. With the exception of the water taxies we were the only ones on the water. We passed outdoor restaurants overlooking the river and could see people drinking coffee and eating bagels. We waved and some waved back, others were way too busy reading the paper or applying some strange app on their iphone to pay attention to the little boat and its strange crew. Even Maggie felt the excitement as she barked her hello to the strangers. The sound echoed off the nearby buildings and caused her even more excitement as she looked for the other dogs on the river.

Our test would come on the third bridge. The Michigan Ave. bridge, also known as the DuSable Bridge, had a height above the water at 17.9 feet. If all my measurements were correct, we should have nine inches clearance above the radar arch of our boat. Had I been more prepared, I could have mounted a PVC pipe on the flag staff on the bow of the boat that would extend slightly above the height of our boat and give us warning if we did not have the clearance necessary to safely go under the bridge. We didn't have any such advance warning device so we slowly motored up to the Michigan Ave Bridge. From the flybridge I could see the construction of the heavy steel structure which opened for traffic in 1920. Maintenance on the bridges had ceased decades earlier and only the necessary work to allow them to open and close a couple times a year was now preformed. The lack of attention resulted in flakes of rust as big as a pie pan. The name plaques were barely readable. People hurried across without attention to us or the poor maintenance. As we approached within a foot or so, I was still not totally comfortable we were going to clear the structure. Just then a water taxi came around the corner and I put *Lifestyle II* in reverse to allow the taxi to pass us and his wake settle before we continued. Denniese and I conferred as I moved the throttle and the boat inched forward. As we moved forward,

I could have easily reached up and touched the rusty beams overhead. I didn't, however, because the thin Sunbrella cover extended over my head and more importantly I was gripping the wheel tightly with both hands. The Admiral made the call. Hanging out from the side, she had a better perspective and said we would clear it. I gently moved the throttle forward so as not to create a stern squat which would raise the bow and possibly the flybridge.

Next the Wabash Ave Bridge, then the State Street, North Dearborn, North Clark, N. LaSalle, N. Wells, New Orleans, West Lake Street Bridge. It went on and on. It was a beautiful, wonderful and lifetime experience but traveling under some 25 to 30 bridges in the span of an hour and a half is just too much of a good thing. We only had to stop once. Amtrak stops for no one, especially a 40 foot trawler. Railroad companies operate by their own rules, always have and always will. I made the phone call and found the operator of the Chinatown Amtrak RR Bridge. That bridge needed opening for sure since it was only 10 feet off the water. The Amtrak bridge operator controlled several other bridges remotely, probably from an office miles away, and was not sure which bridge I wanted opened. He had one name for it, I had another and I was apparently not within view of his camera. We worked it out and as soon as the train passed, he lifted the bridge and we proceeded.

The Chicago Sanitary and Ship Canal has been the subject of books and volumes of articles discussing the project, the effort, the need for the canal and the environmental impact it has on the heartland. The Chicago Sanitary and Ship Canal is 28 miles long, 202 feet wide and 24 feet deep. It was completed in 1900 for the purpose of diverting the city's sewage from entering Lake Michigan which is the same place Chicago collects their drinking water. As a boater leaving Chicago, the first evidence that you are not traveling on just an ordinary stream are the signs posted on the banks every 50 to 100 yards. The one foot square signs read, first in large red letters. "CAUTION" then smaller blue letters state the problem: "This waterway is not suitable for –Wading – Swimming – Jet Skiing – Water Skiing/Tubing – Any Human Body Contact. A web site and a phone number are next and then the statement, "Protecting Our Water Environment". I think it should say "Protecting our water from getting on anybody". Some people refer to this canal as the Chicago Sanitary and SHIT Canal. Others say it is anything but SANITARY. Wikipedia says of the Chicago Sanitary and Ship Canal, "Chicago's sewage treatment system discharges only lightly treated fecal matter into the canals. Because of concerns of the effect of chlorine, Chicago has a rare distinction among major American cities: It does not employ a disinfection stage at its three main sewage treatment plants. The result is canal water with fecal coliform colonies, so the signs along the canals warn that the contents are not suitable for any human body contact". The sewage is combined with the Chicago River, the Cal-Sag Waters, the Des Plaines River and eventually the Mississippi and the Gulf of Mexico.

Floating on top of the Chicago Sanitary and Ship Canal made me wonder, "How am I going to clean this stuff off my boat"? I may have to order a case of sanitary wipes. Maybe if I just spray it down with Clorox I can get it clean. While still considering the effects of motoring down the less than Sanitary Canal, we came upon the next bizarre thing. The Electronic Fish Barrier is located just below the Cal-Sag Channel at Romeoville. It is promoted as the last line of defense to protect the Great Lakes from the invasive Asian carp. Hundreds of millions of dollars have been spent to keep the carp from the Lakes and some say the effort is failing. The Army Corps of Engineers operates the electronic fish barrier and of course has implemented rules for passing through the underwater low voltage barrier. Permission to enter is required and only one boat at a time may proceed through the barrier. An office building is located on the port side bank which houses the Army of carp fighters. We gained permission to proceed and, upon entering, were admonished for towing a dinghy. The radio operator told me, "Only one boat at a time. Next time, bring your dinghy aboard." I answered in the affirmative, no use getting the Army of carp fighters mad at me. My solution to the Asian carp problem would be to put a bounty on the carp. I figure a $2.00 per head bounty for each Asian carp and for a couple million dollars expenditure for a couple of years and we would be rid of the carp once and for all. But then what would we do with that Army of carp fighters? Maybe they could get a real job, start paying taxes and with all the savings and extra money, the government could pay off the National debt. Besides, I'm not all that sure even the Asian carp could live in the Chicago Sanitary and Ship Canal. Maggie, on the other hand, loved the carp. The sound of the engine would excite the fish and they would jump and hit the side of the boat with a thud. Others would jump and clear the water by three feet. Maggie would go from side to side at the bow barking and snarling. Then as we passed over a school of carp she would run to the stern and start the same defensive tactics. She was guarding our home from the invasion of the Asian carp.

By 1600, we were tied up to the Joliet City Wall drinking a glass of red and celebrating the accomplishment of transiting two locks, going under more than 50 bridges and over one fish barrier. We had logged 8.8 hours on the engine and moved onto the river system that would take us to the Gulf of Mexico. Wow it's hot. Now that we are inland we realize it is summer time in the heartland. So far on the trip, we have mostly been riding the wave of spring like temperatures. Except for those few hot days in Canada, we had excellent weather. Like my friend Louis Wade said, "The goal is to be in shorts all year long". Shorts were the appropriate dress for today with high temps in the mid 90s. Throughout the trip, our wardrobe had consisted of shorts and Tee shirts. We did carry aboard one pair of long pants and one dress shirt for Sunday services when we could attend. Thank you, Joliet City, for providing the free wall and free electricity for the boaters.

The next day was again hot. We adjusted ourselves and our activities to being on the closed in river instead of the wide open lake. The Illinois and Mississippi River Canal varied in width and depth at this location. Sometimes we would be in a cut that would be only a couple of hundred feet wide and then a couple miles down the river we estimated the river to be closer to a mile across. Commercial traffic was always a concern. This waterway is the most direct route between the Gulf of Mexico and the Great Lakes. The commercial barges are larger and more frequent than we saw on the intracostal waterway. The tow captains seem less friendly toward pleasure vessels and sometimes failed to answer our call for instructions. In those cases we just stayed out of their way which seemed to work best. To their defense, they mostly work on their own

VHF channel and all the time have their work cut out for them on the river. They also have their own language that must be understood to adequately communicate with them. They usually don't refer to mile markers but instead refer to a point in the river. An example is at mile marker 123 (example only) on the Illinois and Mississippi Canal is a shoaling area which a pleasure boater would refer to as "a shoaling at mile marker 123" and a tow captain would say "a shoaling at Mayo Island". Another difference is communication for passing. Long ago, before VHF radios were standard equipment on commercial vessels, the captains of riverboats devised a signaling system with whistles for passing. A downstream tow has right of way over a barge going up stream and a tow or a vessel restricted in maneuverability has right of way over other vessels. But in any case, communication should be initiated by the passing vessel and agreed upon by both vessels before passing a commercial vessel. With both vessels in sight of one another: One short blast means I am altering my course to starboard. Two short blasts means I am altering my course to port. Rule 34 of the Coast Guard Navigation Rules better explains this and on the VHF it will be referred to as a number one or number two. It is very important to learn this and use it correctly. Unless the tow boat agrees with your request, don't pass. Most times, if a captain of a pleasure craft uses the correct name of the vessel being hailed and the correct location he will receive a tow boat operator that is willing to help. "Chapman Piloting" says it this way: "Big barge rafts (tows) on the Mississippi may cover acres of water, and you should never jeopardize their activities...Stay away from the front of tows. Even modest ones may need a half-mile to come to a full stop." Communication with the tow boats is so important we put a diagram on the dash of the cockpit to use as a quick reference before hailing a vessel. It had the number one and number two examples on it and like our clothespins, for navigational aids, the diagram were referred to often. All commercial vessels are now required to have an Automatic Identification System (AIS) which is modeled after the aircraft TACAS system and is a transponder that broadcast information about the commercial vessel, its speed, position and direction. Recreational vessels are not required to have AIS, but if the boat is going to spend a lot of time on the river system where commercial vessels operate, it is recommended. A commercial captain will then have information about your boat and can initiate communication just as you can.

By that Friday afternoon we arrived at Spring Brook Marina and tied up to the fuel dock at 1500. This was the first marina where the fuel had to be delivered by truck. When they ask how much fuel I wanted, I thought it a bit strange since I didn't see any fuel pumps at the dock. A little while later a truck came up with our 50 gallons of fuel. They assigned us a slip and we were happy to find some fellow Loopers in slips nearby. We talked of our voyage and then took the courtesy van into town to do laundry, eat and stop at the grocery store. By that time in the trip, we could do all three in just under an hour. That was the time most marinas wanted the courtesy car returned.

Saturday morning we felt some relief from the heat. At 0730 the temperature had just reached 59 degrees. A slight breeze from the north made it even nicer. We were in the channel a little before 1000 and reached our first lock at 1100. We locked through with several boats but spent time next to *Jolly Tolly* a 44 foot Tollycraft. Owners Ron and Jan Baysden were lots of fun to talk with while locking through and waiting for our turn in the locks. We reached Starved Rock Lock at 1245 but found a tow locking through. *Jolly Tolly* and *Lifestyle II* rafted together while waiting for the tow to clear the lock. We were enjoying the conversation when we saw a rain storm coming our way. All the boats waiting for the lock scattered like a covey of quail. I didn't see which way *Jolly Tolly* went but *Lifestyle II* headed for the lock wall just under the sign that said NO DOCKING. I just got a line around the metal sign post when the storm hit. Someone later said we had 60mph winds. At the time I was worried about having only one line on the post and the pivoting action the wind was causing on the boat. The storm only lasted about ten minutes, but for those few minutes, we were holding on to that line, feeling lucky we were against the lock wall and not in the middle of the river. After the storm passed, we met up with *Jolly Tolly* again and found they had dodged the storm by tying up to a nearby commercial mooring, those large group of pilings bound together with cables for barges to tie up to and wait for the locks to clear. Neither of us had an ideal spot to tie up to but any port in a storm will do and this event qualified. No one was hurt in the storm but several boaters had a good story to tell.

Our progress had been slow because of the wait for the two locks and the storm but the summer day was long and the river was giving us a push, so we stayed on the river until 1800 and then tied to a free dock at Hennepin. The little town is on a bluff and it had developed a unique approach to constructing a town waterfront. They brought into the bank a large commercial barge, filled it with sand and sank it. Then graded the bank to the barge and even made a road to the barge. Since the barge extended into the river, there was enough water depth to allow a boat or two to tie up to it. So the town in one effort created a waterfront park and a visitor's dock. The only problem is a barge is good for neither a park nor a dock. The steel top is not pleasant to walk or play on and the side of the barge is not friendly to boats or crew. Some boaters, as they travel along the river, tie up to barges but I have always shied away from commercial barges for a couple of reasons. First they belong to someone else and second that someone may want to use it in the middle of the night. Also, barge companies don't like for boats to tie up to their barges for that reason and the liability of having a pleasure boat against a working barge. Barges are not friendly to pleasure boats; the rough steel can have spurs that tear into the gelcoat or puncture a fender. For those reasons I stay away from barges, except in the case of a converted barge such as the one at Hennepin. Even so it was not friendly. The large original cleats remained and they are designed for a two inch line not a 5/8 inch dock line like we carried. So instead of wrapping the dock line around the cleat I tied a bowline and looped it over the cleat. The next obstacle was the metal tubular fence that had been welded to the barge. The fence had been built with children in mind and I'm sure it kept the children or their parents from falling into the water but no thought had been given to the boater that needed to go ashore. No gate or ladder had been provided. Once we overcame the many obstacles to going ashore and figured how to take Maggie ashore, we decided to explore the town. In our cruising guide, it was reported that Hennepin was a friendly little town with a grocery store, a general store, a Laundromat and a couple of bars.

As we approached the front street which was an extension of the road to the barge, we did not see a person. It was Stephen King kind of eerie. Here it was Saturday evening and not a person, a car or a barking dog was to be seen. We approached the grocery store with caution. Maggie drifted behind us, her fur on her back standing up. Maybe she was trying to tell us something. Maybe I should have paid closer attention to the radio for the latest news; maybe something had happened that we should be aware of. No other boats were here; no one was at the park, the stores were all closed up; and the one lone street light was just making its presents known. As we grew closer to the grocery store, we saw a piece of notebook paper taped to the door. It was slightly fluttering in the evening breeze. Denniese, being the brave one, stepped up to the door and read the note. CLOSED, GONE TO WEDDING. Whoever was getting hitched must have invited everyone in town. We walked a couple of blocks to one of the bars hoping to get a burger or wings or something besides boat food. But when we found the bar, the grill was closed. Saturday night is for drinking not eating, I suppose. At least at the bar, we did find some people that were not at the wedding. Back on board *Lifestyle II*, we cooked a quick meal and closed up our little floating house for the night.

Sunday morning we departed the barge before the town woke up. We made good time with the push from the river and since we didn't have any locks to pass through, we arrived at Peoria, IL at 1530. The Peoria Lake is a wide shallow place in the river. Outside the channel the lake is reported to be four to five feet deep. We called East port Marina and requested a slip and ask if the river had enough depth for us to enter. They told us to follow their markers and we should be fine. Approaching the marina, the depth meter flat lined several times and my sphincter muscle got a heavy duty workout. We bumped the bottom, slid through the mud and finally arrived at the fuel dock 1600. We took on only 25 gallons of fuel in each tank for fear that additional fuel would lower our water line and we would have to stay till spring rains.

The next day we slipped through the muck and found ourselves in the channel just after 0900. The temperature was cool and the wind was from the north at 15kts. We saw *Jolly Tolly* waiting at the next lock and we rafted up to them for a visit till the lock was ready. As I entered the lock, the wind caught the stern of *Lifestyle II* and pushed it out from the lock wall. I always carry a 100 foot line on the sundeck, ready for just such an emergency. I tossed it to the lock operator and he made it fast and I pulled the boat in. That 100 foot line has been used many times for just such a need and is always at the ready. We exited the lock at 1230 and *Jolly Tolly* soon was out of sight. They must have been running about 14mph with the wind and the river push because we were doing about 10mph. By 1700, we dropped anchor off the channel behind Quiver Island and saw *Jolly Tolly* at anchor. Ron and Jan invited us aboard for drinks and we accepted after we returned Maggie to the boat from her walk.

Tuesday September 6, 2011 started off nice, sunny but a little cool. We raised anchor and waved good bye to *Jolly Tolly* and within a few minutes we had run aground. Fortunately, we were able to back off and get back in the channel and be on our way. The next thing that happened was the chartplotter, our main navigational instrument, started working in reverse. In the past the chartplotter had gone in reverse mode only to fix itself within a short time or after I turned it off and turned it back on. This time nothing corrected the instrument. It is easy to tell if you are going the right way on the Upper Illinois River because the river is moving at about four mph. Since our little trawler only travels about seven mph, if we got turned around we would be going about two mph. But the chartplotter also gives us information on marinas and navigation aids. It was important to have it working correctly. So as soon as Standard Horizon Company opened for business in California, I called and ask to speak to a tech rep. Shortly a tech rep came on the line and I explained the problem to him and told him our location. Scott (the tech rep) said, "I think I know what the problem is." Then he instructed me how to fix the erratic chartplotter. He said, "Make a fist." I said, "OK". Then he said "Give it a good hard punch in the middle of the screen." I did as instructed with the thought; if I break this thing Scott is going to buy me a new one. SMACK, and it cleared up. I congratulated him on his superior technical abilities and told him I felt I had a flashback to the days I was in the Navy and our saying was "If it didn't work get a bigger hammer."

We scooted through the Lagrange Lock with only a short delay and started talking about a place to stop for the day. This part of the Illinois River is commercial, narrow and not friendly to pleasure boaters. Especially pleasure boaters that need to find a place to walk their dog every day. Denniese was looking through the books and charts trying to find a suitable anchorage. Our first location was too shallow and we had to back out. Our second location was an old barge that had been run up on shore and had several deadheads close to it. We nixed that one. Denniese spotted an Interstate 75 highway bridge and we felt we could get out of the barge traffic at the side of the bridge. I turned *Lifestyle II* into the current and dropped the anchor. It was not the best anchorage we had stopped at but it would do. Just to be safe I dropped a stern anchor to keep the stern from swinging with the passing barge wakes. It had been a long day and the stress of not finding a place to anchor had taken its toll on us both. Most times after setting the anchor we would stop all work, unwind and drink a glass wine before taking Maggie to shore. But this time, we were tired and wanted to get it over with. I looked over at the bank and decided the mud bank would likely suck off shoes or pull-ons. We kept a pair of Aqua Socks in a bucket next to the swim ladder for just such an occasion. Aqua Socks is the brand name for neoprene and mesh slip-ons that grip like socks but have a non-skid sole to protect from rocks or shells. We slipped on our foot wear. I loaded the dinghy and Denniese handed Maggie to me, and then she climbed into the dinghy. I motored the dinghy to shore and as usual I asked Denniese if she saw a good spot to land the dinghy. A good spot was one that I could run the dinghy up on the bank or close to it. I needed a tree or rock that I could tie the painter too. And of course it had to have grass, because Maggie needed her grass.

The bank was wide but had grass behind it. I saw a landing spot upstream about 50 yards and Denniese saw a tree hanging in the water much closer. We opted for the tree. I ran the dinghy up to within a foot or two of the bank. Getting out of the Dinghy was almost as difficult as getting into it. I usually went first to tie the dinghy while Denniese held onto Maggie who was fighting her every move. I secured the dinghy and Denniese stepped into the mud bank and as suspected the mud sucked at her Aqua Socks but we were able to work our way to the grass. Denniese walked Maggie while I worked with the dinghy. After several minutes Maggie was still more interested in looking for rabbits than doing her business. I volunteered to walk Maggie and see if I could get her to concentrate on doing her business. After what seemed like a half hour Maggie finally did her thing and I signaled to Denniese, we had a landing. Denniese was a few paces in front of me as we approached the dinghy when "whoof" She sank up to her thighs in the black, gooey, nasty, sticky mess called river mud. I remembered those old Tarzan movies where Jane would be sinking in quicksand and Tarzan would save her. The leash slipped from my hand and even Maggie was surprised by the situation. Instead of running off, Maggie just sat and looked at Denniese. Neither of us knew what to do. At least Denniese wasn't sinking like Jane. She was just stuck. I tried to pull her from the goo; she tried to push out of the mud. All the time we were both thinking about those signs along the Chicago Sanitary and Ship Canal. "Don't get this stuff on you", was their message. This is downstream from those signs. It was too much for Denniese. She sat down the remaining few inches to the mud and started to cry. I was broken hearted, my darling wife stuck in this mess and I couldn't help her. Finally after several less than graceful missed attempts, Denniese was out of the mud and on the grass. All three of us were covered in the black goo. We tried to clean some of the mud off. What a mess. I was muddy, Denniese was mostly covered with the black goo and Maggie had it up to her belly. How were we ever going to get this off?

We dinghyed back to the boat and the first thing I did was throw Maggie in the river. She hates water but I hate mud more. She swam back to the dinghy and I loaded her back in which only muddied up the dinghy. Denniese and I sat on the swim platform and cleaned mud for the longest time. Our mud shoes were still on, but barely distinguishable from the black goo. We finally stripped off all our clothes and went straight to the shower. Our clothes and footwear were deposited in the bucket for a long soaking.

The crew was served an extra ration of grog, and dinner was just enough to fill our stomachs and we turned in. We did have one high note. We were at the most western point of our voyage. We deserved extra, extra grog.

By the end of the next day, we were docked at Grafton Harbor Marina. We washed the boat, clothes and dinghy. The dinghy had mostly cleaned itself. While underway I always remove the drain plug from the dinghy which allows any water in the dinghy to siphon out the drain. During the day I had dropped my bucket with the line on it into the water and filled the bucket then splashed it on the dinghy. That cleaned the dinghy and drained the water. I repeated that cleaning method until the line to the bucket parted and I lost the bucket. But at Grafton we were able to clean the remaining mud from the boat and our gear. Denniese made a run to Wal-Mart for a new bucket and other supplies. We finished the day with a meal on the porch of the marina restaurant overlooking the dock. We had met a couple aboard a Cytra Bavaria 40 foot convertible named *Bavarian Cream* and enjoyed having supper with them.

Grafton is the place where the Illinois and the Mississippi join and commercial traffic increases. The river is wider and faster, at that time it was running four knots with lots of trash and debris. The river banks were lined with barges waiting for their turn for service. Several barges were moored in the middle of the river. It seemed some were being put together awaiting a tow to attach to them. Others were just moored there because there was no room on the banks. We saw several tows with 15 barges attached to them. Thursday, we got an early start and all was going well until we went into the Melvin Price Lock. We went to tie up to the floating bollard and found it had been removed for repairs, we drifted to the other wall but the wind held us off and we couldn't catch a bollard. Then back to the first wall but there was no place to attach to. The wind was blowing me down on another boat just as the gates opened and everyone made a hasty exit. Luckily the drop had only been 15 feet because we never did attach to anything. That was a first for us, just to drift around while the lock was being lowered. We sailed past St. Louis at a record speed of 12.4mph with the admiral at the helm. Our next stop was Hoppies Marina.

Fern at fuel dock

Chapter 18

Hoppies

BOAT RULE #10: Local Knowledge is everything.

Hoppies!! Hoppies deserves a special place in anyone's record of the Loop or even the Upper Mississippi. Hoppie and his wife Fern have owned and operated Hoppies Marina for decades. Stories are told that their family has been on the river back to the time when markers were lit like a kerosene lantern. Fern says they were called "lamp lighters" and Hoppies dad was a river lamp lighter and Hoppie was put to work as a lamp lighter in his early working career. Hoppies father started the marina in the 1930's and it has been a safe haven for recreational boaters ever since. The marina is not a fancy place with varnished teak hand rails or golf carts available at the dock. No, it is very basic, reliable and needed. The main part of the marina consist of two barges lashed together and connected to land by a walkway that moves up and down with the height of the river. Painting is not a high priority, nor is neatness. Clutter and discarded boat parts seem to be left at the last place they received attention. The two barges have a meeting room, a work shop and a covered lounge. Fuel is available at a competitive rate and trash is hauled for free. A courtesy car is available for transits on a first come basis. Hoppies is not a place to stop for beauty and ambiance. It is a place to stop if you are going up or down the river, need fuel and valuable information about what lies ahead of you. As the season progresses, the transit dock which is the side of the two barges will be full of boats wanting the valuable services they provide. Each afternoon Fern will gather under the covered lounge, also used as the fuel dock and hold court for any boater wishing to take advantage of the years of experience she eagerly shares. Fern tells the attentive boaters where to anchor, where not to anchor, and how to contact the tow operators. Additionally, she discusses a list of cautions to be aware of for the next couple hundred miles if you are going south. The lounge is a covered area but, by the looks of the furniture, the covering does not stop the weather. Worn and torn indoor type chairs are scattered around for the boaters to sit and take notes, ask questions and meet new friends. Many boaters partner up with other boats of similar speed for the next 200 miles and Fern pulls no punches about what is ahead of the boats going south. This is a dangerous section of the river and captains and crew wait for the secrets Fern disperses.

Fern gives the navigational lecture while Hoppie works on the barge/marina or stands by with his pontoon boat ready for a boater in need. Hoppie was injured several years ago from a fall which left him encumbered on the left side. But that does not stop him from jumping in his boat and pushing a wayward barge that has broken off from a tow and is heading toward the marina. Hoppie, Fern or family are available on site 24/7 and many boaters are appreciative for the little barge marina in the middle of the Upper Mississippi and the service they provide.

We were the last boat to tie up to Hoppies on that Thursday afternoon. Not long after we arrived Fern started her lecture. The river was running at about four kts and the river was high enough to allow barges to go in both directions, even at the narrow spots. "Watch out for shoaling at mile marker so and so", or "Look for a reported deadhead at mm so and so", or maybe "Staging for a barge company is here", and Fern would point to a place on the worn chart she used. The boaters would lean in close and make notes on their pad or chart they brought. "Anchor here", and she would point to a couple of locations on the chart. "Don't get out of the channel!! Wing dams are all along here", she emphasized. Back on the boat, I ask Denniese, "What are wing dams",

Little did I know, that in the next few days we were going to have a personal encounter with a wing dam.

It seems back in the 30s a hydraulic engineer came up with the idea of letting the force of the Mississippi River keep the channel open and free itself of silt. By dropping debris perpendicular to the banks and extending it out toward the channel, it would force the flow of the river to move faster toward the middle and scour the channel clean of mud and silt. First trees were used but they would rot and break free and create a hazard downstream. Besides, there were already enough trees floating down the river then and now. Rocks, large and small, became the product of choice and each year more and more piles of rock were added to the river to force the river to do the work that man could not keep up with. Of course these piles of rock lurking just below the surface were a hazard to boaters but the Corps of Engineers issued warnings and the location of the wing dams were marked on most charts. At least in the beginning they were marked. Then it seemed there were just too many to mark and a general statement was issued. "Watch out for wing dams!"

We departed Hoppies Friday morning and said our goodbyes to Fern and Hoppie and the small group of brother adventurers that had gathered at the marina. Our next long term stop was a little over 200 miles away at Green Turtle Bay on the beautiful and calm Cumberland River. But before that, we had to travel the remainder of the Upper Mississippi and the Ohio Rivers. At 1330 we tied up to the wall of the Kaskaskia Lock at mile marker 118. We had traveled only about 45 miles by the time we stopped for the day but our stops along this section of the river were determined by places where it was possible to anchor or tie up as opposed to the miles we had traveled. We were tied to a working lock but it was on a seldom used lock and the lock master agreed to our stay. There was room for about six boats our size but until late in the day we were the only taker. Then our friends from *Jolly Tolly* showed up and we helped them tie to the wall. Later we had drinks and talked about how nice it was going to be to get off the mighty Mississippi.

Saturday (9-10-11) We got an early start from the lock wall. We were away from the wall at 0715. We had taken Maggie for a long walk the night before and felt she could hold it till we found a place at the end of the day. We love our little furry friend but she is a worry, not just the loading and unloading but every docking or anchorage is a consideration. She will not go potty on the boat so we worry about her toward the end of each day. This day was no exception. I watched as she paced the cockpit with that look. At 1600 I told Denniese I was going to find a spot to anchor. The designated anchor spot was still two hours away and we were all tired.

What was it that Fern had said, "Don't get out of the channel." Well I'm smart enough to find a place to anchor even on the Mississippi. I turned to a wide spot in the river and saw the bank where we could take Maggie. I told Denniese I was going to pull over and anchor. I had had enough for one day. I slowly moved out of the channel, carefully watched my depth gauge, and made a clearing turn to make sure I had enough water under the boat to get me out the next day. Everything was going well. It seemed I had about 10 feet of water as I slowly made my circle. One of the basic maneuvers required in aircraft pilot training was called "Turns about a point". The maneuver required a pilot to stay the same distance horizontally from a point on the ground as the pilot makes a 360 degree turn around it. The difficulty in flying a plane is that the wind will push you one way and then the other as you make that circle. A pilot must continue to compensate for that push in order to maintain that same horizontal distance. The fast river current was pushing me as I made my turn for that proposed anchor spot. I had not applied those principals learned in aviation training to the basic turning maneuver of the boat in a four mph current and instead of a circle I was turning an oblong. Then it happened! The boat was on its side and everything was tossed to one side. I knew we had hit something and at first I thought it was a submerged tree. *Lifestyle II* had come to a complete stop and was lying on its side. The prop was still in the water and seemed to be turning free. I put the transmission in neutral and assessed the situation. Denniese was frightened and Maggie was pinned in the corner. I put the transmission in reverse to try to back off whatever we had climbed on, but the force of the current against the 40 foot long keel kept us pinned tight. I could hear the scraping of the hull against rock and gravel but the prop was still free. We were over on our starboard side at about 20 degrees. We had found a WING DAM and it owned us.

I picked up the VHF to make that call every pilot or captain dreads to make. MAYDAY!! But before I made that call I needed more information. Is the boat sinking? What is our location? Can I see anyone to help us? I told Denniese I needed to go below and check for leaks. I rushed below, hanging, climbing, and pulling my way down to the engine compartment. I raised the floor board expecting to see a bilge full of water but to my surprise there was no water and the engine sat purring like a kitten only on its side. I rushed back topside and told Denniese that we were not taking on water but she needed to go below and prepare a "ditch bag". During our years of teaching sailing classes and all of our boating together, I had never used that term- DITCH BAG. Why should I? We never needed a ditch bag before. She said, "A WHAT?" I said, "Put some things in a bag in the event we need to leave the boat." I was thinking, a VHF radio, Maggie's PFD, a couple bottles of water, a blanket and a can of Beanee-Weenees, and the flare kit. Without knowing my thoughts and not having a list of specifics, she rushed below to prepare a DITCH BAG. Maggie and I stayed on the flybridge.

A MAYDAY call is only transmitted when grave and eminent danger threatens life or property and immediate help is required. I did not think our predicament reached that level of emergency. We were not far from that level of danger, but at the present time we were pinned against the wing dam by the swift current and could not sink, because we were already mostly on the bottom. We had the dinghy floating behind the boat and if we started taking on water or lost control of the boat we had that resource available to abandon the boat and head to shore. A level below MAYDAY is PAN-PAN. A PAN-PAN distress call is transmitted when the safety of the vessel or a person is in jeopardy but not life threatening. I made the call to the US Coast Guard on channel 16. When an emergency call is heard on channel 16 all other traffic is to clear the airwaves and allow the Coast Guard and the vessel calling free access to the channel. The Coast Guard responded quickly with a series of questions - NAME OF VESSEL, NUMBER OF PERSONS ON BOARD, LOCATION, TYPE OF EMERGENCY, after I answered the first set of questions, a short delay and another set of questions, age of crew, description of boat, emergency plan, health of crew, each answer was repeated and confirmed by the Coast Guard. By the time the Coast Guard had most of their questions answered several minutes had passed and Denniese had not returned to the flybridge. I needed her to handle the radio so I could help the boat. Time was of the essence and spending time with USCG was not getting me out of this situation. In the middle of all the questions, a boater overhearing the Q&A interrupted to ask, if we had our PFDs on. I responded "Not required as of yet." He interrupted several more times, which is against the rules of an emergency, till I finally reached behind me and donned my PFD, so I could respond with a positive reply to his question. I saw a tow boat with barges in the channel and requested help from them. They all carry a service boat and I was hoping they would send it to render aid. They declined my request. No other boats were within sight. We were in the middle of nowhere, miles from any town and hundreds of miles from a commercial towing service. It was up to us to save our boat and crew. The Coast Guard had no presence near our location. Neither did the Coast Guard Auxiliary or Boat US towing service or Tow Boat US. Boat US contacted me on my cell phone and, while still in touch with the USCG, Boat US was requesting information to try to reconcile the problem.

After several more minutes of conversation with the USCG and Boat US, it was determined that the only service that could possibly help was the local Emergency Management Agency. By that time, I had the VHF mike in my right hand, the cell phone on my shoulder and the boat wheel in my left hand. Denniese finally returned to the flybridge with the exclamation "I couldn't find the right shoes". RIGHT SHOES?? (I didn't think a ditch bag required shoes.) That's OK, I said I think I have it under control. Meaning I didn't think the situation was going to deteriorate and we would not need to depart the boat. The USCG was still worrying me with questions, next of kin, contact number, so I finally said "I haven't got time to answer any more questions, I have a boat to deal with." Then I terminated the conversation.

Martha Nicholson with the Alexander County Illinois Emergency Management Agency called and was the first person that said she would help. She calmly said she would have Volunteer Fire Fighters from Cairo, Il reach me. They had a rescue boat and she already had them on the line. Finally, someone could help!

Now it was my time to stabilize the situation. I told Denniese what my plan was and how I hoped to keep us from being pushed further up on the wing dam or having the rocks pound a hole in the hull from the force of the river. My plan was to take the anchors as far out into deep water and away from the hazard as I could, drop the anchors and use the powerful windless to pull us off the rocks or at least take some of the pressure off the hull. By the time I told my plan to Denniese, the boat had righted itself somewhat. We were still sitting on the wing dam but we were only listing about five degrees. The water was still pushing us just as hard against the rocks, so I still did not have control of the boat. Working from a more level platform was somewhat comforting. Maggie could tell something was not right but being able to walk on the deck was a help to us all. The engine was still in neutral and at idle. The old Ford Lehman was the least of my worries. The Marine Trader is a well built boat and we had made contact with the people that promised to help. So, things were improving or at least not as bad as they could have been. I started the dinghy and then took it to the bow of the boat and loaded the 45lb CQR and a pile of chain in the dinghy. Denniese was to play out the chain as I motored out as far as I could. I was able to motor about 200 feet upstream before the dinghy motor refused to pull that amount of weight any longer. I dropped the anchor and went back to the boat for the large Danforth anchor and placed the rode and anchor in the dinghy and took it out as far as the rode allowed. Back on board *Lifestyle II*, I used the windless to reel in the anchor rodes. I went to the helm as Denniese operated the windless. I gently moved the shift control to forward and listened to hear if the prop was striking the rocks. Denniese had the anchor rodes taut and I revved the engine but nothing happened. We were solid aground.

An hour of working with the engine, the windless and even the dinghy and nothing changed. By that time it was getting close to dark and no one had come to save us. At last Martha called again and said the VFD would not be able to reach us until the next day unless the situation deteriorated. The USCG had stayed in touch but had stopped asking questions. Boat US called back to make sure we were in contact with the local EMA's. Nothing was left for us to do except fix dinner and say a prayer. Maggie looked longingly at us but even she seemed to know we were in trouble. Sorry Maggie, no trip to shore tonight.

After supper we tried to keep our schedule as normal as possible. We showered and went to bed. We were still at an angle but not so bad we could not stay in bed. The bad part was when we laid down and when everything was quiet, we could hear the river sound under our heads. We could also hear the hull grinding against the rock wing dam. We wondered how much damage was being done to our *Lifestyle II*. It was the continuous crunching sound of the rocks along with the water sound, the angle of the bed and the tremendous worry of it all that kept us awake most of the night. We prayed, we listened to the sounds, we prayed some more. We comforted each other and Maggie and we tried to sleep. Sometime in the early morning hours we fell asleep but awoke at about sunrise. When we woke we noticed we were floating level and true.

We went on deck to look around, and although we could not see through the muddy Mississippi, we felt the force of the river and the holding power of our big anchors had combined to push us off the wing dam and we were substantially better off than when we went to bed. Our prayers had been answered. 'Thank you, Jesus!!" We were floating but we didn't know if another wing dam was in front of us, beside us or if any other hazards were near. We chose to stay put and wait for help. The morning was mild and it was Sunday, Sept 11, 2011, the anniversary of the terrorist attack on the twin towers. All things considered, we had a lot to be thankful for.

At 0805 Martha called and said the boat had been launched and should reach us within the hour. We kept a look out for that mammoth rescue boat that would toss us a line and pull us to safety. Just before

0900 we spotted a 16 foot Jon boat with a 35 hp Johnson coming around the bend. I told Denniese some fishermen were coming to talk with us. "Surprise", "Surprise" as Jim Nabors would say. It was our rescue boat? Gene Chrestman and James McWilliams both volunteers with the Cairo Auxiliary Volunteer Fire Department pulled up to our boat. The first thing James said as he looked at the size of the boat he was sent to rescue was, "I don't think we gonna be able to help ya." My feeling was, any help was better than no help, even if it came in the form of two slightly overweight volunteer firefighters in a 16 foot flat bottom boat. So I said, "Wait, I think you can." I told them that my depth gauge showed four feet of water and I needed five feet of water. If they could take soundings for me, I could maybe drive the boat out of the soft mud I was sitting in. I would drop my anchors with floats and retrieve them with the dinghy later, if they could just show me the way to deep water. Denniese and I started the engine and checked out the systems. Everything seemed to be in good working order. James and Gene came back with a report. We only needed to move about a boat length before we would be in 10 feet of water and there were no hazards from that point to the channel. I dropped the anchor rodes with floats and made a mental note as to where the Danforth nylon rode was lying, since my prop could possibly pick it up if I ran over it. Everything was ready and I pushed the gear shift in forward and advanced the throttle. We eased forward as I could feel the 24 inch prop bite into the water and move the slick keel through the mud. Meanwhile, the Jon boat was making a wake to add buoyancy to the effort. After the engine run up, the boat started moving and soon we were in deep water not far from the channel. James and Gene came up in their mighty 16 foot Jon boat and congratulated us for the good plan. They asked if there was anything else they could do for us. We thanked them profusely and asked if they would mind retrieving our anchors for us. I pointed to the floats back where we had started. By the time they had loaded all the nylon rode for the Danforth and the chain rode for the CQR, they were tired. They were not far from us as James leaned over the bow of the Jon boat to pull the 45 lb CQR aboard their little boat. We could clearly hear him say as the anchor approached the surface, "This is a

BIG SONBITCH". Jim was a big guy and clearly strong but this was a challenge for him, but with an extra effort he brought it aboard the Jon boat and within a few minutes the anchor was back home on *Lifestyle II.* We had just stopped laughing about his comment as they came along side to return our anchors and rode. We thanked them again and off they went. We were so relieved to be in deep water that we traveled only to the first designated anchorage and dropped the hook for the well deserved rest. But first we had to take Maggie for her walk on the grass she had patiently waited for. It had been over 40 hours since she had been ashore.

We phoned Martha with the good news and contacted the USCG to cancel our PAN-PAN and report all was well aboard *Lifestyle II.* Later we would send a contribution to the Cairo Auxiliary Volunteer Fire Department and a letter of thanks to the people that helped us during the emergency. Boat US contributed the amount of our annual tow insurance fee to the same organization. I'm sure James and Gene had some great stories to tell about how they saved that 40 foot trawler from washing ashore with just a 16 foot Jon boat.

The remainder of the day we napped and did a few maintenance projects. Denniese cleaned while I checked the engine water strainers. I listened carefully to the engine to see if I could hear any defects. I felt the prop had been knocked out of balance by the grounding and we would have to drive the boat carefully until we could pull it out of the water. We had already scheduled to pull the boat out of the water at our stopover in Nashville. The list of items to be done was long and now a prop check would be added to it.

We woke Monday with a heavy fog around us. Tow boats will run at night but no one runs with a heavy fog. All commercial traffic stops until the fog lifts. By 0930 the fog had lifted and the radio was busy with commercial traffic getting underway. At 1000 we made a left turn onto the Ohio River. We stopped for the day behind Harrah's at Metropolis. Denniese wanted to go into town and see if we could find Superman, but we settled on going to the casino and having a great buffet. Tuesday we traveled the ten miles to the Cumberland River and by 1600 we pulled into a slip at Green Turtle Bay near Paducah, KY.

Green Turtle Bay is a stopover for most boaters going North or South on the Tennessee or the Mississippi Rivers. Each year most of the Loopers stop and stay at Green Turtle Bay before their trip south.

We pulled into our assigned slip at the foot of the marina gazebo at Green Turtle Bay. The Loopers had all gathered there for wine and snacks. As we tied up, they all gave us a cheer and signs of congratulations for getting off the wing dam. It seems they all had been listening to the conversation on the VHF with the Coast Guard and others during our emergency. As soon as the boat was secured Denniese and I with Maggie joined the group for a glass of wine. Everyone wanted to hear the details of the misadventure and how we were able to get off without serious damage. I gave all the credit to a good crew and a sturdy boat. After a couple of days of recuperating, we set off for Nashville. We had a stop for the evening at a great anchor spot in Bumpass Mills and another at the city dock at Clarksville and then we pulled into my old marina in Nashville, at Rock Harbor Marina at 1600 Saturday September 17, 2011.

Mike in engine compartment

Chapter 19

Nashville and Flameouts

BOAT RULE #11: If it ain't broke don't fix it.

Our goal had been to reach Nashville by my birthday, September 19, and we beat it by two days. It had been about 10 years since I had spent much time at Rock Harbor Marina and although the ownership had changed the friendly atmosphere was the same. The next day we pulled the boat out of the water and set it on jack stands for the required maintenance. The first thing I did was inspect the prop. It had several dings in it but not as bad as it could have been. We had the shop pull the prop and send it to a prop shop for tuning. We divided up the maintenance list for the things we could do and the things the marina shop would do. I called my son Jay to come get us. We were going to spend the night in our own bed in our new home in Murfreesboro.

Over the next two weeks Denniese and I washed and cleaned the hull. The marina shop had pressure washed the hull but we did a further cleaning and waxed the hull. At that time Rock Harbor allowed boat owners to work in the yard on their own boat on certain items. We had made an agreement with the management for those items before taking *Lifestyle II* to Rock Harbor Marina. Waxing, cleaning and some painting were permitted. We divided the projects into portions that could be done in a day. Each day we usually put in six or seven hours of labor. Keeping wax on the hull is important and a good gelcoat type wax applied and removed with a substantial power buffer is part of the formula for a successful wax job. At the end of two weeks the prop was returned and it had been tuned and balanced at a cost of $400.00. We were very pleased with the work and the price. Prior to splashing the boat we reapplied a coat of bottom paint. Most of the bottom paint had been worn off when we laid up against the wing dam. We saved the labor cost by applying the bottom paint ourselves. I had also replaced the packing gland while she was out of the water and given the swim platform a couple coats of paint. We moved *Lifestyle II* over to a covered slip and continued the work. I brought in my son Jay, and his friend Jason to remove the teak trim piece I had damaged on the Erie Canal. Both had done trim carpentry in new construction in the past and I felt they would do an excellent job on this project. They removed the damaged trim piece at the seams in about an hour. I delivered it to a teak specialist near Nashville to use as a template to produce a replacement. Tommy Nation is the owner of a specialty shop doing business as Teak World Enterprises in Lebanon, Tennessee. Back onboard Jay, Jason, Denniese and I huddled together to develop a plan on how we were going to remove the green chair. The chair was in such bad shape that it either had to be recovered or replaced. Either would require the removal of the chair. After several measurements and much deliberation, we decided to remove the center window. We had been told that with the removal of that window a full size refrigerator could be brought into the boat. It would be assumed that the opening would be large enough to remove the Green Chair. We removed the window and the hardware and while two people were on the bow of the boat two people lifted the chair to the opening on the inside. While the inside crew pushed and turned the chair Denniese and I pulled from the outside. After ten minutes of pulling, pushing, turning and cussing we could not find an angle that the chair would exit the boat. I was determined to remove the chair but even more convinced that the boat was built around the chair. Time was a wasting! I told Jason who was standing close to a power saw to use the saw to cut it up. Even after cutting off large parts of the chair we still had problems getting it through the window but were successful and soon the green chair found its way to a large green dumpster.

At the end of our dock was a familiar boat, *Coconuts*. We talked to Bru and Sandy and they told us of the replacement shaft and props that were damaged during the storm we both encountered in Canada. They had caught up with us and were enjoying Nashville and all the sights. They were also taking time to have some cosmetic work done to the beautiful dark hulled boat. Other Loop boats came and went as the month passed. Nashville is a good side trip for Loopers.

I picked up the six foot piece of milled teak that Tommy and his crew had prepared to replace the damaged piece. Jay and Jason replaced the piece and I set the screws and put the plugs in and did the final prep work before starting the painting process. The replacement was a very good fit. It was not easy to shape the wood because of the angles and curves, but Tommy made the exact replacement using the damaged piece as a template. While the outside work was being done, I worked in the engine room replacing filters, changing oil and getting ready for the remainder of the trip. Denniese had the inside looking like new with new covers for the seats and pillows in the master suite. Together we varnished the teak and holly sole in the suite. Denniese made a shower curtain and curtains for the windows. Jay and Jason did the heavy lifting of the outside work. *Lifestyle II* had taken a lot of abuse during the continuous travel of the trip, but we had most of the upgrades done and our list was growing short. Our time to complete our trip was also growing short. Fall was here and winter was on the way and we were still in Tennessee. The winter weather patterns change and the Gulf gets a lot more active in the winter and that part of the trip was still in front of us.

Log Book: October 24, 2011 Monday, Rock Harbor Marina, Boat loaded and ready to depart. Departed RHM @0830

The month layover in Nashville was good for the boat and the crew. As we departed Nashville we could see and feel the difference. Like a car after it goes through a car wash, it just seems to drive better. *Lifestyle II* looked good and drove better. The balanced prop and the new paint on the bottom just made it go better. The waxed hull made her slide through the water and beads of water glistened off the white gelcoat.

October in Tennessee is the transition between summer and winter. The trees were showing their fall colors and we could think of no better place to see God's glory than on the river. The unspoiled and unoccupied Cumberland River was just a special place. The river is only about 100 yards wide at most places and runs through rural farmland. The river was flowing only a knot or so and the temperature was about 70 degrees with bright sunshine. The commercial traffic is greatly reduced on this part of the Cumberland. Sometimes a boater can go a couple of days without seeing a tow and then they are much friendlier than any other location. We made our planned destination of Clarksville by 1530. We took Maggie and walked the city river walk which is a credit to the city and the city planners. We were not able to dock at the new city marina which was not scheduled to open for a couple of months. The new city marina and the river walk when connected will combine for one of the nicest small town riverfronts in the south.

We woke at 0600 on Tuesday to see nothing. A thick fog blanket had settled on Clarksville and the temperature was 42 degrees. We went back to bed to give the sun a chance to burn off the fog. After having a breakfast of cereal, we walked Maggie and finally cast off at 0900. The sun was shining and the expected high was going to be in the mid 70's. It was another beautiful fall day on the river. During the day we saw several fishing boats and about a half dozen tows but not a single pleasure boat of our size. At noon I fired the grill and cooked some hot dogs with chili and corn chips. Life is good on the river. Denniese remained at the helm while I worked on the bow rail. I cut the plugs that covered the screws and sanded the large piece of teak. The fit was perfect. Tommy had done a great job reproducing the original piece and Jay and Jason did a professional job of installing it. So far we had about $300.00 tied up in the repair. That is quite a savings from the $2000.00 or so that I was quoted on the Erie. Of course it was still not finished but it would give me something to do as we continued on our voyage. Like I needed another project!

We passed Dover, Tennessee and could see the large cannon that had protected the river and the Confederate fort during the early part of the western campaign of the Civil War. The Northern flotilla of ironclads had been stopped at that place in the river by the cannons at Fort Donelson. The Confederate artillery consisted of one large cannon and a dozen light guns that were well placed on land just above the water line. We motored past the little island the ironclads had hidden behind during the battle and could imagine the fight that ensued as the era's most sophisticated war machines fought each other. This is the location where Andrew H. Foote, Commander of the Western Gunboat Flotilla, was wounded in the foot, no less, and his Flagship *USS St Louis* received heavy damage February 14, 1862. The 13 guns at Fort Donelson held off the flotilla of seven armored boats with over 50 guns. The stationary guns at the fort did not receive a single casualty while the mobile flotilla was halted and damaged. That battle showed the Confederates that well placed stationary land artillery could outdo the state of the art "Ironclad Gunboats". Present at that battle was U.S. Grant who would get his nickname of "Unconditional Surrender" at that battle and Nathan Bedford Forrest who would later use those same artillery tactics to capture the *USS Undine* and become the only cavalryman ever to capture a United States Navy vessel and use it against the United States Navy. Of course I served in the US Navy and I don't remember a single discussion of the capture of the *Undine* during a lecture on the history of the navy. I think they are still trying to forget that a horse soldier captured a mighty naval ship.

We anchored that night at Bumpus Mills. We had enjoyed a wonderful day. The fall colors were beautiful and the temperature was mild. The engine was running great and our floating home looked so pretty, except the port side bow rail that still needed to be stained and varnished. The wax job that Denniese and I had done was repelling the water and helping us slide through the water. The new bottom job just added to our efficiency. As we sat on the sun deck we could feel the slight chill of the winter coming on. The fall colors were gorgeous but we needed to be further south. We had traveled 43 miles today and it was going to be another day before we could even turn south. After the turn south we still had a long way to go before the warm Gulf coast and November was just a couple of days away.

Log Book: Wednesday October 26, 2011. Bumpus Mills at anchor. Up at 0700 temperature 62 degrees. Overcast looks like rain today.

We got an early start and reached the Tennessee – Kentucky state line at 0800. The Cumberland River at this point is wide and shallow outside the channel. The markers are so winding that if you are not careful you will look across an "S" curve and see another marker the same color that you are following and drive your boat across a sand bar thinking you are following the channel. During the spring rains this area tends to collect a lot of trash. During my first trip on this portion of the river, while on my sailboat, my prop hit a small log and shot the log out of the water like a fly ball to center field. This trip the river was lower but this area still takes a lot of concentration to stay in the channel. This wide portion of the river is known as Lake Barkley. In the afternoon we passed the famous Eddyville prison. Built in 1889, it is called the "Castle on the Cumberland" because of the large granite blocks used for its construction. It has a capacity of over 800 inmates and houses mostly maximum security prisoners. It is an impressive site sitting on the water's edge. Seeing the prison signals to us that we are not far from the Barkley Canal that will take us over to Kentucky Lake. Kentucky Lake is part of the Tennessee River which runs north at this point. We will travel south on it until we reach the Tenn-Tom, aka the Tombigbee. The Tombigbee will meander south for another 300 miles before we reach Mobile Alabama and the Gulf coast.

By 1600 we had found a little cove off Kentucky Lake close to the same spot I anchored during my solo trip down the Tombigbee. The days were growing shorter and temperature a little cooler. The trees were still full but had turned their autumn colors. The beauty of being on the water at anchor in the quiet of an isolated cove next to an area known for its remoteness is hard to describe. The world could end and, except for the occasional aircraft headed to Nashville or another place, we would not have a clue about it. The singing of the frogs and chirping of the birds were only broken by the occasional splash of one of our only neighbors, a fish. The Land between the Lakes is so remote that as the night set in we could not even see a house or car light. I turned our anchor light on just the same as required by good boating practices and the U.S. Coast Guard.

We woke at sun up to a wet boat. It seemed we had a good rain in the night but it didn't even wake us. Maggie even slept through it. By the chill in the air I could tell that a cold front had passed through in the night and our day would be a little cooler. I fixed a big breakfast and Denniese tried out our newest addition to *Lifestyle II* that we added at our stop in Nashville, a toaster. While at anchor, we either use battery power or start the generator so we had thought a toaster would draw too much power off the battery and not worth the trouble of starting the generator, so we had never purchased one. With our new purchase, we were going to put our batteries to the test and have toast with our fried eggs and bacon for the first time while at anchor on our trip. After a great breakfast with extra toast and jelly, we got our day under way and lifted the anchor at 0830.

The wind was coming out of the north at about 15kts and had a chill to it. The good part was that the push from the wind was overcoming the upstream run and we were moving along at over six mph. It was still overcast and looked like more rain was on the way. It looked like winter. As the day wore on, it warmed and we took our sweaters off and were enjoying the day until 1300 when the engine failed. The river had narrowed and I saw a tow approaching and I had just picked up the mike to hail him and ask if he wanted a number one or number two pass. Number one and number two are agreed instructions for passing on the river. In this case the tow was the burdened vessel for two reasons. First he was pushing several barges and second he was headed down stream which reduces maneuverability. When the engine stopped, I hailed the tow captain and told him we had lost power. He radioed back and said he would look out for us. The river was not as wide as it had been on the big part of the lake but I felt there was room for both of us to pass if the current didn't push us out in his path. Denniese and I had an emergency plan in place in case of an engine failure and we put our plan into action. We both rushed to the lower helm where Denniese took the helm and reported to me what was happening while I jumped into the engine compartment and started the process for bleeding the engine.

Maggie just watched, not being fully awake from her nap. The current had reduced our forward speed to zero very quickly. That reduced our closure rate on the towboat and his barges, but by having no forward motion we had no water passing our rudder and no steerage. We were dead in the water and at the mercy of the current and the significant tow and barges headed our way. The Ford Lehman, being very sensitive to air in the fuel system, has had so many engine failures due to air in the fuel lines that owners of the engine refer to it as a "flameout." Just like a jet aircraft pilot would call an engine failure a flameout, our first real flameout had occurred at the worst possible time, a current against us, and a tow boat headed our way.

Within 30 seconds after the flameout, we were in our emergency positions and I had the wrench on the bleed nut. I called to Denniese to give me a five second crank while I held the shut off solenoid to help build up pressure in the system. I opened the bleed nut and the air escaped. Denniese reported to me that the barge was approximately a quarter mile in front of us and the current was pushing us sideways. I asked for another five second crank. The pressure built and this time the air sputtered with fuel. One more short crank and the fuel system would be pressurized and ready to start. "Where's the tow now?" I asked. Denniese reported that the tow was closing but the current had started pushing us back and thus reducing our rate of closure. She said this as she pushed the starter button for the third time. I opened the bleed nut and a good stream of fuel shot out. I then tightened the nut and gave Denniese the OK to start the engine and engage the prop. The engine started on the first turn and Denniese put it in gear with plenty of time to avoid the barges and tow. "Thank you, Lord." The entire event took about three minutes during which time we were in a state of sheer terror and stark panic. But with the engine running again, we passed the tow on a number one without ever getting permission to pass. We may have failed the rules of the road for passing but we passed with flying colors the emergency procedures for a flameout! Maybe I should have not tried to fix the fuel system that was not broken while in Nashville.

The engine continued to have fuel problems the remainder of the day. We counted a total of six flameouts before we tied to the dock at

Paris Landing. We got pretty good at the flameout procedure that day and also found that running the engine at lower RPM's would help reduce the number of flameouts. Nevertheless, we were not going to let a little flameout halt our progress. While the engine was cooling, we walked to shore with the official boat dog and discovered we were in the middle of a regional bass tournament. It was misting rain and cool but the crowd seemed to be charged with end of the day weigh-in and posting of the results. Not knowing the least about bass tournament fishing, I asked the guy standing next to me to fill me in. It seems that bass tournaments have become very lucrative. Most return about 80% of the registration money back in prize money and additionally motor and fishing gear companies have gotten in to the game by offering credits to winners for their products. Some of the more successful competitors even have sponsors. It seems that some big bass are to be found in this lake. The previous year's first place winner had a total of almost 25 lbs for his five fish and for that, he received a cash prize of several thousand dollars. The guy standing next to me couldn't tell me the exact amount (something about the IRS having spies around). Looking over the posted rules for the tournament, I could see several rules that would eliminate most of the fishermen that I know: No cussing, no drinking, no obscene hand jesters, no explosives, no live bait except for pork rinds (I wonder what the pig thinks about that) no wading, no parking next to other boats. I found it interesting that the only limit to the engine horsepower was the maximum amount the boat manufacture allowed. I had watched as these guys motored past us the past couple of days and wondered how they could make those boats go that fast. Now I know, it is maximum allowable horsepower.

By the time we made our way back to the boat, the day had cooled and the warm engine compartment felt good. I checked all the fittings and, thinking maybe I had a stopped up fuel filter, I changed the selector valve to the number two primary fuel filter. After checking all the fittings, the "O" rings, the filter seals and gaskets and not finding a problem, I felt that maybe during the transfer of fuel from one tank to the other while in Nashville that maybe I had stirred up some dirt and now that dirt was stopping up my filters. After an hour in the engine compartment, I felt I had solved the problem and we would not have any more flameouts. "Right!"

Friday morning we woke to a cool 42 degrees. Not having a central heating system in the boat, we depended on an electric space heater and a propane camp heater. If we were at a dock Denniese would turn on the electric space heater and come back to bed. But at anchor, Denniese claimed she did not know how to light the camp heater so then it was my job to light the propane camp heater and come back to bed until the cabin warmed above the temperature to where you cannot see your breath. At this dock we had the convenience of city electricity and the boat cabin warmed and the coffee maker brewed and the toaster worked without fear of running the batteries down. We finished breakfast, walked Maggie and finally shoved off around 1000 (ten hundred) hours. The engine ran well until about 1300 when we experienced our first flameout of the day. I bled the engine and it started but quickly failed. We drifted along and Denniese gave me reports while I worked in the engine room. I finally switched the selector back to the number one fuel filter and it seemed to work without a hitch. Maybe the air leak was in the filter selector valve? As soon as we got under way, I called American Diesel and talked to Brian. He told me it sounded like an air problem. Well that's what I thought but with all the trouble I was having I could not rule out anything. American Diesel is the expert when it comes to the Ford Lehman. Brian's dad had been the engineer that helped design the engine for the Marine Trader and after the closing of Marine Trader, Bob opened his own company, American Diesel, and has been helping owners of Marine Traders ever since. With the engine running again, we made our way to our next stop, Pebble Isle Marina. This is the marina where Denniese and I boarded *Miss Poo*, a 36 foot Albin, and traveled for a day while looking to purchase a boat. *Miss Poo* was a good boat, but with a few exceptions, we were very happy with our purchase. We docked *Lifestyle II* on the transit dock and while the engine cooled we enjoyed a catfish supper at the marina restaurant. Before working on the engine again we had time to wash a load of clothes and give the hound a long walk. Back on board I dove into the engine compartment, determined I was going to find that air leak. We had the radio going and while Denniese handed me oil soaks and tools we were listening to St Louis beat Texas in the World Series.

Friday the crew was awake early with hopes that the sun would come out soon and warm our little home. The outside temperature was 31 degrees and the inside temp was 42 degrees. The electric space heater labored to move the inside temperature to the comfortable range of even the 50s. But before long the sun was warming and we cast off the lines and motored to the fuel dock for 100 gallons of diesel. As we pulled out of the marina, I could see to my left the area that in 1864 had been the Union Army's Johnsonville Supply Depot. One of the largest supply depots in the south, it was designed and built to supply the Union Army's needs in their western campaign and specifically to supply General Sherman in his march to the sea. On October 31, 1863, General Nathan B. Forrest captured the *USS Undine*, an ironclad steam driven warship, near Paris Landing. He used the techniques he learned while watching the land/water battle of Donelson, almost two years before. General Forrest placed his cannon so as to attack the *Undine* from upstream and downstream and fired upon the war vessel until the captain ran her aground and attempted to set her on fire as he and the crew abandoned her. The confederate soldiers quickly extinguished the fire and captured the vessel, making it the first and only time a U.S. vessel has been captured and used against the United States. Also the first and only time a Calvary General became the commander of a U.S. Naval vessel. Fortunately General Forrest had a soldier that had been a river boat captain before joining the confederacy and he was able to take charge of the *CSA Undine*. For the next couple of days Calvary General Nathan Bedford controlled the short stretch of Tennessee River between Paris Landing and Johnsonville. An attack on the supply depot by the *CSA Undine* was considered but sitting at the dock were three experienced US Navy gunboats with six more in reserve. All with crew ready to do battle. The Union gunboats quickly drove the *CSA Undine* to shore and she was set afire by the fleeing confederates. The *Undine* was reduced to shreds when her magazines exploded thus ending the short career of Confederate Naval Commander Forrest. Meanwhile Captain Morton, Forrest's capable gunner, was placing his guns across the river from the supply depot and sighting in his cannons. Captain Morton's guns opened fire on the depot completely destroying it along with four gunboats, 14 transports, 20 barges loaded with supplies and 20 pieces of artillery. The destruction of the Federal depot was so massive and complete that it temporarily halted General Sherman's march to the sea.

As we looked at the river today, it is much different. The site where the depot was placed is now under water as a result of the TVA damming of the river. The town of Johnsonville is no longer because of the TVA lake. The town of New Johnsonville sits back about a mile from the original site. The river is much wider but the high banks of the river are still in place and the thought of the accuracy of Morton's cannon is still impressive. A Tennessee State Park is on the West bank of the river where Morton's guns were placed. The park is named for the general that commanded the raid, General Nathan Bedford Forrest.

The day warmed with the bright sun, although the temperature never rose about 55 degrees. The engine ran surprisingly well. The work I did at Pebble Isle must have been what it needed. I was glad to have the flameout problem behind us but would wait a day before I declared victory. At 1600 we dropped anchor behind a little island off the channel. Deasons Island is not large but it is shelter from the main channel and large enough for a couple of boats to find respite for the night. We were enjoying our wine when another Looper came in behind the island and dropped anchor. It was a little too cool to be sociable so we just waved and went back inside our warm cozy floating home. The next morning we woke to an inside temperature of 48 degrees. We were so cold that neither of us wanted to get up and light the camp heater. I finally got up because Denniese claimed she didn't understand the working of mechanical things like thermo couplings. She can be so girly when it serves her. I fixed the coffee in the stainless steel percolator pot and put it on the butane stove because it generated more heat in the cabin than the Mr. Coffee. I was thinking of turning on the toaster to see if that would help warm the boat when the coffee started percolating and took my mind off the cold boat. By 0800 we had finished breakfast and the inside of the boat was all the way up to 50 degrees. A heavy fog was keeping the sun from warming our home. We started the engine at 0900, hoping the fog would lift soon but also feeling the need for the engine heat. By 0930 the fog had lifted to where we had the mile visibility needed to navigate the river. We raised the anchor and headed out. Our Looper friends were staying put for a while. By 1000 the sun had cleared the fog and the warm sun was raising the spirits of the crew. Maggie traded her secure spot next to the upper helm for a warm sunny spot on the aft deck. We were turning 1700 rpms and making about 6.5 mph against a slow current. We were still enjoying the fall colors and nothing could be better. Around noon I put some hot dogs on the grill and started getting our lunch together and just then the engine stalled. It had been doing so well, but now I take back all the good things I said about the blasted hunk of iron. We quickly manned our positions, Denniese was at the lower helm, I raised the floor access to the engine compartment and climbed down, and Maggie sat at the cabin door to watch the excitement. I bled the engine twice and it started up on the first try. Denniese engaged the transmission and we were underway. Not as good as NASCAR #24 (Jeff Gordon) pit stop but not shabby either at about two minutes 30 seconds, flameout to startup. The old girl ran well the remaining part of the day without incident. We dropped anchor behind Eagle Nest Island at 1600 and celebrated the day with a double portion of grog. We had put 7.4 hours on the engine and made 37 miles. That's not too bad since we got a late start and had one flameout.

BOAT RULE #12 KISS; Keep it Simple Stupid

I tried to analyze the flameout problem. Diesels are as basic as combustion engines can be. No electric ignition system, just fuel, air and pressure. The injector motor delivers the fuel into the combustion chamber in an atomized form. The high compression engine causes the fuel to combust and power is transferred to the prop shaft and the boat moves. The heat from the combustion chamber allows the process to continue. So I figured as long as the fuel is getting to the combustion chamber in the atomized form, the engine should work. The diesel engine does not have spark plugs but most have glow plugs to aid in the initial combustion cycle. Flameout occurs when air enters the system and instead of spraying fuel the injector sprays air which is the same as running out of fuel, the engine stops. So if air is entering the system, it has to be entering the system and on the sucking side of the fuel line as opposed to the pressure side of the fuel system. If air was entering the system on the pressure side of the system or past the lift pump (fuel pump), fuel would be visible around the leak. Drips of red diesel would be a clue that I had a leak. The only fuel I found on the pressure side of the pump was the fuel I let out of the bleed plug. So the air leak had to be before the pump. Unfortunately, that is where all the fittings, connections, fuel filters and lines were. OK, that's simple enough; I can solve this flameout problem. Uh, haven't I said that before? OK, I admit it, I needed help. Maybe another portion of grog would help.

Tuesday evening we tied up to Aqua Yacht Harbor. I had called ahead and the nice folks referred to a mechanic, not giving up just requesting some assistance. Diesel Don met me at the dock. He had been working on a boat near our slip. Diesel Don and I talked about the fuel air issue for about 30 minutes and really came to no conclusion. It was late in the day, so he said he would contact me tomorrow. That would work fine since we had to make a run into town to stock up on supplies. While in town, I purchased a five gallon jerry jug and some rubber fuel line. If Diesel Don could not fix the problem, I was going to start replacing copper lines with the rubber line I purchased. Meanwhile, we had the courtesy car, and wanting to make the most of the use of the courtesy car we stopped at the grocery. On the way back to Aqua Yacht Harbor we stopped at Pickwick State Park which is known for its great catfish dinners and home cooking. I love catfish dinners and after staying at the State Park on my first trip down the river in my sailboat, I just couldn't miss stopping for a dinner on this trip. We enjoyed the dinner and it was just as good as I remembered. We even saved some crunches for Maggie. All the state parks in Tennessee that have restaurants have one staple on their menu that is not to be missed. I could never understand how an item so good as peach cobbler could be the very same from Memphis to Johnson City, Tennessee and be so very good. We even got an order of peach cobbler to go and it was not for Maggie.

Wednesday came and went and since I was keeping the engine cool for Diesel Don, I didn't even start the engine. I did take the opportunity to change the oil, oil filter and checked the fuel filters. I checked all the connections again and maybe this time I had stopped the air leak. Maybe?? We did enjoy the off day and since the weather was mild we just enjoyed the day. Around 1600 Diesel Don called and said he would not be able to work on our boat today. He was not sure if he could work it in the following day, so we just said not to try we needed to move on down the river. After all, Diesel engines are simple and I was a licensed aircraft mechanic in a former life and airplanes are a lot more complicated than boats, aren't they?

Thursday we woke up to rain. It was one of those winter rains that bring cold weather and poor conditions to be on a lake in a boat. The weather reports were that the front should pass by noon and the skies should clear. We were excited to be on the next part of the Loop. We were finally going to be on the Tenn-Tom also known as the Tombigbee. This was our link to Mobile and our path to the warm gulf waters. The sky started clearing by 1000 and we cast off 1030. It was a cold wet rainy morning and it seemed we were the only boat on the lake. In spite of being the only boat on the lake, I managed to get into trouble. We passed a small marina on the way to the main channel and although our boat does not go fast, it does cause a small wake at hull speed. Our wake disturbed a woman aboard a boat in the marina and she hailed me on the VHF. I responded to her call and she proceeded to bless me out for causing a wake in her marina. I apologized and slowed *Lifestyle II* down to idle. Looking over through the mist, I saw the marina and the adjacent floating no wake sign about 200 yards to my starboard side. My apology did not satisfy the lady mariner and now that she had identified me she really started in on me. A wake is the responsibility of the person who causes the wake. If damage is done to boats or property, then the boat causing the wake can be held responsible. It is understood by most competent boaters not to cause a wake that could potentially damage property. Knowing that, two things need to be understood.

One, a private "No Wake" sign has little enforcement power and two, getting compensation for damage done by a wake is almost impossible unless it is very serious and documented. A slow boat at maximum hull speed will cause a significant wake, possibly more wake than a fast boat on plane. Unless of course, it is a very large boat on plane and then the wake can swamp a smaller boat or damage a boat at dock or even knock everything off the counter of a boat our size. Even so, our wake was not one that should cause any damage unless a boat was not properly tied. I listened to the lady chew on me for about as long as I could and then politely told her she needed to clear channel 16 and if further discussion was needed, then she could request a VHF working channel. I hoped by reminding her that extended conversations on channel 16 were more egregious than causing an irritating wake. Also, I had no intention of switching channels and listening to her whining any further.

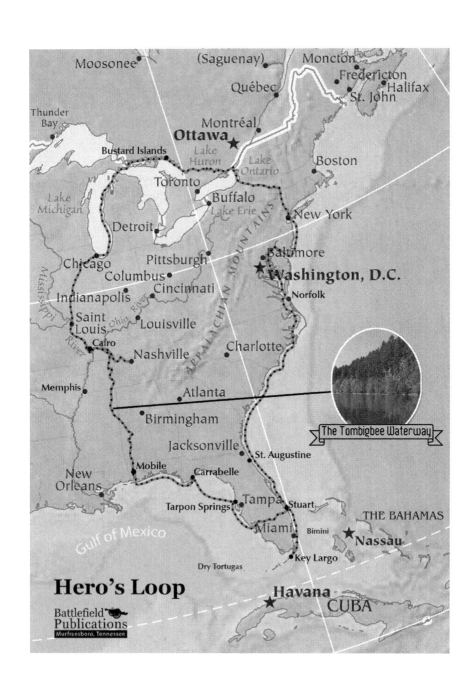

Moosonee　(Saguenay)　Moncton
　　　　　　　　　　　　Fredericton
　　　　　　　Québec　　　　Halifax
　　　　　　　　　　　　St. John
Thunder
Bay　　　Montréal
　　　　Ottawa ★
Bustard Islands　Lake
　　　　　　　Huron　Lake
　　　　　　　　　Ontario　　Boston
Lake　　　Toronto
Michigan　　　　Buffalo
　　　　　　　　Lake Erie
　　Detroit　　　　　　　　New York
Chicago　Pittsburgh　　Baltimore
　　Columbus　　　　　★ Washington, D.C.
Indianapolis　Cincinnati
　　　　　　　　　　　Norfolk
Saint
Louis　Louisville
　Cairo
　　　Nashville　　Charlotte
Memphis
　　　　Atlanta
　　　Birmingham
　　　Jacksonville
New　　　　　　St. Augustine
Orleans　Mobile　Carrabelle
　　　　　　　　Tampa　Stuart
Tarpon Springs　　　　THE BAHAMAS
　　　　　Miami　Bimini
　　　　　　　★ Nassau
　　　Dry Tortugas　Key Largo

The Tombigbee Waterway

Appalachian Mountains

Mississippi River
Ohio River

Gulf of Mexico

Hero's Loop

Battlefield
Publications
Murfreesboro, Tennessee

Havana ★　CUBA

Chapter 20

The Tombigbee

By noon we had turned off the Tennessee River and were approaching the northern part of the Tombigbee. We have only 450 statute miles to go before we reach downtown Mobile where a plaque stands at the convention center announcing mile marker ZERO. The first part of the Tombigbee from the north is called the "ditch" because it is little more than a long wide rip-rap ditch. It was the last cut made in the system and connected the Tombigbee River to the Tennessee River. This section opened in 1985 and looked like a big drainage ditch with rock on either side. Since then, trees and shrubs have filled in and wildlife has once again occupied the remote canal. The Divide Cut is the formal name and it starts from the south at mile marker 418.9 at the north end of Bay Springs Lake and continues some 24 miles. The Divide Cut is 280 feet wide with rock on either bank. There is no place to anchor or stop. If a breakdown occurs, you should move to the side and announce your location. There is no AAA or Boat US service in this area, so a breakdown could be inconvenient at a minimum and disastrous at the other extreme. If a tow boat comes along pushing a heard of barges, that 280 feet will look mighty narrow and the pucker factor will increase by factor of 100. The tow boat captains are just as concerned as you are, so good communication at this point is important. An hour into the ditch I decided it was time to do my S&S tour of the engine room. All was well except I found a vent cap on one of the filters leaking. Could that have been my air problem? I gave it an extra turn and it stopped leaking but after the S&S visit I went back on deck and ordered a new vent cap from America Diesel and had it shipped to the next planned stopping place.

By 1630 we had the anchor down and a glass of wine in our hands. We had found a nice cove next to Whitten Lock and Dam. There was a boat ramp in sight and a grassy area that Maggie was eyeing. The cold front had left us with a day that felt more winter than fall. We put on an extra layer of clothes and started the "at anchor" chores. We started the generator to charge the batteries and give us some electricity for the electric space heater and loaded the dinghy for the nightly walk or rabbit hunt, so Maggie thought. Tonight was a chili supper night along with some left over peach cobbler. Denniese filled the hot water bottle with water from our tank which was still hot from running the engine and placed it deep inside our bed. By the time we turned in, our bed would be toasty warm. We had put 6.7 hours on the engine and did not have one flameout. It must have been that leaking vent cap that was causing all the trouble. Right!!

Log Book: Friday November 4, 2011, at anchor at Big Springs Lake, next to Whitten Lock and Dam. Mile marker 412.

The Tombigbee is marked on the charts by the statute mile (5280 ft.) Reference in the cruise guides are made by the statute mile, so it is easy to find your location. When we reach the Gulf of Mexico we will be back on the Nautical mile which is 6,076 ft. or about one minute of arc of longitude. We had started the day before at Aqua Marine (mile marker 448.7) and ended that day at mile marker 412, which meant we had traveled 36.7 miles that day. At that rate it would take us 12 1/2 days to reach Mobile. That is, if we did not stop for any side trips and I had promised Denniese as soon as we got close to the grandkids we were going to stop. They lived just outside of Birmingham, so each day we were getting closer. We were hoping to reach Mobile for a tradition with Loopers where all who are in the Mobile are to celebrate Thanksgiving together. That was our plan, so our work was cut out for us.

We ended November 4 at Midway Marina at MM 394. We only made 18 miles today but we did make two locks and along the way. I scheduled a mechanic to look at the power plant at Midway Marina. We did not have a flameout that day but this was the only place for miles that had a good diesel mechanic, so I made an appointment. Even if he could not help with the flameout problem we still needed to get the valves adjusted. Diesel mechanics charge about the same rate as a good attorney but you have to take the engine to them or they charge travel time at the same rate. Every day I regret not taking a diesel mechanic course. Why was poetry a requirement in college and not diesel mechanics? The number one mechanic could not get free to work on our boat but sent his helper who he said was excellent. Right! Bubba adjusted the valves and offered no new ideas to the fuel/air issue but did offer not to charge us travel time since he was the helper. What a deal!!.

The next morning the engine started and ran great for the first hour then it died. I bled the engine and it died again. Finally I got the mighty Ford Lehman going and she ran well for the rest of the day. Our guidebook told of a free dock with a view. We tied to the little dock at 1700 at a little park named Blue Bluff. MM 358 for a total of 36 miles traveled that day. The little park was within site of the waterway but far enough that the tows or traffic did not disturb us. The entrance was a challenge because we had to weave our way through stumps of the many trees that were cut or killed when the river was dammed. The dock was just large enough to accommodate one or maybe two boats our size. We were hesitant to pull up to the dock for fear that it would be too shallow or the dock would not hold us. It all worked well and soon Maggie had smelled every blade of grass and christened many of them in the two-three acre park. We were the only visitor and even the boat launch was seldom used. It was wonderful; we had a great little park all to ourselves. The park was operated by the county but this time of year it saw little use by the locals. Across the river and back among the trees was the Aberdeen Marina. We were in a remote part of Mississippi but the city of Aberdeen was about three miles away. We elected to stay at the park and not try to venture into town. We had lots to explore and the bluff had a small dinghy dock and a set of stairs leading to the bluff which was about 40 feet above the water. It looked inviting and we felt the view would be worth the climb to the top.

We loaded the dinghy and motored over to the dock. As we approached the dock, we could see that it was in disrepair. When we tied up to the dock, we climbed over the "Do not Enter" sign onto the dock. Our adventurous spirit was not going to be deterred by a little red and black sign. Maggie was the first to go, with her nose to the ground, or dock in this case; she pulled hard on the leash. As usual, Denniese took Maggie while I secured the boat. The dock was in bad shape and I was careful to find a solid board to tie the dinghy. I climbed on the dock and just as I looked up, I saw Denniese fall. Maggie had rushed over a missing board on the dock without a thought and pulled Denniese over it. The shadows from the trees overhanging the dock had camouflaged the missing board. In the rush to get Maggie to some grass Denniese had stepped in the hole and was only stopped by her knee. Her blue jeans gave little protection. She held on to the leash as she cried in pain. I took the leash and quickly tied it off so I could help Denniese. It was a bad fall and, had it not been for Denniese maintaining her physical regiment, it would have been disastrous. I pulled her from the snare and laid her on the dock. We were both afraid the leg was broken. The pain was intense and as I eased her pant leg up to the wound I expected to see a bulge from a broken bone. Of course that would end our trip, but the trip was not as important as my partner's health. The leg was skinned up pretty badly and bleeding from a small gash. I asked Denniese to move her ankle and toes as I elevated her foot. It was painful but the ankle and toes moved. I lowered the foot and took off my PFD and placed it under her head so she could just lie still for a few minutes.

Maggie seemed to sense the emergency and just sat patiently on the dock, uncharacteristically quiet. We sat on the moss covered dock for a few minutes and the intensity of the pain seemed to wane. A few minutes later Denniese was ready to stand and test the limb. I helped her to her feet and she gently applied pressure to her leg. She winched with pain, but after a short time, she was able to apply her full weight on the injured leg. With my help a step was taken and then another. Maggie was watching and not even pulling on the tied leash. After about 15 minutes from the fall she was able to attempt the stairs to the top for the view we had come to the bluff to see. In the movie "Captain Ron" there is a scene where pirates were attacking the boat; Ron Rico fell down the stairs of the boat into the cabin and faked a broken leg. Upon being discovered that he did not have a broken leg, he stated "I'm a quick healer and I believe in Jesus". Denniese was not faking the hurt but she was a quick healer and I knew she believed in Jesus, so we continued to the top of the bluff. We found a bench and sat for a while before we continued. The view of the river and the little bay were beautiful and the fall colors painted a picture beyond description but Denniese was still in discomfort so we worked our way back to the boat.

Sunday morning we prepared to depart when the engine failed. I bled the engine and it failed again. Well, we were in a great little spot and the dock was free so we decided to spend another day at the free dock. An extra day would give me time to work on the engine and quiet our nerves from the flameouts. I checked the filters and found two out of the four did not have fuel all the way to the top. So the problem was on the tank side of the filters. I worked on and off on the issue, thinking that maybe the fuel pump was not strong enough to keep the engine from starving for fuel. I called Jim, the prior owner, and after talking with him I concluded I needed to work on the fuel pump. After taking the fuel pump apart, I found the rubber membrane diaphragm was stiff and needed replacing. At last, I had found the problem, I thought. I put the fuel pump back together with a new diaphragm, filled all the filters and started the engine. The mighty Ford Lehman started up and ran for a half hour. I shut it down concluding I had solved the problem and needed a break. It was cool outside but the sunny afternoon was inviting, so we took a nice walk. Denniese was moving about better and she felt a walk would work some of the soreness out of her leg. With all of our problems solved, for this day anyway, we poured a glass of wine and sat on the sun deck and enjoyed the cool afternoon.

Monday morning we departed our little free dock and entered the Aberdeen Lock and Dam. Entering a lock adds a degree of stress to the life of a boater. You have to drive the boat to the right spot along the lock wall, next to the wall but not too fast or hard so as to hurt the boat, catch a bollard or cleat or rope or whatever the case may be and stop the boat. Then communicate with the admiral that you have your end secured. She reports back that the line is attached and then I announce to the lock master that the boat is secure. With the floating bollard, a boater can just tie off on the bollard at the center of the boat and let the fenders at the bow and stern keep the boat off the wall. If the boat is going down, as we were, it is a little less turbulent than if you are being raised. Each lock system has its own set of specific rules about how they want things done. On the Erie Canal, we were pretty much on your own and most time we didn't even see a lockmaster. He stayed in the control room and communicated with you over the VHF. In Canada, the locks were well maintained and landscaped with pride. The lock master would come to your boat and hand you the line, but in Canada the lock master required that you shut off your engine while being raised or lowered. The TVA system required that you wear your PFD while in the lock, but don't care about the engine. If they have time, they will come out and socialize with you. All lock masters are helpful and a great source for local information.

We entered the Aberdeen Lock at 0745 and the lower gates opened at 0800. We were just past the lower gates when the engine failed. The exiting of a lock is a time of caution. Many times the water is turbulent from the exchange of water and the space is limited. Past the gates are the wooden fenders that are made of rough cut lumber the size of small trees. They are built to fend off boats and are not meant for boats to tie up to or even lay against. Remembering the event I had with the lock on the Erie Canal, I was feeling the stress. I was exiting the lock at a very low speed and had reached the wooden fenders section when a flameout occurred. We quickly manned our stations. Fortunately, no other boats were in the lock so we had the water to ourselves. Even knowing that no other boats were near did not remove the fear and anxiety that we felt as we rushed to our "Flameout Stations". Once in the engine compartment, I bled the air from the engine and it started on the first try, only to stall again within a few seconds. By that time we were dead in the water and drifting toward the giant wooden lock fender system. I was completely frustrated. The engine failures were taking their toll on my psyche. I was second guessing everything I knew about engines. I felt defeated. What else could I do? I wanted to park the boat and go to a safe warm house where my main worry was what time the mail arrived. Oh for the comfort of sitting on my porch and watching as the world goes by. Denniese had been so unwavering. She depended on me to make good decisions and take care of our boat and get us safely to our destination. She stood by me and was my help mate in everything I did. Even when I was in the engine compartment, she stood by waiting for my request for a tool or a part. These engine flameouts were driving me crazy. I was stronger than this, I could not walk away. I had to fix the engine. I had to continue! I had never been weak in my decisions. When in business, I felt even a bad decision was better than no decision because you could at least learn form a bad decision. Little could be learned from no action. Even against substantial odds I would forge ahead with action. While serving in the Tennessee General Assembly, I took on the powerful tobacco industry and was successful in bringing the first legislation negative to the tobacco industry in the history of the state to the floor of the House. At the time tobacco was a significant cash crop in the state. One fellow legislator stood on the floor of the House and said to me while the bill was in debate, "You may think tobacco is bad, but in Green County it puts shoes on our children's feet". That bill was defeated by the strong effort of the tobacco industry, but the next year a bill was passed and today Tennessee is leading the nation in tobacco free legislation. I could overcome this engine problem. I had to, I had no choice!!

I picked up the VHF mic and called the lock master. I ask him if we could re-enter the lock and return to Aberdeen Marina. His response caught me off guard. He said "I'll have to charge you". While in Canada I made the same request but for different reasons. In that case I could not find a place to park the boat and remembered I had passed several places on the way to the lock. In Canada they do charge for locking through in a different direction. In Canada it was a one way pass I had paid for. The Canadian lock master allowed the passing without a charge because he could see there was no place to stop the boat. In this instance it was a mechanical problem. I needed a place to repair the boat. Not thinking through his response, I snapped up the mic and falling back to my aviation days, I responded curtly, "This is an emergency!" His response was just what we needed. He said "Just kidding". It broke the negative spell that had been cast on the boat and crew. Denniese and I both laughed out loud. I called back and said "Sorry and Thanks". Within a few minutes we had locked through and we were tied up to the Aberdeen Marina. I climbed down in the engine compartment. I pulled the fuel pump off and disassembled it. My plan was to redo all the work I had done over the past couple of days and locate the problem. This time I replaced the pump, tested all the lines, filled the filters, pressurized the system and looked for leaks. All looked good and no leaks were found. I popped my head up from the engine compartment and saw Denniese waiting patiently for my next request. I said, "Let's give the old girl a try", just like Charlie Allnut (Humphrey Bogart) said onboard the *African Queen*. Before we started the engine, Denniese handed me a cup of warm coffee that she had warmed up on the camp stove. She had added to it a jigger of Tennessee sipping whiskey also know as Jack Daniels. The coffee and the break were needed. We sipped the coffee and enjoyed the warmth it generated. We started the engine and motored to the fuel dock and took on 50 gallons of fuel. We called the lock master and asked permission to lock through for the third time in a little over two hours.

As we pulled up to the wall and laid the line over the lock bollard, we noticed a herd of turtles approaching the lock. Turtles are slow boats like *Lifestyle II*. Most of the boats were Loopers that we had seen or visited with along the loop. *The Cooper* was one of the boats and we had not seen or heard from them since the Bustards in Canada. We exited the lock and fell into last place in the herd of turtles but listened to the group on the radio as they conversed with each other about which dock they would next stop. We followed the herd and ended up at Columbus Marina at Mile Marker 335. At the end of the day we had only gone 23 miles but the first three hours of the day we had gone through the same lock three times, changed a fuel pump and taken on 50 gallons of fuel. Such is life on the river.

Columbus Marina is located not far from Columbus Air Force Base and the runways are only a couple miles away. I could see lots of planes flying, mostly trainers. I spotted that famous T-37 and some T-38's and a couple of heavier Air Force planes. I ask someone about all the aircraft traffic and was told that because of the training base, this was not only the busiest Air Force base in the nation but the activity ranked it as being one of the busiest airports in the nation. It was right up there with Atlanta and Chicago with the number of takeoffs and landings. So from our sundeck we could watch as the pilots made their required number of take off and landings or as it was called when I was in training to be a private pilot, "crash and burns". Maybe the level of precision at my flight training school was not as high as the United States Air Force.

"T" Caldwell is the marina manager of Columbus Marina and has a reputation up and down the river as one of the best on the river. He waited at the fuel dock with Jimmy his capable assistant and fueled the Loopers and assigned slips for each. With all the potential confusion of nearly a dozen boats driving into the marina all at once, he was able to manage each boat and its crew as if they were the only boat around. We didn't need any fuel so we went to our assigned slip and soon had the boat tied to the floating dock and our electricity hooked up. We heard that the docktails (boaters cocktails with significantly less formality) would be held at *The Cooper* at 1700. Denniese had a dip prepared for the event and we grabbed a glass of wine and headed out. At docktails a boater must bring his own wine or liquid refreshment and a dip or snack for others. The dock soon became crowded with Loopers and even a few locals that wanted to join in on the fun and stories. But by 1800 most of the Loopers were ready for a real meal and wondered off to their boats. Some of the Loopers were heading out the next day and some had found a great place to stop and catch up on laundry and shopping or as always is the case, some needed boat repairs. We made reservations for a car rental for the next day, had a great pasta salad for supper and turned in early.

Columbus Marina is a full service marina and a sponsor for the America Great Loop Cruising Association but one additional feature that we appreciated was the Enterprise Car Rental company located only a short drive away. They had the car delivered to our slip on time and we loaded up for a drive to the historic areas within a short drive of the Marina. Just driving a car and getting away from the boat for a while made us almost giddy.

After moving aboard our boat in February our boat had been our home for the most part of a year so it was a treat just to drive around in a car like normal people do every day. I had spent some time in the area, mostly Alabama, in the late 60s and early 70s and wanted to see if I could still find my way around. We enjoyed the ride, and as expected I could not remember much of anything, especially about the road system. Of course when I drove the area, the interstate system was not completed and only a few divided highways ran through the area and, just think, that was just three or four decades ago. I do remember that the area had benefitted from World War II prisoner of war camps. The story goes that the prisoner of war camps were located in the rural south and away from any large town so there would be no way a prisoner could escape and find his way back to Germany to fight in the war again. Camp Aliceville in Aliceville, Alabama was the largest of the camps and housed mostly Germans troops from Rommel's elite African campaign. The prisoners sent to Camp Aliceville numbered in excess of 6000 and created a local boom to the economy of the area. Also the prisoners were hired out to local farmers who needed the manpower to grow the food to feed the war effort. The prisoners were treated so well by the people of Alabama that there were even complaints to congress that the prisoners had a higher standard of living than the people of the community. The POWs formed sports teams, a camp newspaper, attended camp college and even had a marching band that marched in the local parades. At the end of the war, many POWs chose to stay in the area and make it their home and marrying many of the local farm girls. The community has benefitted from the hard work of the Germans and the love they have for their new country. King Cotton is no longer King and corporate farms have put many of the local farms out of business. The economy has suffered and evidence of better times can be seen on many of the closed store fronts. But at least in Aliceville the community seems to be getting back on its feet. The few industries seem to be doing well and a recently built Federal Woman's Prison has just opened.

The county seat of Pickens County is Carrollton, AL and has a population of just over 900 where Aliceville also in Pickens County has a population of over 2000. Carrollton has the distinction of being known as the courthouse with the face in the window. The first courthouse was burned by Union troops in 1865. The next one was destroyed by arson. It seems the present courthouse was built in 1878 and housed the suspected arsonist, a black man by the name of Henry Wells. As he waited in the courthouse jail for his trial, it is said an angry mob gathered on the courthouse lawn with the intentions of lynching Henry Wells. While watching the mob, Henry Wells pressed his face to the window; just then lightning struck the courthouse and left the image of his face on the window. The impression of his face can still be seen today. I never heard the fate of Henry Wells, but I can guess.

The touring of the country side ended with the usual routine of grocery shopping and of course trying to find a NAPA store to buy filters for our mighty Ford Lehman's fuel system. Before turning in the car, we treated ourselves by eating at a restaurant, one that had linen table cloths and waiters instead of order takers. What a day we had, driving, touring and eating at a real restaurant.

Wednesday, November 9 we checked out of Columbus Marina and sat and waited for the rain to stop. The rain was light but the weather looked like a winter day so it felt good just to stay tied to the dock for a few extra minutes. By 0830 the engine was on and we pulled into the lock at 0915. Several Loopers had joined the parade into the lock. I took my position at the back of the line and exited the lock at 0930. At the back of the line moving downstream, we just passed the end of the lock when the engine died. All of our friends motored off as Denniese and I took our flameout positions. Like all other marina stops since Nashville, at Columbus I had taken the opportunity to make sure all the fittings, "O" rings, gaskets, bleed nuts and filters were leak free. So why did the engine flameout? That question was running through my mind as I dropped down into the engine room. Denniese stood at the lower helm watching and giving me reports. I bled the engine just as

Denniese reported that we were drifting out of the channel. Since the fittings, gaskets, "O" rings and other areas had been checked, I also switched the primary filter switch to the new unused primary filter. The engine started up and off we went.

By 0950 we were turning 1400 RPMs and moving downstream at 6.2MPH. OK, so was the problem a leak or a stopped up filter? Our Ford Lehman engine has three filters that filter the fuel before it reaches the engine but it does not have a vacuum gauge to tell when the filters are stopped up. The prudent skipper will know to switch filters before they become a problem or make the investment of a vacuum gauge. So without a vacuum gauge, it was just a guessing game. This time I must have guessed correctly because the engine ran well the rest of the day. The flameouts will drive you crazy. It makes you second guess all the work you do. Of course not having the experience working with diesel engines made what I did just a guessing game. Maybe the problem is something different. Maybe the engine is starving for fuel. Could a line be crimped? Could the cam that drives the fuel lift pump be worn down? What else could it be?

By the time we got underway again, the fast turtles had motored beyond our sight. At the end of the day we found an island off the channel, and dropped the anchor. To keep the boat from swinging out into the channel, I took the dinghy over to the bank and tied a line to a tree. Safely secured it was Maggie's turn. Since we had this small island almost beside the boat, why not make use of it? It will be perfect for Maggie. She can't run off, she hates water so she will not swim to shore and she needs the exercise. Besides, there may even be a rabbit on the island and what trouble could she get into on an island? We loaded Maggie into the dinghy and made our way over to the island. After looking it over we decided it was a good place to let her run. We released Maggie from her leash and she immediately found a scent she wanted to pursue. We stood back and watched as our beagle dog scoured the little island for a rabbit. Back and forth, up and down, long ways and crossways she ran. Finally after about an hour she had worn herself out and we were tired of watching her so we called her to come to the dinghy. She was even ready. She came walking up and took a short jump into the dinghy. We looked at her and quickly surmised that even on an island she can get into a mess. She was covered with stick-tights. Stick-tights are a weed that goes to seed in the fall and is credited with being the idea for Velcro. The hook like barbs on the seed pod will attach to anything, especially beagle fur. We got Maggie back on board *Lifestyle II* but would not let her go below before we picked all the stick-tights off her.

After supper we called the lock master of the nearest lock and told him we anchored at mm 302.4. He in turn would hopefully let the tows know we were anchored beside the channel and not run us over in the middle of the night. It was good to call but we were in a wide straight section of the river and pretty far off to the side so we felt safe. Before bed I used some tubing that I had purchased at the NAPA store and made a DAY TANK. A day tank is a small fuel tank used to carry enough fuel for the day or to supply fuel in the event the main tank is suspect of contamination or leaking. Our day tank was a five gallon jerry jug that I could put to use after leaving Columbus. I felt the air leak could be circumvented by using the day tank. The problem with a day tank is the small amount fuel, the reason it is called a "day tank". At 1600 RPM's the engine will consume about one and a half to two gallons per hour. That means the five gallon jug will last a little over two hours before it has to be refilled or discontinued. The fuel for the day tank was drained from the port fuel tank to a five gallon day jug. That jug was then hooked up to the suction side of the fuel pump with fuel grade rubber hoses without getting air in the system. I first tried two jugs by swapping out one jug as it got low of fuel. Moving a five gallon jug of fuel around in a hot engine room with moving parts and lots of hot things that would burn my arms when accidently touched, proved a bigger problem than I first thought. Next, I left the five gallon jug in place and would service it with one gallon jugs using two at a time. That would last about two hours. Meanwhile Denniese is doing all the boat handling duties while I'm in the engine compartment trying to keep the engine running. If we could just make it to Demopolis we could stop and fix the problem…Right!

We pulled into Demopolis Yacht Haven at noon on Saturday November 12. Now I could fix the fuel system once and for all. But first we needed to reserve the courtesy car and make a run to Walmart and a local pizza shop for a late lunch. Back on board we celebrated our arrival at Demopolis, the last marina we will stop before Mobile. Maggie did her part in the excitement by miscalculating the distance between the boat and the dock and falling into the water. We pulled her out of the river water and dried her off. She even seemed embarrassed by her miscalculation. The new Demopolis Yacht Haven is located behind the old facility and is state of the art in every way. It has a floating dock with pump out stations at every slip and a boater's lounge that is the best in the nation. It has lots of washers and dryers, a large screen TV and showers all tiled and clean. The new dock is just behind the old dock but a long way to walk to the office so golf carts are provided for the boaters.

We had finally reached a marina where we could stop and work on the boat. I was determined to solve the flameout problem. I had been reading about the problem, talking to American Diesel and asking every boater I could for his opinion on the subject. The suggestions were as varied as the people I ask. The engine ran fine as long as it had fuel. The jerry jug system worked, but that meant a lot of manual work and circumventing the primary filters. So, it would seem the problem was in the primary filter system. But I was not satisfied with the obvious simple solution; I opted for the more complex. I blew out the fuel lines, and again changed out the fuel filters. One of the suggestions I had was that my fuel tanks had become contaminated. Sometimes a boater will say he has bought some contaminated fuel. Most times the fuel is good but it is the tank that is contaminated. Contamination occurs when the air inside the tank above the fuel cools condenses and water is formed. Water is heavier than fuel so it works its way to the bottom of the fuel tank. Most tanks have a sump where the water will settle. If the water is not drained out of the tank over time it will rust a steel tank or grow microbes that can feed off the fuel in any tank. The microorganisms can grow and multiply until the water becomes milky or slimy with the little buggers. Everything is OK until the boater takes the boat out onto some choppy water and the microbes and water get bounced around and become sucked into the fuel lines and OOPS the engine stops. The cure is to drain the tank or kill the microbes or both. Just killing the microbes can also cause the fuel lines to stop up. Another solution is to filter out the contaminates. At our present location in the trip we had used up enough fuel that I felt contamination was not the problem. If any water was in the tank, I surely had filtered it out. Plus the problem did not start until we left Nashville. The flameout problem must be air getting into the system. So after changing out the fuel filters, I checked all the fittings again.

While in Demopolis we were about as close to Denniese's grand children as we were going to get on the boat trip and she let it be known that she needed a side trip to visit the kids. I called the marina office and ask for a recommendation for a car rental company in Demopolis. There is no car rental company in Demopolis was the answer. That was hard for me to believe. I thought every city had a car rental company of some sort. So I started calling around. I even called the used car lots and ask if they would rent a car to me for a couple of days. I was turned down at every request. Finally I found a fellow boater who had a car that I rented for the same rate that we had paid in Columbus. The road trip was on.

We made the road trip to Hoover, Alabama in about three hours and had a wonderful visit. The kids were glad to see us and we were happy to see all of them. We returned the next day and cleaned the borrowed car so as to leave it better than when we borrowed it. Unfortunately, it had rained while we were gone and the road to the dock was one big mud hole so all our cleaning work was in vain. The owner didn't seem to mind after I gave him a crisp hundred dollar bill for the single night usage. By Wednesday, morning we were ready to depart Demopolis and make our way to the coast. We started to call the lock when we heard loud blasting of sirens. They were not just any siren but tornado warnings. We turned on the VHF and found we were in the path of a tornado. We could not take any evasive action, just hope and pray it didn't strike the boat dock. The wind picked up and the rain poured down and within a few minutes we heard additional sirens and emergency vehicles. The tornado had hit the town but bounced over the marina. The damage to the town was minor but the power was knocked out to the town and the dam. We waited another couple hours before canceling our planned departure. The power was restored the next day and we were able to transit the dam.

By the time the dam was back in operation a group of Loopers and other boaters had gathered in Demopolis waiting for passage. It all worked out to our benefit because several in the group were slow boats like us and they made for good travel companions. We spent the next four days traveling with them and enjoyed their company. One special boat was *Jeremiah*, who we had met several times along the way. *Jeremiah* was a 38 foot Bristol Trawler with a white top and a black hull. The owners Jeff and Linda Brinker took really good care of the boat and it showed. Molly and Snickers were their boat dogs. Molly was a chocolate lab and Snickers was a mixed poodle. Each evening Jeff would launch his dinghy and motor over to *Lifestyle II*. I would load Maggie and the five of us would make our evening poop run. We had lots of fun and the three dogs seemed to have more fun than we did.

Convention center and the start of the Tombigbee

Chapter 21

Mobile

Monday morning we pulled up the anchor at mm 12.2 and by 1000 hrs we had downtown Mobile in sight. By 1100 hours we reached the convention center and spotted the tall channel marker placed on the grounds of the convention center designating the start of the Tenn-Tom waterway. The waterway we had been traveling for the past 18 days and 425 miles.

Across the bay from Mobile is Fairhope, Alabama, an upscale community with improved downtown and wide streets with manicured lawns. We called and found an open slip at Fairhope Yacht Club. The others Loopers went to the marina across the inlet from the yacht club. We later found out that they were paying about $.50 a foot per night to dock there while we were paying only $15.00 per night. That's just one more reason to join a yacht club. The Fairhope Yacht Club is located in a large new southern style building with a veranda that runs around three sides and is a perfect place to watch the sun set. We were welcomed as if we were long lost relatives and shared stories until the club got so busy that we could not hear others speak and then we retired to our boat. Another advantage of the club was that it was on the town side of the inlet and within walking distance of downtown, while the other marina was across the inlet. In order to get to town from there, the boater would need to walk about four miles to get to downtown. We felt we had been lucky in our choice but the real reason the Loopers stopped at

Fairhope was the traditional Thanksgiving dinner hosted by one of the Golden Loopers. Everyone was required to bring a dish while Bob and Vicki Riggs provided the place and several types of meat. Their boat was named *Si Como No* which is Spanish for yes of course or something like that. He is retired Navy and is full of great stories about the Loop and the Navy. It was great to spend Thanksgiving with the Riggs and the fellow Loopers. We ended the day with a picture in the front yard of the Riggs home with all who had partaken in the celebration.

While at Fairhope I had worked on the engine, bled the lines and changed the fuel filters again. We were ready to shove off when Friday morning arrived. A cold front was approaching and Mobile Bay is not friendly to boaters when the wind is over about 15 knots. We started the engine at 0645 and pulled away from the yacht club dock at 0715. The engine was running good and waves were small. We were hoping to get off the bay and into the intracoastal before the water got rough. Even with a good plan, we were the only boat to leave the dock and once out on the bay, we were the only pleasure boat within sight. Everything was going great for about the first 15 minutes and then we had a flameout. The wind was strong enough that it made it rough to just drift and the water was shallow in the direction it was drifting, so I tossed out the anchor. With the nose of the boat pointed into the wind and waves, the boat settled into a slow roll over the waves. I climbed into the engine room as I told Denniese that this was no way to start a trip. Then I realized what day it was. It is Friday!! I shouted, "Sailors never start a trip on Friday. That's just plain bad luck!" Of course I'm not superstitious, not a bit. Let me think, we made the proper toast to King Neptune before we started the voyage, we changed the name of the boat according to legend, even though we could not find any virgin urine to sprinkle about, we did pour a substantial amount of good quality champaign into the water to acknowledge King Neptune. We did not have any cats aboard. No one was allowed to whistle aboard *Lifestyle II,* we always boarded the boat with the right foot first, never with the left foot. And besides all of that I have forwarded every one of those emails that promises good fortune, if you forward it to four of your friends. I can say I'm not superstitious because I adhere to all the necessary protocols to avoid these mishaps. Except this one really slipped up on me. "Starting a trip on Friday is a big No-No," I stated. The Royal Navy had trouble getting sailors to depart on Friday so they set out to disprove the legend. The *HMS Friday* was the vessel that was going to prove that the bad luck surrounding Friday departures was a myth. The English were going to lay to rest the Friday superstitions by laying the keel of a boat on Friday, launching the boat on Friday, assigning a Captain named Friday and setting sail on Friday. That Friday was the last time anyone saw or heard from the new ship, *Friday*. Yet here we were bobbing around in Mobile Bay with an engine that would not start on a Friday morning. Once again, I bled the fuel lines and after several tries, it started. Should we turn back? Should we venture out on a Friday? We were almost within sight of the yacht club. We could be back tied to the dock in another 30 minutes and wait another day to start the trip. No, we don't go back! We pulled up the anchor and headed south.

The engine only ran for a few minutes before it stalled. The wind had increased to about 20kts and as expected, it was on our nose. Mobile Bay is only about 10 to 12 feet in most places so a three foot wave and a four foot draft left only a few feet margin for that old tree stump or boat hull lying on the bottom. After another flameout we switched to the jerry jug and the engine ran fine. Everything must come to an end even weather on your nose. We made the turn into the channel at 1200 hours. With a new heading of 100 degrees and the protection of the channel, we had a smooth ride on the intracoastal all the way to Barber Marina. Barber is a new marina and we felt special because we were one of only about six boats in a marina that had space for about a hundred. In addition to the in-water marina, they had a large dry storage and couple of travel lifts for taking larger boats out of the water and taking them into a hanger like repair facility. The marina was all first class and had a most interesting display of antique outboard motors displayed throughout the marina office. The only negative was their location. By water the marina was just off the intracoastal but by land it was close to 20 miles to a grocery store. The marina did have a courtesy car and we reserved it for the next afternoon. An approaching cold front dictated that we stay put for a couple of days. We reserved the extended stay until the front passed and the wind calmed a bit. It would also give us time to work on the fuel problem and visit one of my nearby favorite spots.

Lula's is a marina and tourist hot spot close to Barbers. Lula is reportedly Jimmy Buffett's sister and just the mention or association of the name "Jimmy Buffett" attracts boaters and wannabe boater of all types. I have stayed there, even eaten there but it is not my favorite place along the Orange Beach Coast. My favorite place is Pirates Cove, a small marina located next to the Florida – Alabama state lines and the real lifestyle of Jimmy Buffett enthusiasts. They serve cheeseburgers and a couple other items but most people order the cheeseburger. It is mostly an outdoor bar but if you need to get in out of the weather, seats inside are available. The small marina is located behind the restaurant and is just as rustic. The first time I sailed into Pirates Cove I ask for the electric power hookup for my boat. I still remember what the bar-tender/ cook/harbor master said "Yea, the electric outlet is behind the coke machine." Sure enough plugged into the wall outlet behind the coke machine were several boat drop cords and the coke machine. Everyone gives the place great reviews, not only for the food and atmosphere, but also for the dogs. A sign tacked to the wall says "If you don't like dogs maybe you shouldn't be here." It seems the owners and staff have adopted all the stray dogs in the area. The boaters and the dogs know the rules, "No growling or biting." All the dogs are well behaved and fed by the many people that stop to enjoy the place. We had two reasons for visiting Pirates Cove. We wanted one of the great cheeseburgers and I wanted to see *Lifestyle I*. A friend told me he saw her docked there and I wanted to just say "Hi" to my old sailboat and reminisce for a few minutes about all the good times I had over the years I had owned her.

The drive over to Arnica Bay was a pleasant one and always nice to get off the boat for a while. I only got lost once and didn't even feel that my masculinity was threatened when I stopped to ask directions to Pirates Cove. The place has been destroyed by several hurricanes over the years but it is always built back and looks mostly the same each time. The exterior is rough cut wood without paint and decorations seem to just happen as opposed to a real plan. We enjoyed the food and the ambiance. We also enjoyed the visit with my old sailboat. She was in pretty good shape, although the teak was not as bright as when I owned the boat, otherwise the new owner seemed to be taking good care of her.

We returned to Barber marina and scheduled the marina mechanic to meet me aboard *Lifestyle II* and discuss the fuel/air problem. He came aboard at the scheduled time and we started the process of eliminating the source of my flameouts. He found two suspect areas. A fitting at the lift pump was loose and the copper line from the primary filter to the lift pump showed areas of corrosions. After replacing both items, I started the engine and it purred like a happy kitten.

By Monday November 28, we were ready to cast off the lines and continue our trip. The front had passed and we woke to an outside temperature of 45 degrees. Even the north part of the Gulf Coast gets chilly in November. We crossed the Florida state line at 1030 hrs. The engine was running well and the wind was from the west which gave us a good push. We had a report that the next stop had a good price on fuel. At 1300 we pulled into Little Sabine Bay and spotted the fuel shack on our port side. The wind was still blowing hard from the west, but since we were pointed south, the wind pushed us up against the dock. No one was available to take our lines but the wind was holding us fast against the dock. From the flybridge I could see a small sign taped to the fuel shack window, "Closed on Monday, Tuesday, Wednesday starting November". "Well that sucks", I said. Denniese was still trying to get a line on a cleat when I saw Maggie jump ship. I let Denniese know and off they went across a parking lot and behind some buildings with Denniese yelling her now familiar yell for Maggie to stop. I was still in the flybridge and had a good view of the area including the high tailing rabbit dog. I called Denniese on her cell phone and gave her directions. Even with high tech reconnaissance effort, Maggie was still able to avoid capture. After about 10 minutes Maggie found a friend that invited her into a car and delivered her back to Denniese. The nice lady had spotted Denniese with the leash in hand running down the road and when she saw Maggie with a significant head start, she "cut Maggie off at the pass." Another angel came to our rescue. A few minutes later Denniese came walking back to the boat with the crazy dog in tow.

With no one to help, it was up to the crew to get the 40 foot single screw boat with no thruster off the dock while a 25kt wind pushed us against the dock. To make matters worse the boat in front of us was backed into the slip perpendicular to us and had his bowsprit hanging in our path by about five feet. The challenge was to turn our boat to starboard against the push of the wind and against the prop walk. A spring line with a loop back to the boat was the answer. I only needed to figure out the pivot point of our boat and the thrust of the engine without pushing us forward. I ran a line around a forward pole and made it fast at one end to an aft boat cleat. Denniese held the bitter end of the line and made it temporarily secured on the same cleat. I put a fender at the port side aft, at the stern of the boat. This works best if the wind is pushing the boat off the dock but we made it work even with a wind holding us against the dock. I centered the helm and put the boat in reverse. The bow did swing out but as soon as I put it in forward, the wind pushed us against the dock. After about four tries I told Denniese as soon as the bow moved out from the dock drop the line and bring it in. I put the transmission in forward and turned the wheel hard to starboard. Our boat moved off the dock but it also moved forward. The 65 foot sailboat with an eight foot shinny teak bowsprit with a large chrome plated plow-type anchor was dead ahead. Our little rudder caught and held the pivot against the dock and we moved past the anchor and the sailboats rail with inches to spare. From the flybridge I looked straight down on the polished bowsprit. Fortunately, the owner was not present or he would have had a heart attack.

We motored over to the transit dock and slid into a slip for the evening. After we secured the boat to keep the crazy dog from escaping, we walked up the strip and had a supper of Redfish with Bubble and Squeak. Denniese was raised by a very English and proper mother who served many weird sounding meals. Bubble and Squeak is one, an English dish of mashed potatoes and cabbage. I was reluctant to have such a meal but Denniese insisted and it turned out to be very good. Maybe those Irish genes were coming out in me. Best of all, when our check came we were given a discount because it was off season. After all, it was late November.

The next morning we woke to 38 degrees at our dock in sunny Florida. The good news was it was only down to 50 degrees inside the boat. We motored across the intracoastal and took on 80 gallons of fuel at the Santa Rosa Yacht Boat Club. We discovered the club would have been a much better place to stop, with better rates for transients and competitive fuel rates. But if we had stayed there, we would have missed the dog chase, the sailboat with the chrome anchor and possibly the Bubble and Squeak.

For the next couple of days the engine ran great. No flameouts and our travels east were very nice. The sun kept the temperatures comfortable but of course on a boat nothing works all the time every time. Now it was the GPS giving us trouble. We could live without the GPS Chartplotter as long as we had the paper chart. We had over 100 pounds of charts and books on board that we had been progressively using as we did the Loop. The flip chart of Florida was the last book we would need. The Florida chart book would take us all the way to Stuart, Florida which would connect the circle. We pulled into the Panama City Marina at 1430. The weather had improved and the outside temps were up to 60 degrees. It was the first time in almost a week that we had been warm without a jacket. It was time to check our fuel filter supply and make sure we had what we needed to get us to Carrabelle. We needed a couple of each type of filter to get us to that point. A good marine parts store was within easy walking distance from the city dock. We locked Maggie in the boat and headed out for a nice walk. The first marine store was out of the filters we needed but were told that a NAPA store was only a couple miles up the road. By the time we found the NAPA store and returned to the boat we had walked about four miles and it was more than I had planned. I was tired and having strange feelings in my lower abdomen. I had first noticed those feelings when we ran aground on the upper Mississippi where I had pulled and hauled on the anchors trying to get us off the grounding. But now after a four mile walk, it was not just a feeling but a visible bulge there in my left groin. I had a real life hernia. We showered in the marina shower and then back onboard, I went to bed to get some needed rest.

The following day was Friday and with past experience and now a hernia giving me trouble, we decided to stay in our slip for the day. It also gave us a chance to have dinner with some other Loopers who had gathered at Panama City Marina. We took the short walk over to Bayou Joe's for a good seafood dinner and fellowship with our boating friends. It was already December and we still had the Gulf crossing ahead of us. We had to move along if we were going to make a crossing this year. The weather patterns make it more difficult to cross the gulf with the Canadian cold fronts driving the jet stream down to the panhandle and beyond. Saturday we shoved off from the Panama City Marina while all the other Loopers stayed put. That seemed to be the case most times. We made decisions based on what was good for our boat and crew and didn't wait for another boat or crew. If we met along the way and were able to travel together that was good but we couldn't slow down or even wait a day for another boat. Our boat was slower than most, our needs were somewhat different and our time table was our own. After all Denniese had taken a year leave of absence from work for this trip and as soon as we returned, I had a house to finish.

We needed to connect the dots on this trip and get back to the real world. I guess each boat and crew had their own goals and desires but it seems most of the others were more concerned with group travel or the social side of the trip than we were. The engine was running well and it seemed that I had solved the fuel/air problem. But, I think I had said that before. With the days shorter and the temperature cooling in the evening we started looking for spots to anchor earlier, remembering that once we set the anchor we still needed to walk the dog, fix supper, do boat chores and then get ready to start all over the next day. About 1300 we found a recommended anchor spot but decided against it because it was all swamp and there was no place to walk Maggie. We saw some fishermen in a small boat and ask if there was a launching ramp or park nearby for us to drop anchor for the night. One of the men said yes, "there is a ramp a couple miles that way", pointing east. That would work out great, I thought. It was still early and we could maybe get an early start in the morning and make Carrabelle by the following afternoon. We thanked the locals and headed off. Two hours later we still had not found the ramp. In fact it seemed we had found nothing but more swamp. Denniese looked in the cruise books and searched the banks and side streams for a suitable anchor spot. Port St. Joe, it seemed, would be our next best stop, although it was out of the way by about six miles. Just then we found a spot next to a bridge at White City. The only distinguishing thing about White City is that it is exactly on the line between the Eastern Time and the Central Time.

The road and the bridge divide the time zones and the residences. The really nice thing about White City is they have provided a really nice park, pavilion and free dock for the traveling boaters. They have an area cut off the river that has parking for about a dozen boats our size. In addition, picnic tables, restroom, grass for the dogs and even a store to buy worms or beer within walking distance. You could buy gas for your outboard motor and send a letter off from the post office in the back. What a great place. "We need to move here", I told Denniese. When a boat ties up to the courtesy dock it seems it is big news and the locals come to visit. The community is so small that most of the residents own a golf cart to go to the store or the river, the only two spots to visit. After we tied the boat and Denniese walked Maggie, we visited with locals and the few boaters who had chosen White City to spend the night.

Sunday looked to be a good traveling day weather wise, but with the nice free dock we decided to stay put for the day. *Lifestyle II* was tied port side to the floating dock, which is just opposite the way we usually tie her and it gave me the opportunity to do some work on the port side. I replaced an engine compartment vent that had been smashed in one of the many locks we had gone through and the repaired port rail needed a final coat of varnish. It was a good day to take care of those items and enjoy White City. Denniese walked down to the store to mail a letter and discovered that it may be the only post office in America open on Sunday. In fact the whole place reminded me of a bar that I once visited in the Caribbean. It was on Yost Van Dyke in the British Virgin Islands. Yost Van Dyke is such a small island that it has no airport or bridge, so there is only one way to get there. The bar was called Ivan's and it was the last remaining "Honor Bar" in the Caribbean. The title Honor Bar has nothing to do with the people that enjoy a brew but how they pay.

When you entered Ivan's you put your name and the name of your boat in a log and proceeded to get a beer or drink from the bar. When you departed you settled up with Ivan. If you get too drunk and stagger off to your boat without paying, Ivan will remind you the next day. He said it cut down on the help stealing drinks and money from the place. I once asked Ivan did he ever lock up and go home. He said, "Look MON, I got no doors." I think White City could be the same. I would not be surprised if most of the residences did not know where the key to their house was. Just like Ivan's may have been the last Honor Bar in the Caribbean, White City may be the last "Honor" spot in America.

Monday we got up at 0700 Eastern Time. If we backed the boat up about 100 yards we could sleep in for another hour and get up at the same time. Instead we had breakfast and checked the outside temperature. It was 58 degrees but the weather forecast predicted warmer temps in the Florida panhandle. We motored past Apalachicola at noon and thought about stopping for lunch at one of the many good restaurants there, but we continued on and arrived at C-Quarters marina in Carrabelle at 1700. We fueled up and were assigned a slip at the west side of the marina. In front of our slip and across the parking lot on the other side of the highway was an Ace Hardware. Next to the Ace Hardware was an IGA Grocery store. Both stores were within sight of our boat. During the trip from White City the motor had stalled a couple of times, so it seemed I had not solved the fuel/air problem. It looked like the Ace Hardware would come in handy. This time I planned to build a pressure system to attach to the fuel line to find the leak and fix it once and for all. Right!!

Tuesday we started preparing the boat for the crossing. We do not own a life raft and did not intend on purchasing one so the next best thing is to use the dinghy as boat of last recourse. Denniese and I took the motor off the dinghy and drained the fuel and ran the little engine until all the fuel had been used up. The new fuels with 10% ethanol are bad on the small engines. If you leave any fuel in the system for any extended time, the fuel will do lots of strange things to the engine. Corrosion, rust and degradation of the fuel lines are just some of the problems associated with this fuel the EPA thinks is so wonderful. If you have a higher percentage ethanol fuel you are going to get to know the small engine mechanic real well. We stored the dinghy engine on board and pulled the dinghy on to the swim platform. The 12 foot RIB is heavy but I attached two lines on the swim platform and passed them under the dinghy as she floated abeam and aft the swim platform. I then passed the lines to Denniese waiting on the sundeck. I climbed back on the sundeck and together we pulled the dinghy onto its starboard tube and it pivoted over and sat on the swim platform. It could have only been easier if we had spent several thousand dollars for dinghy davits system. But we have a beagle dog that must go ashore every night so mounting the dinghy even on the swim platform is something that we will only do when we are making a crossing. With the outboard motor stowed and only two lines holding the dinghy, we had a suitable life raft in place. After all, the trip is only 26 hours and we will only be out of sight of land for a short time. Additionally, the panhandle is so shallow I'm not sure the boat could sink. The rule for abandoning ship is, you step "up" into the life raft. With the dinghy secured we had that part done. Next was the engine work. After all, we didn't want to have a flame out crossing the gulf. A single engine boat in a big body of water could be in real trouble if the engine failed. If the engine fails on a sailboat you raise the sails. The sails drive the boat through the water but they also steady the boat and keep it from getting sideways to the wind. A trawler like ours does not have a sail to keep it steady and we would be at the mercy of the wind and waves. A large wave broadside could broach the boat and she could be swamped. To eliminate any possibility of any of that, we will make sure our engine is working properly and we will not cross when the weather has a chance of creating problems for us.

By Wednesday C-Quarters and the next marina Moorings were full of Loopers waiting for the weather window to cross the Gulf. We had supper with some of the boaters we had been traveling with and talked about the crossing. Our check list of things to do before crossing was getting small. I had purchased a pressure gauge from Ace and some tubing and pressurized the fuel system to 20 pounds and held it for an hour. Before that I had replaced another fuel line and added a shutoff to the generator. Since the fuel system is normally only a 6-10 pound system I felt I had overcome the problem. Right!! The boat was mostly ready. I had ordered a EPIRB from a rental company that would add another degree of safety to our trip. All the Loopers at both marinas were getting antsy. Everyone wanted to get on the other side of the Gulf. Tarpon Springs was the destination for most but a few were planning on going a few miles south to Clearwater. Clearwater would add a couple hours to our trip so we were planning on the shortest and most direct route for the crossing which would be Tarpon Springs.

A few of the boats were fast enough to cross in one day and they would leave at first light and make Anclote River with the sun to their backs which would help spotting the many crab traps. The crab traps are so numerous that most experienced captains do not recommend going into Tarpon Springs at night. I have never been in there at night but during the day a sharp lookout is necessary to avoid hitting one. Of course hitting the floating ball is not the problem. Grabbing the line with your prop, rudder or keel is the problem. I have a friend who was in a sailboat race in the area and picked up a trap and wondered why his boat kept losing ground. The crew adjusted the sails, balanced the boat and watched the wind but still they were going slower than their competitors. It was not until one of the crew looked aft and saw the float bobbing in the water behind the boat that they discovered the cause. It was then necessary for a diver to go into the water and cut the line connecting the float to the crab or lobster cage and clearing the line. If the engine is running as it would be in a trawler and line gets wrapped around a prop, it can cause serious damage to the prop or drive train. In a serious sail boat race after the crew cuts the line, the captain has to make a decision whether the crew in the water is worth picking up or should the captain try to make up the lost time by leaving the guy in the water. That's always discussed by the crew and the captain but I don't know of anyone who has been left in the water, just sailor humor. Several products are available to attach to the prop shaft, which are designed to cut the line. I have never used one but I always think of them as I motor through an area littered with pots. I just keep a watch out for them and have yet to snag a pot.

The month of December is not a good month to make the crossing. In the winter cold fronts are more frequent and more intense. Even knowing that, boaters do make the crossing. All responsible boaters who venture out on the unsheltered waters of the Gulf, do so with lots of information, especially in the winter months. Most boaters have their favorite place to get predictions of the weather for a crossing. The Loop Group has its own volunteer weather watcher. During the winter months he announces his own prediction each morning for the crossing from Carrabelle to Tarpon Springs. Tom's weather musings can be viewed from the Great Loop home page. Moorings Marina at Carrabelle has their own prognosticator. My favorite is a web site that looks at the weather and sea buoys in the gulf. Windfinder.com will give present and predicted winds at a certain weather buoy. The buoy I look for is located 106 miles NW of Tampa and gives wind, waves, tide and weather forecast in time steps of three hours and are available for seven days in advance.

Thursday morning we woke to outside temps of 35 degrees, ice on the deck and high winds predicted for the next seven days. We quickly made a decision. We were within an eight hour drive of our house and with Christmas on the way we decided to leave *Lifestyle II* at C Quarters and drive home. I signed a month to month contract with C Quarters and made arrangement for a rental car. Carrabelle has no rental car agency but a local guy will drive you to the Tallahassee airport to pick up a rental, for a fee. With the decision made to leave the boat for a while it was a good time to have a project contracted that we had been putting off. The isinglass or plastic windows in the flybridge were old, brown and cracking. Not being one to waste anything, comes from my days as a sailor, I waited until duct tape was needed to close the windows before I considered replacing them. I asked the locals for a reputable canvas man. Brooks Bryan arrived at the boat that afternoon and took measurements. His bid was lower than the bid we had received in Nashville, so I gave him the go ahead. Next I called the EPIRB rental and cancelled the unit just as the postman was picking it up. After that we went down the list of things we needed to remove from the boat and checked off the list of valves and switches that needed to be adjusted before we departed.

Friday morning, December 9, we departed for Murfreesboro with a packed rental car with just barely enough room left for Maggie. I surmised that leaving on a car trip on Friday did not count as a bad omen. I figured that naval superstitions did not carry over to land travel. And besides I'm not superstitious, anyway.

During the winter months I was able to get the GPS repaired for the second time, Brooks replaced the plastic and I was able to continue the work on the house. Denniese started back to work and ended her leave of absence. The group she works with was glad to have her back but it was a difficult transition for her. She loved her coworkers and the work was rewarding but living on a boat for the most part of a year gives a person a different perspective on life. We visited the boat a couple of times during the winter but as spring approached we started thinking about connecting the dots for our conclusion of the Loop adventure. By March the weather patterns were starting to moderate and we set a date to move back aboard *Lifestyle II*.

Ralph and June Vaughn

Chapter 22

Ralph and June

St. Patrick's Day was March 17 and it was the day we chose to move back and continue our trip. We arrived in Carrabelle at 1630 with a car full of supplies and a happy boat dog. Maggie was happy because it had been a long time since the last pee break. I don't know what goes through a dog's brain but they are about the most adaptable animals on the planet. She seemed to recognize the boat and I'm sure the smells were recognizable. She found her comfort spots that kept her out of the way while we loaded the boat, cleaned the boat and made the adjustments necessary to live aboard again. Maggie seemed to accept the fact that we were back on our boat home to stay for a while and that was OK with her. Our plan to continue on the trip after the break had a positive side. We had now obtained some creditability. Many of our friends had been following our Blog story at Blogspot.com and the local paper had done a story on our trip. We even had people wanting to join the ride with us when we continued our trip. In the South we say "Talk is Cheap" and that proved to be the case when we gave folks the time frame we had planned for the last leg of our trip. We didn't find anyone who wanted to cross the Gulf with us but that was OK because we wanted to do the most difficult part of the trip solo, just like we had completed the other parts. We did find one of our favorite couples that were eager to join us for a week's worth of travel where ever we could work it in.

Ralph and June Vaughn joined us in Carrabelle on Saturday, March 24, 2013. They had flown into Panama City airport where we picked them up. They were not going to cross with us but serve a very important service; drive the car to Tarpon Springs. We were close enough to the finish line that we had brought the car with us to drive home when we finished. Moving a car is simple enough except the car is never where you want it. It is always either at the next stop or at the last stop or if it is at the same place as the boat, then you are worrying about how you're going to get it to the next stop. But we can't do without them. When we were moving every day we would plan our stops on which marina had a courtesy car or near to stores where we could bike or walk. The last couple hundred miles we would be playing leap frog with the car.

Monday, March 26, all the reports said it would be a good day for a crossing. We were the only boat left at the marina that wanted to cross. All the other Loopers had found a window and a buddy boat to make the crossing and had departed. We liked Carrabelle and would miss it. We had everything we needed at Carrabelle. We even found a Baptist Church to attend which was only a couple blocks from the marina. The people at the marina were very nice, although, sometimes the morning meeting beside the burn barrel started a little early for us. The burn barrel was a 50 gallon drum where all the cardboard and other things were placed to be burned. The locals had their coffee around the burn barrel on cool mornings. When the wind was blowing from the east the smoke was not pleasant. Other than that, "What's not to like?" As we motored out of the harbor the wind was calm the temperature was about 58 degrees. By 0900 we had passed the sound and were officially in the Gulf of Mexico. Ralph and June were in our car and had planned on doing some sightseeing and then meet us in Tarpon Springs the following day. We did not have a buddy boat and there would be little or no moon that night so we were going to be all alone for the 170 statute mile trip unless another boat was spotted or some strange sea creature found us. The engine was running great and we were making good time. By 1600 we were only about 114 miles from Tarpon Springs and about 56 miles from Carrabelle.

So far it had been a great day. Denniese and I had adapted to the roll of the gulf and were even able to eat some light meals. Maggie found a sunny spot and caught up on her dog naps. The GPS was working well, the auto helm was working great, the boat was going through the water like she had missed *the open sea*. The crew was not sea sick so all was good in the world of *Lifestyle II*. 1615: FLAMEOUT!!. The alarm sounded and we manned our stations. There is only one thing worse than having a dead engine on the open water and that is having a dead engine and not having a working radio to call for help. No worry there, we had two working VHF's, two working cell phones and even an air card for our computer, all in great working condition. Only problem was, we were out of range for all of them! A satellite phone would have been nice or a buddy boat to render aid or relay a message, but none of that was available either. We did have the rented EPIRB that we could turn on in case of an emergency. We weren't at the emergency stage yet so we didn't fire off the EPIRB. We just did what we had been doing since leaving Nashville last October. We bled the engine of air and it started back up. We were again underway at 1640. At 1645, the engine died again. I bled the fuel system and started the engine and it ran and then it died again. It was getting close to dark. I didn't want to be out in the middle of the Gulf on a boat without a working engine, remembering the night we spent on the Upper Mississippi, hard aground, heeling over and scared. I didn't want to go through that again and I didn't want Denniese to go through it again. Denniese was depending on me to solve any problem that arose. The burden was heavy and the sea was lonesome. The good part was it had happened so many times before that neither of us panicked. Maggie was still sleeping. I made the decision to hook up the jerry jug system which I had kept aboard even though I felt sure I had solved the fuel air problem when I pressurized the system in Carrabelle.

By 1745, we were under way again with the two jerry jugs serving as our fuel tank. I could switch out the tanks as we used the fuel but it would mean a constant watch on the jugs to make sure we didn't run one dry and suck a ton of air into the system. We watched as the sun set over the Gulf and we turned on the running lights. There was not a boat or a light within sight. The sky was mostly overcast and very few stars could be seen. There was no moon. It was dark! We checked the chartplotter, the auto helm, and moved to the lower helm. As soon as we reached the lower helm I checked the compass heading and logged it as it became our main navigational instrument at the lower helm. Our course over ground according to the GPS was 138 degrees True and the lower helm compass gave us a reading of 150 degrees magnetic. Both were correct and by holding that course we should get to the Anclote Isle marker at Tarpon Springs at about 0900 the next day. I lowered the dining table and made a watch bed so we could nap and still be near the helm, the jerry jugs, the engine and each other. Maggie found her spot on the carpet close by. The only light that could be seen was the small glow from the compass, the reflection of our navigational lights on the water and the florescent glow of our bow wave. Occasionally during the night we would be sitting at the lower helm chair with the cabin door open, and we could hear a porpoise breach and look in on us amateurs to make sure we were OK. The first time I heard a porpoise surface and blow next to the boat on a night watch it scared the fire out of me. But then I realized their good intentions and accepted the break in the dark night's silence as just another friend saying hello.

The night wore on and we each tried to sleep in between navigating, filling fuel jugs and worrying about our precarious situation. At 2145, I went topside and checked the GPS and found even with the difficulties we were making reasonable headway. We were only 72 miles from Tarpon Springs. Denniese was sleeping and our little craft was heading for our destination. At 0200, I woke Denniese and she took the helm as I changed out the jerry jugs. She settled in at the helm and climbed into the watch bunk we had set up on the dining table. It was good to get a couple hours of sleep before the engine would demand a new supply of fuel. It seemed like only a few minutes later when Denniese put her hand on my shoulder and said "Its time". I raised up wide awake and ready to climb down into the engine compartment and transfer some more fuel. By 0500, we were only 23 miles from the Tarpon Springs marker. Soon I saw a faint red glow of the sun trying to come up and on the eastern horizon and then I could see the tall power plant smoke stacks marking the town. They were a welcome sight. Sunrise was set for 0635 and low tide was at 0800. We followed the markers through the cut that took us around Anclote Island and into the Anclote River, then finally into the harbor at Tarpon Springs. The cut is narrow and the water is shallow outside the cut. Navigating to the mouth of the Anclote River is difficult with that as the only duty. But now we had fuel issues, the sun was blinding us and we were on a falling tide. The falling tide is not normally an issue if you stay in the channel since we only draw 4 foot. The real problem is dodging the crab pots. They are hard to see in normal light but with the sun reflecting off the water and in our eyes at the same time, it was almost impossible to see all of them. We dared not get out of the channel. It would be better to catch a pot than run aground. Denniese watched for crab pots as I steered the boat. We had moved to the upper helm as soon as it was light enough to see our way. It is much easier to see the crab pots from the upper helm and just one of the many reasons to have a boat with a upper helm. Denniese would call out "one at twelve o'clock, three in a row at eleven o'clock." And I would make adjustment to our course. We made it safely to the river by 0930, and by 1030, we were tied to the dock at Turtle Cove. "Thank you Lord"

Twenty six and a half hours from dock to dock, several flameouts, many change out of five gallon jugs and no potty break for Maggie but we had made the dreaded Gulf crossing. As soon as the boat was tied to the pilings, Denniese helped Maggie off the boat and onto some welcome grass. The crew of *Lifestyle II* had sacrificed to make the crossing from Carrabelle to Tarpon Springs and Maggie had done her part. I checked in with the office at Turtle Cove Marina and then settled down for a well deserved nap. That afternoon feeling reasonably well, I started in on the jobs that needed to be completed prior to our guest arriving and the continuation of the trip. The hot water heater element had gone out in Carrabelle and the replacement element had leaked and now the replacement to the replacement was also giving me trouble seating. Denniese cleaned the inside of the boat, did laundry and fixed lunch while I worked on the hot water heater. At 1500, I announced that the hot water heater was repaired. I tested it and found it to be water tight. The engine maintenance was next and then a well deserved meal at MaMa's Real Greek restaurant. We were in bed by 2200 and glad to be tied to a dock and back on a reasonable sleep schedule.

The next day Ralph and June joined us and were all excited about their first pleasure boat trip. Neither were boat people but both were adventurous and took all the inconveniences of boat life in stride. While tied to the dock, energy management is not an issue. But once away from the dock, energy and supplies are to be carefully watched. In the Caribbean, the locals have made an enterprise from the wasteful Americans. While at anchor early in the morning a boat would suddenly appear at your swim ladder selling fresh bread and for just a dollar more per bag they would carry off your garbage. You soon learn to stuff the bags really full before handing them over the side of the boat to the garbage scow. The same small boat would find you in the afternoon and sell you a bag of ice. If you happen to tie to a mooring ball that same local would collect the mooring fee. Each mooring field offered much the same service. So when guests arrive aboard *Lifestyle II* I have a talk with them about some of the differences they will encounter aboard a boat. Electric usage is a biggie. Although we have a generator we still use electricity carefully and of course the generator uses diesel fuel to make electricity. Water management is next in importance. In addition to the two 125 gallon tanks of water we also carry a gallon per person per day of drinking water usually in gallon jugs. We purchase distilled water at the grocery so we can have good quality drinking water and a reserve for our battery maintenance. If we find good drinking water at a marina, we refill some of those jugs being careful to mark them so as not to use them for the batteries.

Garbage and refuse management takes some ingenuity. Just remember don't store that bag of garbage in the engine compartment. You may have to work down in the hot stuffy compartment that particular day. Trying to convince the first time boater that the head does not operate like the toilet at home is difficult. A good way to get their attention is to get them to imagine a half dollar coin. Then tell them that everything that goes into the toilet has to go through a pipe the size of a half dollar. If that does not convince them to be careful then tell them "if you break it you fix it." And next show them the backup toilet which is a two gallon plastic bucket. The size of the boat's holding tank can become an issue with several folks aboard and a long trip. Remember the harrow stories of the cruise liners when the generator failed and the toilets did not flush. Most boat toilets are now electric and that is a concern. One of the first sailing adventures I had was in Mexico and the sailboat owner did not allow toilet paper to be flushed down the toilet. Rather, he provided a paper bag in the head and the toilet paper was deposited in the bag and then taken ashore. I still adhere to that rule only now I provide a box of plastic sandwich bag wraps in the head and then they are placed in the garbage container. It sounds gross when it is first explained but all my guests over the years have willing adopted the idea when I offer them the choice of the zip lock or the other choice, "you break it you fix it."

So before leaving Tarpon Springs, I had such a discussion with Ralph and June. We went over emergency procedures, fire extinguisher locations and some basic safety precautions and most importantly "man overboard" procedures. I showed them where the throwable life ring was located and demonstrated that the first person to spot a man, woman or dog over board is to yell "Man Overboard" and point to the overboard victim and not take their eyes off the location in the water. The other crew members are responsible for stopping the boat, turning the boat and the other demands of the rescue effort. Ralph being the serious person he is was listening intently. I next explained that everything that comes on the boat has to be consumed or later taken off the boat. It takes energy to bring it aboard and energy to remove it. Water is the consumable I was thinking of at the time. I said, "When taking a shower water has to be pumped to you for the shower and then pumped overboard afterward. So wet down, soap up and rinse off and then pump the water overboard. The water is pressurized by a small 12 volt pump that is kept in the off position except when needed to pressurize the water system." We were going to be away from the dock for about a week and I knew all the supplies would be low by the time we reached a marina.

Before leaving Tarpon Springs, we motored around the harbor and looked at the working sponge boats. Fewer boats are needed these days because few natural sponges are used. Most sponges used today are synthetic. But, a few working boats can still be seen in the harbor with the crew washing the live sponges and hanging them in rigging to dry. Our 30 mile trip south to Boca Ciega Bay was great and enjoyed by all hands. We had one flame-out but it was handled so smoothly that our guest hardly realized the potential hazard that had been diverted. We were traveling on the Intracoastal looking at all the expensive homes and boats and I was able to tell stories about my many trips to Clearwater and all the little towns as we passed them. The bridges were a constant concern. With our antennas down we figure we needed 21 feet of clearance. Bridges have their height marked on the charts and it is measured at high water. Most bridges have waterboards with large numbers that sit in the water at the side of the bridge fender that marks the bridge height. Bascule bridges are measured at the bridge fenders to the lowest structure of the bridge. Since the bascule bridges are curved at the bottom, which allows for a couple extra feet of clearance in the middle. But just in case we would call the bridge tender to let him know our needs and intentions. We came upon one bridge that by the chart we could clear by a couple of feet. It was a wide bridge and because of our angle I could not see the far side of the bridge. As we approached, I could see the waterboard showing 21 feet clearance. I made my courtesy call to the bridge tender and told him we did not need a lift, we could clear 21 feet. By the time he responded to my transmission we were within a boat length of the bridge. It was then that he told me he had a painter hanging from a boatswains chair under the bridge at the far side and he needed to notify the painter to come up and bring his chair and paint. The next minute or so was filled with activity. I slowed the boat to an almost stop but the tide was pushing me into the bridge fenders so I needed to maintain some headway.

The painter and his crew scrambled to get off the boatswains chair which was hanging down about four feet from the bottom of the bridge and had to bring all their supplies up as was a very excited bridge master talking to me on the radio. We motored under the bridge just as we saw the painter and equipment hauled over the far side. My surprise to them did not go unpunished. For the next several weeks I found and cleaned up small aqua blue spots of paint from the white gelcoat, the same aqua blue as the color of the bridge.

We arrived in Boca Ciega bay by wine time and celebrated a beautiful day and successful trip from Tarpon Springs. Ralph and June were still elated by the new adventure. Gulfport has many good restaurants so we all loaded up the dingy and headed into town for a good local meal. We returned some time later and since we had walked Maggie when we first arrived, we decided to forgo her night time walk. She was happy without the walk since she had already visited the new place to smell and besides she had new friends aboard her boat. We enjoyed coffee on the sun deck and watched as the darkness closed in around us. I had my chores to do so I excused myself to turn on the anchor light and run the generator to charge up the house batteries. Soon we were all ready to turn in, and since we only have one shower on board I told Ralph he was honored with the first shower. I asked him to let me know when I could pump the shower water out because the float switch on the brown water reservoir was sticking, and instead of fixing the switch I would just turn it on and off as needed. He had listened carefully that morning and took all the instructions and cautions to heart. It wasn't but a few minutes later that he returned and said the shower reservoir was ready to pump out. I commented that was a quick shower. It was not until the next day that I found out that I had failed to turn on the water pump and the little bit of residual water pressure allowed him only to get wet and soapy before the water stopped flowing. Ralph never complains about anything, and thinking that was all the water allotted to him, just dried off, dressed and returned to the sundeck.

Log Book: Saturday March 31, 2012 At anchor off Gulfport in Boca Ciega Bay. On board Mike, Denniese, Maggie and guest Ralph and June. We woke to a nice breeze and 72 degrees. We enjoyed an egg and bacon sandwich on the sun deck and watched the little community of Gulfport wake up.

Gulfport has gone through several identities. When I was a kid in Tampa we made fun of this little town next to St. Pete. We called it the elephant burial grounds. We thought it was the place old folks came to spend their last days in the sun and warm weather. Those that migrated to Gulfport were the ones who could not afford the higher prices of Clearwater beach or the even higher prices of the communities further south. The quiet little artisan community of today still offers a lot for the dollar and the blue clear protected waters of the Gulf are ever inviting. Boca Ciega Bay will always be a favorite of mine and a place of such found memories. I was glad Ralph and June were able to spend a few days with us on this trip and especially here on Boca Ciega Bay. Ralph and June were flying out today and our enjoyable anchorage would soon end as we would be on our way for the last leg of our crazy trip.

We loaded up the dingy and made two trips to unload the crew. We waited with Ralph and June until the cab arrived and then said our sad good-byes and watched as they drove out of site toward the airport. Denniese, with Maggie in tow, and I found an outdoor café to have lunch and enjoyed watching people.

The streets were blocked off and a craft fair was in progress. After lunch we walked the street and marveled at all the interesting items for sale. Maggie enjoyed meeting a large black lab that smelled so good. We made our way back to the dinghy about three o'clock and noticed a large black cloud on the horizon. Of course nothing works all the time on a boat, so today it was the dinghy motor. After pulling the crank for about 10 minutes I started taking things apart. Just as I was thinking of dumping the thing in the water, the boater tied next to us showed up. It was the local Sheriff's Marine Patrol. I ask him if he would tow us to our boat and he agreed. We were back on board *Lifestyle II* just minutes when the thunderstorm moved over the bay. We wondered what was happening to the craft fair in downtown Gulfport, but had no time to even look up as we worked to tie gear down, add some scope to the anchor, and close all the hatches. The wind picked up and we watched a sailboat drag anchor. The boat slowly passed down the middle of all the boats at anchor. Amazingly it didn't snag an anchor or hit another boat. When the storm ended, the sailboat had drifted about a half mile without incident. I'm sure when the owner returned he had to wonder where he parked his boat.

After the storm I went back to working on the dinghy motor fuel system. I knew the problem was the fuel system because it would start with starting fluid and run as long as I feed it fuel manually. The small fuel lines were stopped up; unstopping them was not a talent I possessed. Satisfied that the motor was in need of a mechanic, I climbed back aboard *Lifestyle II* and started the check off of the items prior to departing the next day.

Sunday was a beautiful day to be on a boat. The anchor spot was gorgeous. It was going to be hard to leave this perfect spot, but this trip was never to be completed if we stayed at each beautiful spot. The temperature was about 70 degrees and with no wind. The sunny Boca Ciega Bay was about as good as it gets. Even so we pulled up the anchor and pointed our boat south. We only had one flameout on our trip to Sarasota Yacht Club. The clubhouse at Sarasota Yacht Club is new and beautiful. It is hard to find a place with more to offer; beautiful landscaped grounds surrounded by new buildings and a fabulous pool. Maggie especially liked the manicured grass. After docking we called the restaurant and made reservations for dinner. We would move here but I don't think we could afford the dock fee much less the required bar bill for members. Sarasota Yacht Club offers a discount for visiting yacht club members which is about the only way we could afford the dock space.

We cast off early on Monday morning and quickly ran aground. I guess our clue should have been the small boat at anchor with a couple fishermen waving at us to go the other way. We were out of the channel by about a hundred yards, but we were able to back off the grounding and relocated the channel and continue on our way. At 1230, we had a flameout but we were able to bleed the system and be on our way within a few minutes. At 1530, we dropped the anchor behind Inglewood Beach.

Only a narrow sliver of land separated us from the Gulf. We could not see the Gulf from our anchor spot but we thought we could hear it. So even without a motor and only one oarlock we all made it to the landing spot behind a nearby house. Most neighborhoods have dedicated access or rights of way between homes for people to walk to the bay or the beach. We found one and landed the dinghy and walked the short distance to the Gulf beach. Maggie hates water and has no affection for sand either. I guess if sand rabbits would appear she would have a different attitude but for now she hated every minute of this outing. We dragged her to the edge of the water. Her paws touched the water and that was it for her. She has her standards. Her heritage dictates her actions. She is a scent dog and not a retriever. Yes, she has her standards.

The next couple of days were some of the best in our Florida travels; anchoring behind islands or in small bays, watching beautiful sunsets and sleeping by the sound of small waves. By Wednesday we had made our way to Cape Coral City Marina. We had finally made the turn east. The closing of the circle was almost in sight. If all goes well we should cross the line at Stuart, Florida by the weekend. We just need to make that cut across the lower part of the state. After Cape Coral, we would pass through down town Fort Myers and then on to the feared Lake Okeechobee. Granted, Lake Okeechobee is full of gators and snakes but the real fear is the depth of the lake. Ten feet is considered deep across the 730 square mile lake. Two routes are available, across the lake or around the rim. The rim is the shallowest while the cut straight across is the shortest, it can be rough as a cob. It doesn't take much wind to blow up a two or three foot wave with skinny water and a long fetch. We would refer to our Bible for direction. Proverbs: 12:15 "… a wise man seeks advise." We would seek advice from many sources. Among them, all of our weather forecasters, the Corps of Engineers lake information, other boaters and lastly call a friend. Little Man was the beloved dock hand at Rowland and Martin Marina in Clewiston. Little Man has been on the docks for years and boaters of all sizes have come to love him and respect his advice. His advice was to take the rim. "There is enough water for you on the rim and the center of the lake is gonna be rough for the next week." That would be our course, the rim.

We checked in with the dock master at Cape Coral City Marina and told them we were only going to stay one night. We were anxious to close the gap and conclude our Loop adventure before the end of the weekend. From our slip I looked across the water and saw a familiar Loop boat. *Seeya* owned by Dave and Peg Miller had wintered in Cape Coral, Florida. We had first met them at Aqua Marine back last October where we had shared information about the loop and he recommended Diesel Bob who advised me on my fuel/air problem but could not help otherwise. I walked over to say Hi to Dave and within a few minutes he offered his car for our use. We had intended to bike to the store for our supplies. After making the drive to the store, we appreciated the car even more. It was a long car ride to the store and a bike ride would have been exhausting. We prepared the boat and stocked the groceries and waited for a front to pass. The afternoon storms were building and we could see that it was good to be in a slip for the approaching storm. I used the time to check the engine and prepare it for the last 140 mile leg of our trip. By this time in the trip, I had given up on trying to find the fuel/air leak. I would just bleed the fuel of air often and hope and pray the engine would not fail in a critical spot. The storms finally passed over us about midnight and the winds rocked the boats but the secure marina received no damage. The morning came and by 0700 we had walked the dog, had breakfast, started the engine and the dock lines ready to bring in. The day was starting off cool but the clouds were moving off and it should be a nice day.

By 1100 we had made the first of the last set of locks we would transit on our Loop adventure. We were on lake water now and the scenery changed. We were still in a tropical zone and the plants were natural and ornate but the ground was taking on the appearance of swampland. We stopped for the day at the free dock at Labelle. The city has provided a nice stopping place to passing boats. They even offered free electricity and water. All they ask is that you sign in at the kiosk at the end of the dock and dock your boat stern in. Signing in at the kiosk and visiting the city library at the end of the street would be the fun part. Looking over the names in the sign-in book was fun and we even saw several of our boating friend's names and their comments. Backing in to the dock, now that's a different story. There was, at the time we arrived, a slight current, a light wind in the same direction and a 24 inch prop to contend with. The plan was to drop the anchor upstream while Denniese let the rode out and I would smoothly back the boat to the dock. The wind and tide were to bring the stern of *Lifestyle II* neatly to the worn but friendly dock. What a wonderful plan I had. On the first try I reached the end of the anchor rode short of the dock by about 30 feet. The second time the wind picked up and I found a patch of lily pads and a bunch of mud for the prop to dislodge about ten feet downstream of the dock. The third time is a charm, right? Wrong, the additional power to overcome the wind and current walked the boat to the other side of the dock, beam first. The next couple of docking attempts were variations of the first three attempts. Finally, all the commotion woke the boater already tied to the dock and he came out to either protect his boat or help us. He took a line that we tossed and pulled us into the dock stern first. Maggie was the real hero because I am sure it was all her barking that woke the poor fellow. I felt bad about disturbing him so I told him I would buy him a drink of his choice if he knew a place. We walked Maggie which quieted her to the relief of the neighborhood, fed her and tied her to the aft rail where she could guard the boat. Denniese and I, with our new best friend, walked to the nearest restaurant and enjoyed a meal, drinks and sailing stories from our new neighbor.

We left the free dock at Labelle a lot easier than we had arrived and were underway by 0745. We exited our first lock at 0950 and out of Moore Haven lock at 1205 and by 1430 we were pulling into Rowland Martin's Marina. It is a good place but somewhat expensive. Little man was there to take our lines and help settle our boat in. Denniese had visited this place in the past to purchase bait for a fishing trip on the lake. Her parents wintered in Clewiston and a fishing trip on the lake was maybe the only thing to do here in the big town of Clewiston. But on the other hand, they do catch some great bass on that big lake. Little Man suggested that I not try to get out without his help when we left. As I looked over to the opposite bank, which was only about 50 feet away, I could see the bank had been stabilized by large boulders and riprap reducing the turning area by about 5 feet. Later, I went to the office, handed them my credit card and saw that the restaurant was open for business. I settled up for the one night stay and walked next door and placed an order to be delivered to our sun deck. With wine glass in hand we watched the waiter deliver our supper to our boat. We didn't even have to put on our deck shoes to enjoy the meal. Now that is great service.

The next morning, Good Friday, true to his word Little Man was on the dock waiting for me to disconnect the electric and get underway. I queried him about the best route for crossing the lake. He reported that today, it would be best to take the rim route. With the route determined, we made plans to turn the boat. Since I only had about 45 feet to turn the 40 foot boat, Little Man showed me a wide spot at the end of the dock. He walked to that spot to coach me from the dock. I slowly made the ten-point turn with the help of the prop walk, to do the 180. I was really proud of my success of turning the boat without nicking the prop or scratching the gelcoat. I motored out of the narrow harbor with my head held high, until Denniese suggested I slow the boat so she could untie the dinghy. The dinghy was still in its nighttime tie down position with both bow and stern lines tied to the stern of the boat. We were pulling the dinghy sideways. I slowed the boat before the dinghy was swamped and caused a multitude of problems. With the dinghy in its proper configuration we again cranked the speed up to about eight miles per hour. A couple miles down the stream we slowed again, but this time out of respect for retired Master Sergeant Benjamin B. Caldwell who had served his country with distinction and upon his retirement he fished this very spot. Ben Caldwell or "Gentle Ben" or "Pappy" as he was often called was Denniese's dad. She had fished this very spot with him and our slowing was to give her time for those sweet memories to be reflected upon and which actions cannot be enjoyed again.

We passed through Port Mayaca Lock at 1500. Only one more lock and we would be finished with the up and down and in and out of locks. We lost count of the locks we have transited during this trip but I believe it is close to one hundred. At 1645 we tied our little craft to the wall at Indiantown Marina. We had put 8.5 hours on the engine and transited one lock. We had gone all day without a flameout. Maybe the problem was salt water. No, that can't be right, the problem started on the Cumberland River. We tied the boat and walked the dog as we usually do. Indiantown is just south of nowhere, so you can understand how surprised I was by all the activity. I found out it is the drop-off place for many Canadians and others returning from a winter in the Bahamas. They want to deposit their boat in a safe hurricane hole and go home for the summer. The place was a bee hive of activity. Boats were waiting in line to be pulled out washed off and stored on jack-stands in a nearby field. We walked Maggie over to the grass boat yard and marveled at the boats. I guessed there were close to 50 acres of boats of all sizes and design. All were strapped down with special straps that were anchored in the ground. We found out later that Indiantown Marina required the use of only their jack stands and tie downs. Of course they rent those at an extra charge. The will also shrink-wrap your boat, add moisture absorbers to your boat and even service your batteries while you are away, all for an additional charge. We were just spending the night so we didn't have time to see all the sights at the marina. They have welcome back parties for the boaters going and coming. It looked like the marina staff were getting ready to have a cook out as we perused the area. It would have been nice to sit and relax but we were too close to our goal. Just one more day and we could cross our line.

Crossing our wake

Chapter 23

Gold Flag Day

Easter Sunday April 8, 2012. We had sunrise service on the sundeck in the form of coffee and Denniese's delicious pancakes. The temperature was a bit on the cool side but we had so much to be thankful for we didn't mind a bit. We didn't depart the marina until 1030 hours because the wind was blowing even in the inlet we were in. At 1330 we entered our last lock, St Lucie, and exited at 1340. As we exited the lock, we could see some of the familiar sights. We weren't there yet but if we wanted to we could probably have thrown a rock to our starting point. We saw a marina that we had driven past and a restaurant that we visited and liked. We looked out in the bay and the wind was blowing up some waves. Only the fast boats and wave runners were daring the blow. We looked to our left and could see Loggerhead Marina, the place our outboard motor was stolen and we were so depressed that I considered just going home. We could see the dock where we met Neil Adams the Canadian who helped us purchase a new motor and would not take a cent for the effort. We called him our angel. We briefly relived the fears and anxiety we both had shared as we started the trip. We laughed at how little we knew and how naive we were about this Great Loop Adventure, and then we saw it, the straight line of buoys that marked the entrance to Loggerhead Marina. The same channel markers we had motored out of on May 3, 2011. We had crossed our wake!! We did it!! Denniese took the helm and made a circle over our wake and then stopped the boat in the middle of the channel.

I dropped the anchor and we celebrated, just the three of us. We were hoping for a large flotilla of boats, maybe a fireboat with all nozzles spraying water, maybe the Coast Guard would supply a cutter for the occasion. But, not so, we sat in the bouncy bay and watched the few jet skis wander off in a different direction now that we were not providing a wake to jump. The three of us gathered at the bow with a glass of cheap red wine to mark the occasion. We took a few pictures and I ceremoniously removed the old and worn white AGLCA burgee. The white burgee had flown almost continuously from the bow, except when we were in Canada, when we flew a courtesy Canadian flag. I then attached a new bright gold burgee signifying that boat and crew had completed the Loop. We took a few more pictures then raised the anchor and motored back the way we had come a few minutes before, with our new gold burgee blowing in the breeze. The jet skis soon joined in behind us and everything seemed right in the world, at least for a few minutes.

Conclusion

What do we do now? For a few minutes we seemed lost, a boat and crew without a purpose or destination. We headed west but didn't have a destination or goal in mind; we were now on a pleasure cruise with no set destination. Then reality hit us. We had a house to complete, Denniese had a job and Maggie had some unhunted rabbits in the park behind our house. Our plan all along had been to buy a boat, do the Loop, sell the boat and return home to complete the many undone items we had left. We decided we needed to put our plan into action. We located a nearby dock and started the cleaning, sorting and removing a year's worth of stuff. It took us three days to clean the boat and get it ready for our departure.

We decided since the boat was going to be left unattended for a while we need to find a safe marina. We decided Indiantown was the best choice. It was in fresh water, it had a complete shop and it was an acceptable hurricane hole. We contacted a broker and arranged a meeting with him at our new slip in Indiantown. The papers were signed and our friends from Tampa delivered our car. We drove out of the marina and looked back to see *Lifestyle II* sitting high in her slip. From the bow rail I could see the listing broker's sign was swinging in the breeze, the same rail that held so many memories, so many adventures, and so much love. We had removed all our personal gear and we were headed home. It was a sad day, thinking we would quite possibly never, ever board her again. She had become our second home and place of refuge from the stresses of everyday life. A place to hide and heal, not mention a cocoon surrounding and protecting us for nearly a year while on the water. Would we ever see our little lady again?

September arrived and we had not had a reasonable offer on our beautiful little boat. Our broker said, "It was a bad time, not many boats selling." We decided we needed to visit our friend. We drove to Indiantown after a stop in Clearwater to visit our friends Robert and Cherolyn Buzby. We walked to our slip and were taken aback by the appearance of *Lifestyle II*. Some people said Indiantown has the black crud from the sugar cane fields that are burned at the end of the growing season; others say it is swamp crud that grows on anything. In addition to those things the boat was sitting next to the active travel lift and each boat that was raised had its bottom washed and, if the wind was blowing from the west, the spray would deposit the dirt on our boat. She was almost black. In the five months of sitting in the slip at Indiantown, she had more dirt and growth than many of the derelict boats that had been sitting in the field there for years. It was sad, we almost cried. Well, it had to be cleaned.

After a two day trip, we were not up to the task but it had to be done or we would need to find a motel. The thought of sleeping on a dirty boat was only slightly better than sleeping in a motel in Indiantown. I asked some of the liveaboards if they knew of some one that would clean our boat. I even asked the marina staff but it was the weekend and no work was being done by the staff. Finally, we realized we would have to clean her ourselves.

Someone had mentioned a sailor who was working on a boat in the yard and he might be willing to help. I knocked on the hull of the sailboat sitting high on jack stands. The owner appeared and climbed down to great me. I introduced myself and I told him of my predicament. He stood about 6 feet 5 inches and looked to be about my age but in very good physical shape. He said his name was Raivo Rooneem, but everyone called him Rye. He was Canadian and had retired here to work on a sailboat he had purchased at this marina. He agreed to help me clean the boat but would only take a beer for payment. After almost two hours of hard cleaning, Rye and I had the outside clean enough to move aboard. Denniese had worked during that time on the inside and it was much improved. The three of us in wet and dirty clothes drove to the only pizza place in Indiantown and enjoyed a large pizza and several beers. Rye had once been a semi-pro hockey player and had retired from the Canadian Government as a barrister. He was another angel.

The next couple of days, we continued to clean the boat and hound the marina management about moving us to a new slip. They finally got tired of my complaining and found a slip for *Lifestyle II* at the end of the slips far away from the travel lift. We tied *Lifestyle II* down and found our new neighbor walking his dog. Bob, Norma and dog Sissy lived aboard their trawler *Firefly*. Sissy was a Vizsla, a Hungarian pointer. A beautiful light brown medium size dog and one Denniese recognized as a potential prize winner. We all became instant friends and enjoyed the shared experiences of living aboard a boat. Bob agreed to look after our boat and I canceled our listing.

We had forgone the completion of the upstairs of the new house in order to buy the boat. The upstairs could wait a little longer. After all, there is an advantage to living in a one bedroom house. We did have a blowup mattress for anyone wanting to spend the night, although we had few takers. We made the decision to keep the boat and put off the upstairs a little longer. Denniese said it best when she said, "We could afford the boat while I was not working, so we can certainly afford it when I go back to work. We will keep our boat."

Over the next 12 months, we would move the boat from Indiantown back to Nashville. Denniese would schedule vacation time from her work to move the boat and in-between I worked on the upstairs. I even found time to have the hernia repaired. Long weekends were spent at some remote marina cleaning and fixing on our boat. We enjoyed some of our favorite spots along the way and developed stronger friendships and even found one last angel.

Before we departed Indiantown I told Bob of the flameout problem and how it had plagued us for a third of our trip. Bob was one of those guys who had done it all. He was an excellent mechanic and at each stopover he would seek employment in that endeavor. He had been an Army Ranger and used that experience as an aerial assault firefighter and even a jump master for the team. So when he said, "I can fix it", I had no doubt he could. The following day he brought a stainless steel bottle somewhat like a garden sprayer aboard *Lifestyle II* and said, "This will do it." He hooked up the pressure rig to the fuel lines just before the primary filters and pumped the handle. We sat back and waited and in a few minutes we saw the red diesel fuel seeped from around two fittings. Bob tightened the fittings and declared the problem solved. I said "Right." We started the motor and didn't have another flameout for almost a year. I don't think Bob has been described as an angel many times, but he was an angel to us.

We found our way back to Boca Ciega Bay aboard *Lifestyle II* and spent some time there. Bob and Norma joined us in Tarpon Springs and while Norma ferried cars, Bob, Denniese and I made the 26 hour Gulf crossing, without a flameout. We met Bob and Norma at Lulu's in Gulf Shores, Alabama after they had moved their boat there and signed a yearlong contract for the slip which was a long commitment for Bob and Norma. We found our way to Lulu's aboard *Lifestyle II* and joined them in fun and food. We used Lulu's as a staging point to ferry the car, this time to Columbus, Mississippi, which would be our last long stay before the trip to Nashville. While in Columbus, I had the start batteries replaced and tuned up the genset. We departed Columbus Marina on Sunday October 13, 2013 and said our goodbyes to our friends there.

We were scheduled to arrive at Pebble Isle Marina in New Johnsonville, TN in one week and pick up another crew member to help us complete our last leg. Duane is the college ministry pastor at our church and a boat lover. Our departure from New Johnsonville with Duane aboard started with a near collision with a tow pushing about eight empty barges. I had told Duane how uneventful the trip would be and how he would have plenty of time to catch up on his reading and studying. Over the next six days, besides the near encounter with the tow, I would run us hard aground, have to drop the anchor and bleed the engine to cure a flameout and in the middle of one night, I had to call all hands on deck to bring the anchor up and relocate the boat after a very windy storm almost blew us up on the bank. Duane loved every minute of it even though I was apologizing for all the extra activity. We arrived at Rock Harbor Marine Saturday October 26, 2013 and officially ended our Great Loop Adventure.

The driveway may never get paved, we may never have a new car, but we do have an extra bedroom in our finished upstairs for any guest and of course our HERO, *Lifestyle II*, is sitting under a covered slip in Nashville waiting for our next adventure.

THE END

Made in the USA
Columbia, SC
10 November 2020